Guide to Efficient

Burner Operation:

Gas, Oil, and Dual Fuel

Second Edition

Guide to Efficient Burner Operation:

Gas, Oil, and Dual Fuel

SECOND EDITION

Edward A. Faulkner, Jr.

Published by
THE FAIRMONT PRESS, INC.
700 Indian Trail
Lilburn, GA 30247

Library of Congress Cataloging-in-Publication Data   LCC:85-45872

Faulkner, Edward A., 1925-
   Guide to efficient burner operation.

   Bibliography: p.
   Includes index.
   1. Oil burner. 2. Gas-burners. I. Title.
TH7466.06F38   1986   697'.044   85-45872
ISBN 0-88173-016-5

Guide to Efficient Burner Operation:
Gas, Oil, and Dual Fuel

Second Edition

Published by The Fairmont Press, Inc.
700 Indian Trail
Lilburn, GA 30247

ISBN 0-88173-016-5   FP
ISBN 0-13-369471-2   PH

While every effort is made to provide dependable information, the publisher,
author, and editors cannot be held responsible for any errors or omissions.

Printed in the United States of America.

Distributed by Prentice-Hall, Inc.
A division of Simon & Schuster
Englewood Cliffs, NJ 07632

Prentice-Hall International (UK) Limited, *London*
Prentice-Hall of Australia Pty. Limited, *Sydney*
Editora Prentice-Hall do Brasil, Ltda., *Rio de Janeiro*
Prentice-Hall Canada Inc., *Toronto*
Prentice-Hall Hispanoamericana, S.A., *Mexico*
Prentice-Hall of India Private Limited, *New Delhi*
Prentice-Hall of Japan, Inc., *Tokyo*
Prentice-Hall of Southeast Asia Pte. Ltd., *Singapore*

Acknowledgements

The author gratefully acknowledges the helpful criticism and encouragement of the late Wilfred D. Hoyt, Hoyt–Grant Company, New Haven, Connecticut; and of Robert Cotter, retired foreman, HELCO Division, Northeast Utilities Company. Special thanks to Guenter K. Toska, then manager Special Products Department, Cleaver–Brooks Division, Aqua–Chem, Incorporated, who did a technical review of the original manuscript.

Appreciation is also given to the many companies and associations who kindly furnished and permitted the presentation of data, drawings and photographs of their products. Among them: Dunham–Bush, Inc.; Cleaver–Brooks Division; The Foxboro Company; Brook Motor Corporation; Betz Laboratories, Inc.; Honeywell, Inc.; General Electric Company; Improved Risk Mutuals; Sun–Ray Burner Manufacturing Corp.; Electrol Burner Manufacturing Co.; Babcock and Wilcox; American Petroleum Institute; Jamesbury Corp.; ITT General Controls; Maxitrol Company; Dwyer Instruments, Inc.; Ray Burner Company; Preferred Utilities Manufacturing Corp.; Fisher Controls Co.; Gordon-Piatt Energy Group; Gulf Research and Development Co.; American Gas Association ; and Electronics Corporation of America.

Finally, an expression of heartfelt thanks to my daughter Cheryl, who greatly helped with the illustrations.

Edward Faulkner

Shelton, Connecticut
May 1986

Preface To The Second Edition

At the time the manuscript for the first edition of *Guide* was nearing completion, Electronics Corporation of America (Fireye) introduced the D Series flame safeguard control. There was no reason to believe it would be anything but a coup for ECA, where upon production of the conventional C Series programmers was curtailed. The new control expanded on the modular concept by incorporating a plug-in solid state timer for the first time. Unfortunately I was unable to gain any experience with the unit before press time. Therefore, in keeping with my philosophy that the text be based as much as possible on my own field experience, I elected not to make reference to it. As it turned out, I got more hands-on time with these controls than I needed or cared for.

Speaking for the technicians who got the service calls at 2:00 o'clock in the morning, the premature introduction of the D Series programmer was a megablunder. To those less directly involved, and inclined to be more charitable, it was just a blooper. ECA took their lumps, stood behind their product, and eventually got the return rate under control.

Meanwhile, Honeywell came out with their solid state offering, the BC 7000, which introduced the microcomputer to combustion control. Not to be outdone, and none the worse for wear, ECA bounced back with their own microcomputer-based programmer, the E Series, and carried diagnostic annunciation to a new plateau.

The second edition devotes no more space than this to the Fireye D Series programmer since the field service procedure for this control can be summarized in two words . . . *replace it*. The text does describe the new microprocessor based technology and evaluates it with respect to efficient burner operation while maintaining due regard for traditional or conventional flame safeguard systems.

In my opinion the Fireye 26CF6 5022 and the Honeywell R4140L 1006 are years away from extinction.

Edward Faulkner

Shelton, Connecticut
May 1986

Contents

Chapter		Page
1	Introduction to Dual–Fuel Burners	1
2	Fundamentals of Fluid Flow	14
3	Pressure Losses and Gas Pipe Sizing	23
4	Valve Capacities and Flow Measurements	32
5	PRV Selection and Performance	39
6	Flow Valve Characteristics	51
7	Coordinating Fuel and Air Input Rates	57
8	The Oil Transport System	68
9	The Oil Circuit	77
10	Oil Viscosity and Its Effect	91
11	Oil Heating Methods	101
12	Principles of Oil Atomization	110
13	Atomizer Types	114
14	Oil Firing–Rate Control Methods	125
15	Air Atomizing Systems	135
16	Flame Volume Dynamics	147
17	Flue Gas Analysis	165
18	Interpreting Flue Gas Data	177
19	The Chimney and Its Effect on Modern Boilers	187
20	The Realities of Air Pollution	196
21	Electrical Considerations	207
22	Input Modulation	219
23	Safe Operating Limits	228
24	Flame Detection and Programming	236

Chapter		Page
25	Introduction to Troubleshooting	245
26	The Operating Sequence	257
27	Starting and Running Problems	265
28	Microcomputer-Based Integrated Combustion Control Systems	275
29	Support Systems	281
	Bibliography	297
	Index	299

1

Introduction to Dual-Fuel Burners

The evolution of combination gas and oil burners can be traced back nearly as far as the commercial oil burner itself, with early burners having been built and installed more than 70 years ago by such pioneers as the Babcock and Wilcox Company and the Hauck Manufacturing Company. Most of these burners were developed to utilize the by-products of certain manufacturing processes, with either coal or oil as the primary fuel. Blast furnace gas, and coke-oven gas, for example, resulting from the distillation of coal in the manufacture of iron and steel, were recovered and used for power generation in specially constructed boilers. In the 1920s and early 1930s, natural gas was also used to some extent in power generating stations by utility companies in localities where it was available. However, it was generally conserved for domestic purposes such as cooking and water heating.

The boilers used for power generation, which were fired alternately with natural gas or oil, utilized unsophisticated manually-controlled multiple burners. The gas burners were each capable of handling but a fraction of the total boiler capacity and were little more than larger versions of the domestic appliance burners of the day. Combustion efficiency was not good, as an excessive amount of combustion air was necessary to operate these combination fuel boilers.

The development of the commercial oil burner of the same period had progressed to the point where combustion efficiencies of more than 80 percent were obtained, equalling those experienced even today. In many plants which were traditionally fired with coal, oil fuel made significant inroads by offering some labor-saving advantages and conveniences over hand-fired coal systems in the generation of steam. At very high firing rates, however, with improved mechanical stoker equipment, the efficiency of coal surpassed that obtainable with the early oil burners. This was, and still is due, in part, to the fact that industrial grades of fuel oil require heating to remain fluid during storage and handling. This consumes some of the steam generated by the boiler, reducing the net heat output of the oil burner.

The modern combination burner, Figures 1-1A and 1-1B, embodies the components of the mechanical gas burner and the oil burner in the same housing. The burners share the same combustion air supply and ignition system, and are sometimes designed to burn gas and oil simultaneously. However, the combination burners discussed in this text use one fuel or the other as a stand-by fuel and have their control systems especially arranged so that the main burner can fire only one fuel at a time. Furthermore, the text confines itself to combination burners commonly employed in commerce and industry and makes only passing reference to the very large field-erected, utility-company-type boilers.

Combination burners are *variable-input* burners as contrasted with so-called *fixed-fire* burners commonly found in domestic heating applications. A variable input is one which can be increased or decreased while the burner is operating—within certain limits. Fixed-fire, or on-off type burners, ignite at full fuel input rate, run until the load demand is satisfied and shut off. "Low fire start," on the other hand, is an example of variable-input operation where the burner starts its heating cycle at reduced input then increases the flame size automatically after safe ignition has been established. Once load demand has been satisfied the burner stops until the next heat demand. "Modulation" is a further refinement of this operating mode where the burner automatically returns to low fire instead of stopping when the load demand rate has been reached. The flame size is reduced rather than extinguished. When the load demand again increases, the firing rate controller increases the flame size ac-

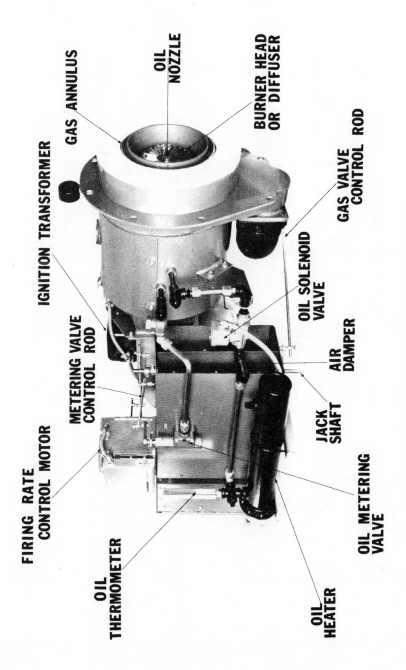

FIRING RATE CONTROL MOTOR

IGNITION TRANSFORMER

GAS ANNULUS

OIL NOZZLE

BURNER HEAD OR DIFFUSER

GAS VALVE CONTROL ROD

METERING VALVE CONTROL ROD

OIL SOLENOID VALVE

AIR DAMPER

JACK SHAFT

OIL METERING VALVE

OIL THERMOMETER

OIL HEATER

Figure 1-1A. Gas/Oil Burner (courtesy Iron Fireman)

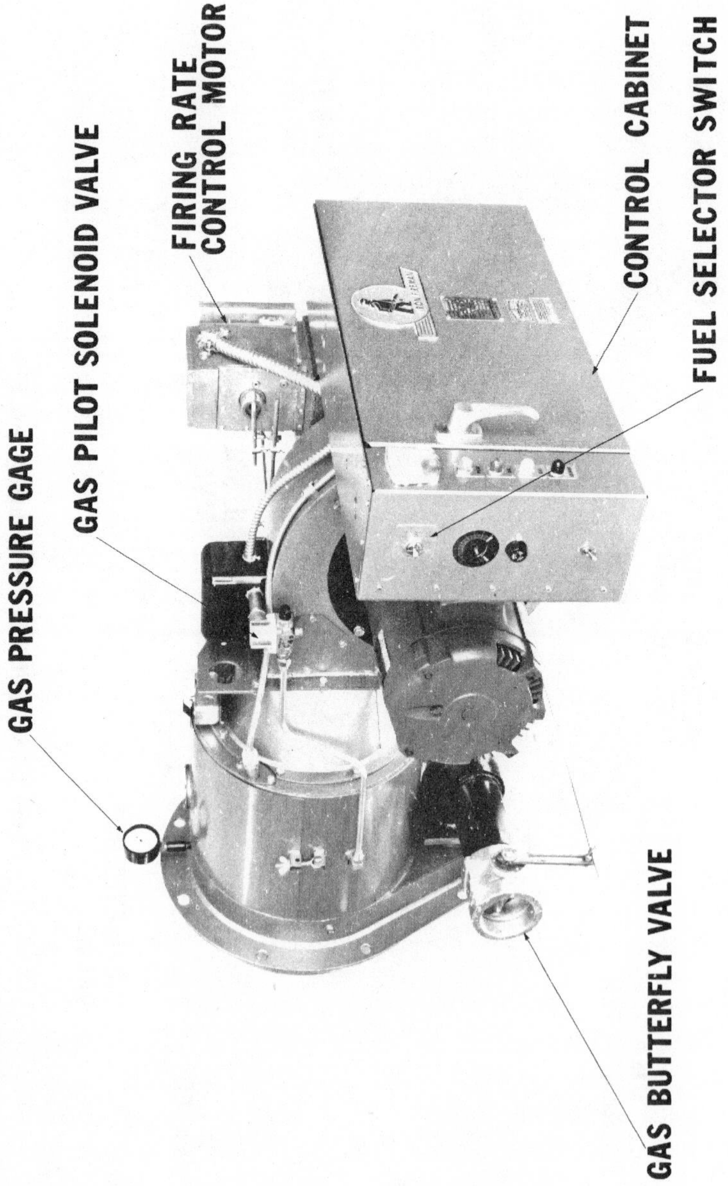

Figure 1-1B. Gas/Oil Burner (courtesy Iron Fireman)

cordingly. The flow of fuel and air is mechanically controlled by a motor–driven linkage system (Figure 1-2). In this type of burner the air damper is connected to a driving arrangement called the *jack shaft,* which is also connected to the gas–fuel- and oil–fuel–rate control valves. As the jack shaft is moved by a pneumatic or electrical motor which is responsive to changes in the load on the boiler, the gas (throttling) valve control linkage moves also. The oil rate control (throttling) valve responds in like manner, since it, too, is connected to the jack shaft. The fuel selector switch in the control panel, of course, assures that the fuel flows through only one of these valves at a time, by closing an electric shut–off valve in the unused supply line. In that way, even though the oil–flow–rate control valve may be going through operating motions, without oil fuel flow it does not figure in the operation when burning gas. Conversely, the same applies to the gas valve when oil is being burned.

The configuration of the combination burner is heavily influenced by the requirements of the oil fuel. It is as though the gas burner components have been hung on the oil burner as a kind of afterthought. In part this is true, because the combustion of gas is so straightforward when compared to the combustion of fuel oil. Much more hardware goes into the makeup of an oil burner. This is also true of burners that handle solid fuels, such as pulverized coal, sawdust and certain other volatile industrial wastes.

The mechanics of the combustion of solid and liquid fuels essentially involves injection of fuel into a swirling air stream. However, it is the nature of carbon, which is the primary source of heat in commercial fuels like petroleum, natural gas, and coal, that it gives up its energy reluctantly. It must be in the gaseous phase and in the presence of sufficient oxygen in order to release its heat energy. The main function of burners that fire solid or liquid fuels is, therefore, to *prepare* the fuels so that they will vaporize (gasify) prior to ignition. Basically, this requires reducing the physical size of the unit–fuel as it comes to the burner in its natural state, heating it, and mixing it thoroughly with air. In other words, preparation of the fuel for combustion is the heart of oil burner technology. Once the

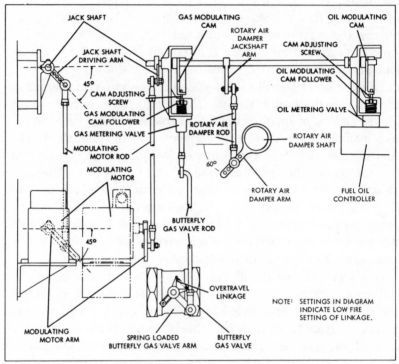

COMPLETE LINKAGE ASSEMBLY - COMBINATION GAS AND OIL

Figure 1-2. Complete Linkage Assembly (courtesy Cleaver–Brooks)

liquid fuel has passed into the vapor phase, its theoretical behavior in the combustion process conforms to the same laws of chemistry as do other fuel gases.

THE FLAME ZONE

The flame does not burn *in* the combination burner but in a *combustion chamber* within the pressure vessel to which the discharge or front end of the burner is fitted. The terminus of the burner at this point of union with the combustion chamber is described variously by manufacturers. For example, the front end of a horizontal rotary–type oil burner is called a *snout,* whereas the front end of a gun–type oil burner is the *burner head* or *diffuser.* Steam–atomizer and some air–atomizer oil burner manufacturers use the term *air register,* while still others merely call this area the *throat.* It is not surprising to find that much of the traditional oil burner nomenclature has passed over into combination burner terminology without much standardization, especially since some combination burners are little more than oil burners modified to burn gas as an alternate fuel. Be that as it may, the discharge end of this hybrid burner obviously provides an air passage and fuel conduit into the combustion space. More important, however, its unique design largely affects the character and efficiency of the flame produced.

Referring to Figure 1-1A, if we compared the combination gas–oil burner head to a wagon wheel, the oil nozzle would be located at the hub; the spokes would represent the louvers of the burner head where the air discharges; the gas manifold or annulus would be compared to the rim of the wagon wheel. The configuration of the burner head has an aerodynamic effect on the flame zone which is twofold. One, by means of its total effective flat plate area, it offers a specific resistance to the flow of combustion air which results in a relatively low pressure area immediately downstream of itself. This lee area of turbulent air currents tends to retain the flame in suspension or *stabilize* it close to the burner head. Two, by means of its louvers or turning vanes, it imparts a tangential or revolving motion to the fuel–air mixing process. (See Figure 1-3.) Since the individual fuel delivery systems are arranged to discharge into this area, the gas or oil fuel is immediately swept up or captured by the high velocity air stream.

Combustion air–handling parts in general, and front ends in particular, have undergone considerable evolution in an effort to improve oil combustion, resulting in oil burners that release more heat from the oil in a smaller flame volume. This has come about as a result of the delivery of higher air velocities and pressures to the burner head, which facilitates maximum dispersion of oil droplets in the air stream.

These conditions of velocity and pressure, although not required for the successful combustion of natural gas, do not work any unusual hardships when the combination burner is firing

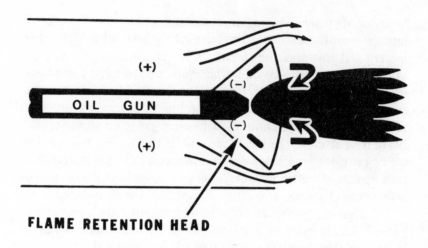

FLAME RETENTION HEAD

Figure 1-3

the gas fuel. There are some flame characteristics, however, which differ from the typical blue flame burner associated with domestic gas appliances, in that the flame is generally not as quiet, is more luminous (yellow) and vigorous.

The main advantage that improved oil combustion has presented is that the compaction of the flame volume makes it possible to reduce the overall size of the combustion space, namely the furnace. This in turn makes it possible to reduce the size of the pressure vessel itself. For example, an early burner where a typical oil firing rate and combustion air volume produced only a minute air pressure drop across the burner throat and a very lazy flame characteristic, required a furnace 20 feet long. A modern pressurized combustion system, firing at the same oil input rate but taking a high air pressure drop across the burner head, requires only a 7–foot–long furnace! Obviously, a shorter, wider pressure vessel design has come about as a result of this improvement in oil combustion. However, designers have traditionally considered it prudent to provide more furnace volume per unit fuel input with oil than with natural gas, inasmuch as it was felt extra time was needed to vaporize the liquid oil. Actually, gas is the slower burning of the two fuels and generally exhibits a larger flame volume per unit input. Nevertheless, gasification of the oil droplet must be complete before contact is made with relatively cool water-backed surfaces; otherwise the burning process will not go to completion, and smoke and soot formation result.

THE FUNDAMENTALS OF AUTOMATIC FUEL FIRING

Combustion of hydrocarbon fuels, like fuel oil and natural gas, is a steady-state reaction. That is, fuel and air enter the flame zone at a given rate, react with one another, and the products of their combustion leave the flame zone at the same rate, according to fixed laws. However, unlike natural gas, firing liquid fuel is a multistep *physical and chemical* process involving:

1. breaking down of oil into tiny droplets, called *atomizing;*
2. heating and vaporizing of these droplets, called *gasifying;*
3. mixing with air and actual firing, called *autoignition;*
4. formation of entirely new compounds that make up the products of combustion, called *dissociation.*

The process is further complicated by the role the discharge air pattern of the burner plays in relation to the shape of the oil mist after atomization has been accomplished. The latter, in turn, is related to fuel-atomizer or orifice geometry and cleanliness, as well as to the pressure, viscosity, and surface tension of the oil.

Air for automatic combustion processes is supplied mainly in two ways. *Primary air* is introduced through or with the fuel and *secondary air* is introduced to the flames issuing from the fuel. The gas burners employed in domestic heating appliances, for example, are generally of the nonluminous or blue-flame type. Some of the air required for combustion is aspirated, or drawn in, as primary air into a burner mixing tube by venturi action (see Figure 1-4) where it mixes with the gas prior to ignition at the burner ports. Since the primary air is seldom sufficient to support complete combustion, additional air—secondary air—is brought into the appliance and around the base

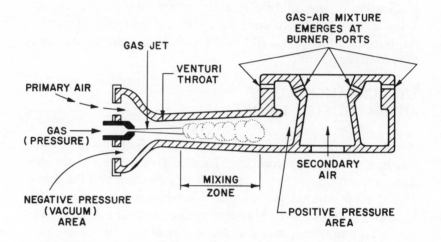

Figure 1-4. Atmospheric Gas Burner (courtesy American Gas Association)

of each separate burner flame by the expansion effect of the issuing mixture of gas and primary air, and by the natural draft created by the heat of the flames. These burners are characterized as atmospheric or natural-draft burners.

The combination burners discussed in this book are mechanical draft burners which are not solely dependent upon the heat of the flames and a chimney to create a draft. Mechanical-draft systems often create fuel-air pressures in the flame zone that are considerably higher than atmospheric.

Historically, mechanical draft has been used in a limited way, in conjunction with the draft induced by the chimney. The burner fan provided the force to move the air through the burner and the natural draft provided the force to move the products of combustion through the boiler flues and out the chimney. Even where a fan was installed on the exhaust stack or breeching between the boiler and the chimney, it was intended merely to induce secondary air into the combustion chamber and carry away the products of combustion. On the other hand, modern forced-draft boilers (more accurately called pressurized boilers) which, with their customized combustion systems are manufactured and assembled as *packaged units,* require only a vent to atmosphere for the combustion products. See Figure 1-5. Their combustion air–handling systems are designed both to move the air through the burner and provide the force to move the hot gases through the boiler and out the breeching without the aid of chimney draft.

The roles of fan, blower, and chimney in modern combustion systems are discussed in considerable detail later in the text. At this point it is important to recognize that no matter what method is used to bring combustion air into the flame zone, or what is the final furnace pressure at which the flame burns, it is the secondary air which supplied the momentum and most of the oxygen needed to mix the fuel and air in the combustion chamber of the combination burner. Flame–generated motion accounts for but a small share of the mixing process, whereas the jet–entrainment effect of converging fuel and air streams and the character of the resulting *interface* determine fineness of mixture. The process takes place, however, external to and downstream of the burner hardware. The fuel is aspirated

IRON FIREMAN PACKAGED STEAM BOILER
(GAS/OIL FIRED)

Figure 1-5. Dual-Fuel Packaged Boiler (courtesy Iron Fireman)

by the air stream, instead of the other way around as with the typical gas burner described in Figure 1-4. The flame thus produced is usually vortex–shaped and has a motion that may be roughly compared to a spinning pinwheel. The visible light emitted varies from sun–like brilliance when oil is burned to semi-luminous transparency when gas is burned.

The combination burner head is subjected to more heat when firing with gas than when firing with oil. This is due in part to the fact that the head is in intimate contact with the gas flame. The oil flame front, however, is specifically designed not to impinge on the metal burner parts and is stabilized farther downstream in the combustion space. The area between the burner head and the flame front is called the premixing and heating zone. It is especially crucial to the successful combustion of oil fuels. The oil droplet is vaporized in this zone. The faster this is accomplished, the smaller will be the physical distance between the flame front and the burner head. Compacting the flame volume up close to the burner head is the objective of good burner design, and is referred to as *flame retention* (see Figure 1-3).

Preparation of the gas fuels for combustion does not involve a change from their natural gaseous state. Therefore, introducing the correct amount of air and raising the temperature of the mixture to its ignition point is the main function of the gas burner. There is no vaporization of the fuel required since it is already a gas. Combustion takes place practically at the burner ports, as with the appliance burner. However, the amount of mixing of the air and gas that actually takes place before ignition largely determines the color of the resulting flame. Precombustion mixing of air and gas produces a blue flame. However, it will be seen that flame color has little to do with efficient gas combustion.

The ignition energy source for combination burners is supplied by a high–voltage electric spark. The high voltage is produced by a step–up transformer. Except in a few cases, the spark lights a small pilot burner whose fuel flow is controlled separately by a solenoid valve. The pilot flame then lights the main burner flame at the proper time in the burner starting sequence. The fuel commonly used for the pilot burner is either natural or propane gas, but occasionally light oil is used when the main burner fuel is also light oil.

In combination burners designed with fuel inputs under about two million Btuh, the pilot burner is sometimes omitted and the main burner is lighted directly by the electric spark. This usually necessitates one set of spark electrodes for the oil burner and another set for the gas burner. The same ignition transformer is used for both firing modes, however; and operating personnel must manually connect the high–voltage ignition wires from the transformer to the appropriate igniter, according to the fuel in use.

The conventional combination fuel burner uses the same gas–electric pilot burner to light either the oil or gas main burner flame. The air for the pilot burner is supplied from the main burner combustion air system and may have its own manually adjustable air volume control which can be regulated while the pilot is operating. Many combination burner pilot systems cannot be adjusted except when the complete system is off, because the main burner must be removed to gain access to the pilot burner. Then, too, often the pilot burner air is supplied from the main burner combustion air stream in such manner that adjustment of the main burner air damper also affects the pilot burner air flow.

2

Fundamentals of Fluid Flow

It has been stated previously that combustion of natural gas is comparatively straightforward inasmuch as little or no preparation of the fuel is necessary prior to its ignition. Furthermore, no elaborate fuel transport system is needed since gas is supplied to the customer's premises under pressure by the utility company. As a consequence, many more of the technical aspects of the satisfactory operation of the combination burner, especially in the gas mode, are grounded in the elementary physics of fluid–flow rather than in the complex chemistry of combustion.

Fuel pressure regulation, for example, is more crucial to the operation of the combination burner when gas rather than oil is fired. This is because a very narrow and precise pressure differential relationship must be maintained at the fuel–air interface. This area, at the leading edge of the flame zone just downstream of the burner head, is where stirring and heating of fuel and air take place. Furnace pressure is a dominant factor here, not only affecting how much pressure is needed to propel the gas fuel to the flame zone, but also the velocity needed for the successful entrainment of the fuel in the combustion–air vortex. In the case of petroleum, the pressure at which the liquid fuel is brought to the flame zone is governed by the method of droplet formation and the physical composition of the oil fuel.

Modern packaged boilers with combination fuel burners generally have pressurized combustion systems. That is, the furnace is under positive pressure relative to atmospheric pressure. Atmospheric pressure can be considered as the pressure of the air which surrounds and fills the boiler room. It is considered as zero gage pressure. Pressures above zero gage are called positive pressures, and below zero gage, negative or subatmospheric pressures. In combustion technology, where there are often deviations in air and gas pressures of less than one pound per square inch (1 psi) above or below zero gage, the units of measure are *inches of water column*, abbreviated *in. WC* or *in. H_2O*. Where liquids are subjected to subatmospheric pressures, the units of measure are *inches of mercury* (in. Hg), or simply stated as so many *inches of vacuum,* "of mercury" being implied. Table 2-1 illustrates the relationships of the various units of measure to one another.

Table 2-1. Common Pressure Conversion Units

in. WC X 0.557 = oz/sq in.	oz/sq in. X 1.732 = in. WC
in. WC X 0.0361 = psig	oz/sq in. X 0.0625 = psig
psig X 27.71 = in. WC	psig X 16 = oz/sq in.
psig X 0.49 = in. Hg	in. Hg X 2.016 = psig

Conversion of in. Hg to psig is seldom required in gas burner work but is performed regularly in sizing fuel oil piping for oil burners.

The pressurized packaged boiler's combustion air fan (or blower, as it is also called) must do double–duty. It must deliver the required volume of air to the flame zone for complete combustion of the fuel. At the same time, it must be capable of raising the pressure of that volume of air high enough to overcome the resistance of the boiler flue passages so that the products of combustion can be forced out the vent stack. The volume of combustion air which the burner system must deliver to the flame zone is determined mainly by the quantity of fuel being burned. The pressure of the combustion air, on the other hand, is primarily determined by pressure vessel design and secondarily by the configuration of the burner head.

In analyses of fluid motion in combination fuel burner systems, air and other gases as well as liquids, are treated as incompressible fluids. That is, when calculating such values as pressure losses in piping systems, flow rates, fuel–air mass velocities and the like, gases are treated as though they are liquids. The volume of a particular mass under consideration may be given as cubic feet, or it may be expressed in gallons or pounds. The technician should be able to convert from one unit of measure to another accordingly.

The rate of flow of liquid or gas (as it passes a given point in a flow system) is the product of its mass or volume per unit of time. An example of mass flow rate is gallons per minute (gpm). An example of volumetric flow rate is cubic feet per hour (cfh).

SOME FACTORS AFFECTING
FURNACE PRESSURE

In any given boiler, operating furnace pressure varies approximately as the square of the firing rate. The length and area of the flue gas passages and the changes in direction which the gases make in traveling through the boiler also affect furnace pressure (see Figure 2-1 with explanation). According to boiler design and firing rate, furnace pressure can vary from a few hundredths of an inch to several inches of water column. Comparing three steel tubular boilers of different design which contain the same heating surface area and are fired at the same input rate, demonstrates the effect the number of fire tubes and a more circuitous flue gas path has on furnace pressure (see Table 2-2).

Generally, furnace pressure increases as boiler capacity increases. At several size increments, however, where the pressure vessel diameter does not change but the number of tubes is increased, the operating pressure may actually be somewhat lower. Nevertheless, the furnace pressure has a direct bearing on the pressure to which the gas fuel must be subjected before it comes to the flame zone. Gas pressure must be higher than the maximum furnace operating pressure in order for the gas to exit the burner ports. In any flow system, a pressure difference must exist between its entrance and exit points sufficient to overcome the frictional resistance of the system itself.

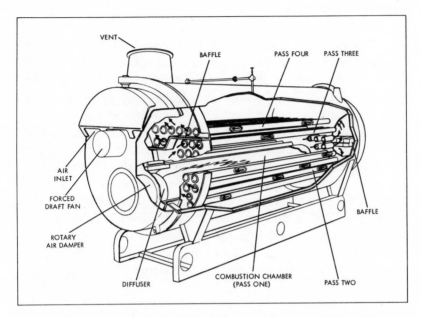

VENT

BAFFLE

PASS FOUR

PASS THREE

AIR
INLET

FORCED
DRAFT FAN

BAFFLE

ROTARY
AIR DAMPER

DIFFUSER

COMBUSTION CHAMBER
(PASS ONE)

PASS TWO

THE FOUR PASS CONSTRUCTION OF A TYPICAL CB GENERATOR

Combustion air enters through the air inlet. The Forced Draft Fan forces air through the Rotary Air Damper and the Diffuser into the Combustion Chamber. The Main Fire Tube or Combustion Chamber, constitutes Pass One. Baffling allows gases to pass to the front of the Generator only through Pass Two; here a baffle allows gases to pass to the rear of the Generator only through Pass Three. From the rear the gases are forced through Pass Four to the vent.

Figure 2-1. Four Pass Design (courtesy Cleaver-Brooks)

Table 2-2. Three Types of Tubular Boilers Compared*
(Each with 1072 sq ft heating surface, 5.5 sq ft/BHP)

Boiler Type	Furnace Pressure, in. WC
Firebox	0.38
2–pass Scotch w/2½ in. tubes	0.12
3–pass Scotch w/3 in. tubes	0.83

*Adapted by the author from data supplied by Dunham–Bush Inc.

THE GAS TRAIN

The gas pipe, valves, and fittings installed on the packaged boiler–burner unit at the factory are collectively referred to as the gas train. Figure 2-2 shows a gas train with the various components labeled for identification. Depending upon the insurance company or other agency requirements at the particular boiler destination, a number of extra safety features may be added to the gas train at the time of assembly at the factory. An additional main gas cock or an additional motorized shut-off valve are examples of extra safety features, as are dual gas pilot valves, vent valves, test cocks and pressure switches. A very important item is the pressure reducing and regulating valve (PRV); see Figure 2-3. It is the function of the PRV to hold a predetermined pressure at the entrance to the gas train over a wide range of gas–supply pressures and burner–demand rates.

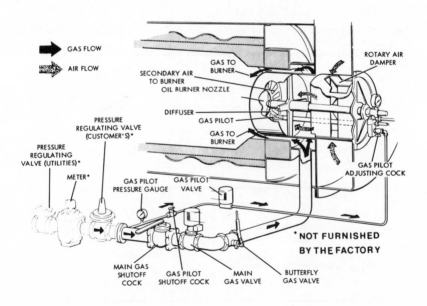

Figure 2-2. Standard Gas Train (courtesy Cleaver-Brooks)

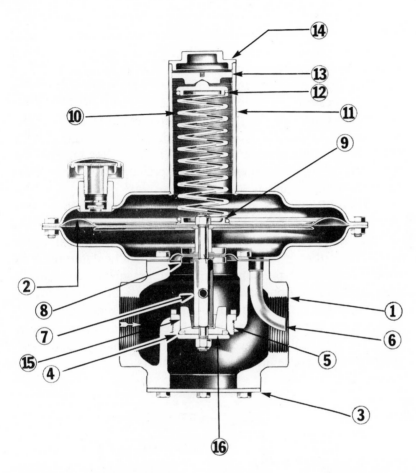

KEY NO.	PART NAME	KEY NO.	PART NAME
1	VALVE BODY	9	LOWER SPRING SEAT
2	MAIN DIAPHRAGM	10	SPRING
3	BOTTOM FLANGE	11	SPRING STACK
4	O-RING	12	UPPER SPRING SEAT
5	SEAT RING	13	ADJUSTING SCREW
6	PITOT (SENSING)TUBE	14	CLOSING CAP
7	VALVE STEM	15	VALVE GUIDE
8	SEAL DIAPHRAGM HEAD	16	VALVE PLUG

Figure 2-3. Gas Pressure Regulating Valve
(courtesy Fisher Controls Company)

Just as a banker is a middleman between the money supply and the borrower, so can the gas pressure regulator be considered a kind of middleman between fuel supply and burner. It actually engages in a borrowing and lending process, and even becomes overdrawn at times. In order to maintain a relatively constant pressure at the entrance to the gas train, the PRV must borrow pressure from the gas service line connected to its inlet and lend it to the gas train. At the proper time it must make collection and repayment to the lender. The following brief explanation of the components of total pressure will demonstrate the basis for this analogy.

Total pressure is the combination of *static* and *velocity* pressure, and is expressed in the same units. It is an important and useful concept because it is easy to determine, and although velocity is not easy to measure directly, it can be determined by subtracting static pressure from total pressure. The subtraction need not be done mathematically; it can be done automatically with the instrument hook-up shown in Figure 2-4 which shows a Dwyer pitot tube (pronounced pee-tow) and manometer. The pitot tube arrangement shown is primarily used to calibrate other pressure measuring instruments.

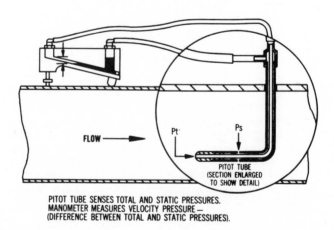

PITOT TUBE SENSES TOTAL AND STATIC PRESSURES.
MANOMETER MEASURES VELOCITY PRESSURE —
(DIFFERENCE BETWEEN TOTAL AND STATIC PRESSURES).

Figure 2-4. Standard Pitot Tube (courtesy Dwyer Instruments, Inc.)

In a flow system, such as a gas train or burner combustion-air delivery system, static pressure (SP) is the pressure against the inside walls of the pipe, as the pressure of air in a balloon. Velocity pressure (VP) is pressure due to flow, as one feels when the wind blows.

In practice, when the fuel rate controller drives the butter-fly valve toward open, SP in the gas train begins to decrease as the VP (fuel flow) increases. Reduction in SP is sensed by the pitot tube built into the PRV (Figure 2-4) and transmitted to the lower diaphragm case. This upsets the balance that existed between the tension of the spring on one side of the diaphragm and the *regulated* gas pressure on the other, so that the valve moves toward open. With the help of additional pressure thus admitted (or borrowed, if you will) from the upstream service pressure, action of the spring is once more counterbalanced at the new valve position. Each new demand for more gas velocity by the butterfly valve causes a further momentary imbalance which would lower the static pressure in the gas train, were it not for the fact that *simultaneously* more pressure is borrowed from the service line as the regulating valve drives farther open. Ideally, what we have is high *velocity pressure* without having sacrificed the *static pressure* we started with. As a result, the *total pressure* in the gas train often approximates two or more times the measured static pressure at maximum flow rate.

As the fuel rate controller returns the burner to low-fire position, the butterfly valve begins to throttle against the force developed by the total pressure of the gas acting upon it. It is important to understand that the pressure observed on a direct-reading gage or manometer attached to the gas train is static pressure, and is only part of the total pressure inside the gas piping. Only when flow is completely stopped or *locked-up* do the total pressure and static pressure have the same value.

When the butterfly begins throttling, it is in effect *convert-ing* the velocity pressure of the flow back to static pressure. As a result, the gage reading rises. The static pressure upstream of the butterfly is increasing while the static pressure downstream of the butterfly is decreasing, so that we say the *differential* pressure across the valve is increasing. Stated still another way, the *pressure drop* across the valve is increasing.

There is no convenient way in the field to measure the total pressure in a gas line while gas is flowing. One can get a pretty good idea what it is, however, by causing a sudden shut-down of the burner, and observing the locked-up pressure on the gage. Because the test would blow the water right out of a simple *U-tube manometer,* the use of a conventional pressure gage with a 0–15 psi scale is recommended. A typical 400 horsepower boiler with an input rate of 14,500 cfh, requiring a net regulated pressure of 14 in. WC at the entrance to the gas train, might lock-up at 2 psi (55.4 in. WC) or more under emergency fuel cut-off conditions. This is the kind of total pressure the PRV must handle during turn-down from high to low-fire fuel input rate.

During return of the butterfly valve to the low-fire position, buildup of static pressure under the diaphragm of the PRV begins to lift it against the spring tension. As the diaphragm inflates under the influence of the increased *backpressure* caused by the disc in the butterfly valve, the valve plug to which the diaphragm is connected reduces the area of the port in the PRV through which the high-pressure gas supply has been entering the gas train from the service line. Each movement of the butterfly toward low-fire results in a corresponding movement of the valve plug in the PRV, thus converting more velocity pressure to static pressure. As the static pressure thus regained is added to the total pressure in the gas train, a like amount is repaid by the throttling action of the PRV to the upstream service pressure. The net effect is to keep the static pressure at the entrance to the train relatively constant while the velocity pressure in the train goes from one extreme to the other.

Repayment to the service line of all velocity pressure by stopping flow completes the regulator action. However, the butterfly valve is not designed for tight closing, and actual cutoff of fuel flow is done by an electric shutoff valve. For that reason, some velocity pressure will convert to static pressure at time of lockup, therefore it is advisable to adjust the firing rate controller so that it is in low-fire mode when the heating load demand is satisfied. That way there will be no sudden release of high pressure when the burner begins another firing cycle.

3

Pressure Losses and Gas Pipe Sizing

In a flow system, pressure loss due to friction is usually expressed in one of two ways: in units of pressure or, in the case of piping systems, in Equivalent Feet of Pipe (EFP). In the latter case, the pressure loss through valves and fittings is expressed in terms of the length of pipe of the same nominal pipe size that creates the same friction loss. Table 3-1 lists the equivalent resistances of commonly used valves and fittings. The table can be used for sizing oil and gas piping systems providing the characteristics of the specific fuel are taken into consideration.

The size of the gas main from the meter set to the contractor's connection point on the boiler gas train (often referred to by utility people as the *house line,* to differentiate it from their piping which they call *mains)* is crucial to the satisfactory operation of a variable input burner; all the more so if, due to physical limitations or code restrictions, for instance, the gas pressure that is available at the outlet of the meter is marginal; that is, available pressure is only slightly higher than the pressure specified by the manufacturer of the gas burner. In anticipation of such conditions, the respective locations of meter and boiler should have been determined early in the job–planning stage, so that interconnecting piping and flow–control components were sized, specified, and laid out accordingly.

Subsequent deviations from the piping plan during installation, necessitated by unforeseen circumstances, are sometimes made without due consideration to the effect these changes have

**Table 3-1. Equivalent Feet of Valves and Fittings
(courtesy Iron Fireman, Division Dunham–Bush, Inc.)**

EQUIVALENT RESISTANCE OF FITTINGS

NOMINAL PIPE SIZE INCHES	LENGTH STRAIGHT PIPE IN FEET							
	SCREWED FITTINGS				VALVES		90° WELD ELLS	
	45° ELL	90° ELL	TEE ANGLE FLOW	TEE STRAIGHT FLOW	GATE	GLOBE	RADIUS = DIA.	RADIUS = 2 DIA.
$1\frac{1}{4}$	1.61	3.45	6.90	2.30	0.81	38.3	1.84	1.03
$1\frac{1}{2}$	1.88	4.02	8.04	2.64	0.94	44.7	2.14	1.21
2	2.41	5.17	10.3	3.44	1.21	57.4	2.76	1.55
$2\frac{1}{2}$	2.88	6.16	12.3	4.15	1.44	68.5	3.29	1.85
3	3.58	7.67	15.3	5.00	1.79	85.2	4.09	2.30
4	4.70	10.1	20.2	6.73	2.35	112	5.37	3.02
5	5.88	12.6	25.2	8.30	2.94	140	6.72	3.79
6	7.07	15.2	30.4	10.1	3.54	168	8.09	4.55

on fuel-flow regulation at the burner. Extra pipe and fittings used for a more circuitous route around an obstruction, or to a more distant meter location than originally planned, can cause burner operating difficulties when the allowable pressure drop for the circuit was calculated to be only a few ounces.

Problems are most apt to be encountered on so-called low-pressure gas applications where, for one reason or another, maximum service pressure available is on the order of 6–8 in. WC, which is the nominal pressure supplied by utilities for residential heating, cooking, and water heating. Regardless of the cubic foot per hour capacity of the gas service line, the *available pressure* at the meter obviously places a limit on the size of the forced draft boiler it can accommodate. For as we have seen, the boiler's furnace design pressure resists the flow of gas to the combustion zone, as does the gas pipe and fittings used to get it there.

Except for the gas pressure supplied for residential use, there is no standard establishing "available gas pressure" for large burner installations. By "large burner," we refer to a burner that operates with a furnace pressure in excess of 3 in. WC or an atmospheric burner whose fuel consumption rate exceeds the capabilities of the utility service line in a given locality. Therefore, in most commercial applications, the gas company makes available service pressures in an intermediate range of from one-half to 5 psi, judging each service application on its own merit.

It is important to recognize that the difference between available pressure at the meter and *minimum net regulated pressure* at the entrance to the gas train, is the *maximum* allowable pressure drop for the house line. The sum of all the friction factors that combine to resist the flow of gas—the pipe, the elbows, the tees, the shut-off cocks, and regulating valves—must not exceed this figure. The smaller this differential pressure, the more carefully the house line must be sized, and the more diligently the piping plan followed. See Figure 3-1.

In the case of the packaged boiler–burner unit, the "net regulated" gas pressure required at the entrance to the gas train is specified by the manufacturer. He has taken into consideration the resistance of the valves and fittings on the gas train

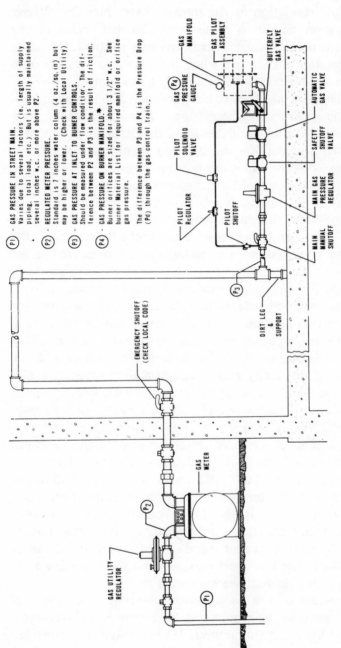

TYPICAL GAS PIPING INSTALLATION

*MANIFOLD PRESSURE DEPENDS ON BURNER MAKE AND MODEL

Figure 3-1. (Courtesy Peabody Gordon–Piatt)

and the pressure against which the gas must be delivered to the flame zone. However, unless the manufacturer has been informed in advance of boiler shipment what the available gas pressure is, he might opt to leave selection of the PRV to the installer. The necessity for a properly sized and installed PRV at the boiler between the gas train and the house line cannot be overemphasized.

HOW TO CHECK GAS LINE SIZING

In order to know the capacity of a particular gas line, the technician needs to determine the following:

1. The gas pressure available at the meter outlet or at the start of the main to be sized.
2. The maximum gas flow rate in cfh needed for the burner.
3. The gas pressure required at the inlet to the burner manufacturer's gas piping.
4. The heating value and specific gravity of the gas in use.
5. The length of the main to be sized.
6. The number and type of fittings used in the main: Ls, Ts, valves, etc.

A typical pipe sizing problem might work out like this:

Required input: 1,645,000 Btuh
Gas (natural): 0.70 specific gravity, 1100 Btu/cu ft
Main: 2–in. pipe, 110 ft long with six 90° Ls and two side
        outlet Ts
Pressure required at the burner piping: 6 in. WC
Solution:

The gas flow rate required is

$$\frac{1,645,000 \text{ Btu/hr}}{1100 \text{ Btu/cu ft}} = 1,495 \text{ cu ft/hr}$$

The equivalent length of the fittings, from Table 3-1:

6 Ls @ 5.17 ft	31 ft	
2 Ts @ 10.3 ft	20.6 ft	
Equivalent length for fittings	51.6 ft	

Actual length of main   110   ft
Total equivalent length of main 161.6 ft
                                            (Call it 162 ft.)

Where the initial line pressure is 7 in. WC and the pressure required at the burner is 6 in. WC, a difference of 1 in. is available for friction loss in the piping and pressure regulation.

Referring to Table 3-2, the quantity of gas that can be carried through various lengths and diameters of pipe is listed for two pressure drops, 0.5 in. and 1 in. The table shows that with 1 in. pressure drop, the 2-in. pipe will carry only 1370 cu ft/hr for 150 ft or 1270 cu ft/hr for 175 ft. The 2-in. pipe, therefore, is too small for the 1495 cu ft/hr required.

Making a similar calculation for the next larger size pipe, 2½ in., the total equivalent length of the main would work out to 172 feet, and the capacity of the larger pipe, referring again to Table 3-2 would be 2082 cu ft/hr for 175 ft; adequate for the assumed conditions in the example.

The table does not show the actual pressure drop for the pipe size and flow rate used in the example, merely indicating that the 2½-in. pipe size will result in less than the 1-in. allowable pressure drop. If the actual pressure drop is required, the value can be calculated from the data in the table. The pressure drop increases or decreases with the square of the flow rate and directly with the pipe length. Thus, if the pressure drop is 1-in. WC at 2082 cu ft/hr and 175 ft (from the table), the drop at 1495 cu ft/hr and 172 ft (from the example) would be:

$$\left(\frac{1495}{2082}\right)^2 \times \frac{172}{175} \times 1.0 = 0.5\text{-in. WC}$$

Where fuel gases other than natural are used, specific gravities and heating values can be approximated from Table 3-3. The multipliers obtained in Table 3-3 can then be applied to Table 3-1. Tables 3-4 and 3-5 are for use with other design pressure losses and equivalent lengths of the main.

On commercial and industrial installations where the gas pressure is available in the street, so to speak, and utility company policy permits, the house line might be sized for some intermediate pressure, in the range of ½–5 psig. The higher

Table 3-2. Gas Pipe Sizing
(courtesy Iron Fireman, Division Dunham–Bush, Inc.)

GAS PIPE SIZING — INITIAL PRESSURE UNDER 1 PSI

CUBIC FEET PER HOUR - 0.6 SPECIFIC GRAVITY

PIPE SIZE IN.	PRESSURE DROP "WC	TOTAL EQUIVALENT LENGTH OF PIPE, FEET											
		40	50	60	70	80	90	100	125	150	175	200	250
1¼	.5	598	535	490	453	423	399	380	339	309	286	268	240
1¼	1.0	847	760	691	642	598	565	535	480	438	405	380	339
1½	.5	928	832	760	703	657	620	588	525	480	445	416	322
1½	1.0	1312	1175	1070	993	927	878	833	743	678	630	588	525
2	.5	1875	1680	1530	1420	1330	1250	1188	1062	969	897	839	749
2	1.0	2650	2375	2165	2005	1875	1770	1680	1500	1370	1270	1188	1062
2½	.5	3080	2750	2515	2335	2180	2050	1950	1740	1585	1475	1378	1230
2½	1.0	4350	3900	3545	3290	3075	2905	2755	2460	2250	2082	1950	1740
3	.5	5590	4900	4680	4230	3960	3740	3545	3175	2895	2680	2510	2240
3	1.0	7920	7100	6470	5990	5600	5290	5010	4480	4090	3790	3545	3175
4	.5	11720	10500	9600	8870	8280	7810	7430	6650	5950	5620	5240	4700
4	1.0	16600	14820	13530	12520	11700	11040	10500	9360	8560	7930	7430	6650
6	.5	34800	32200	27250	26250	24600	23100	22100	19430	17390	16640	15570	13920
6	1.0	49150	44100	40200	36950	34800	32800	31200	27850	25400	23550	22050	19700

Table 3-3

CFH MULTIPLIERS FOR OTHER SPECIFIC GRAVITIES

SPECIFIC GRAVITY	.40	.50	.60	.70	.80	.90	1.00	1.20	1.40	1.60	1.80	2.00
MULTIPLIER	1.23	1.10	1.00	.926	.867	.817	.775	.707	.655	.612	.577	.547

Table 3-4

CFH FOR 10% PRESSURE DROP, 100 FEET LENGTH, 0.6 SPECIFIC GRAVITY

INITIAL PRESSURE PSI	PRESSURE DROP " WC	PIPE SIZE, INCHES				
		1¼	1½	2	2½	3
1	2.8	1090	1650	3210	5180	9260
2	5.6	1590	2410	4700	7580	13540
5	14	2740	4140	8070	13010	23240
10	28	4330	6530	12720	20500	36610

Table 3-5

CFH FACTORS FOR OTHER LENGTHS

EQUIVALENT LENGTH, FT.	50	75	100	125	150	175	300
FACTOR	1.414	1.152	1.00	0.895	0.815	0.755	0.707

(courtesy Iron Fireman, Division of Dunham–Bush, Inc.)

available pressure enables the designer to take advantage of certain economies offered by reduced pipe sizes, which can be considerable. For example, if careful engineering and installation can avoid the use of pipe sizes 3 inches and larger, there are significant savings to be had in fabrication, erection, and suspension costs on the basis of the weight of the pipe alone. Furthermore, it is considered sound engineering practice to design for up to 10 percent pressure drop per 100 feet of the house line when the available gas pressure is more than one pound.

4

Valve Capacities and
Flow Measurements

The resistance or friction loss of the valves and fittings on the gas train of an approved (by code or insurance company) large boiler can be 40 or more inches. The manner in which the various valves are rated and cataloged by the manufacturers is considerably more sophisticated compared to the way pipe sizes are determined. Friction loss is expressed in gallons per minute, whether the valve is intended for use on liquids or gases and, by convention, most manufacturers suscribe to this rating method.

Valve Coefficient, (C_V, and spoken C sub V), is determined by testing, and represents the rate of flow in gpm of 60° F water through the valve, when the downstream pressure is one psi lower than the upstream pressure. A valve restricted (or ported), which passes one gpm of liquid with a specific gravity of one (water) with an accompanying pressure drop of one psi is assigned a rating of C_V=1. Similarly, a valve with a C_V=2 has twice the flow capacity with the same pressure drop.

Table 4-1 was compiled by the author from data supplied by the manufacturers of several electrically–operated gas shut-off valves commonly found in the field. Selection and application of these valves is done on the basis of their flow capacities in terms of valve coefficients (C_V). The fact that the coefficient was determined with water as the medium is of no consequence.

Table 4-1. Composite Table of Valve Coefficients (C_V)

| Valve body pipe size | Honeywell | | ITT Hydramotor | | | Maxon | General ITT |
	V5055	V48	H117	H118	V710	5000	S251
1¼	26	39	51	25	28	44	34
1½	31	44	75	35	34	53	37
2	67	77	151	67	70	86	80
2½	79	94	244	86	85	127	110
3	97	103	320	125	104	173	135
4	189	NA	510	168	NA	551	NA

Manufacturer and Model

Although the manufacturer rates his valve while maintaining a constant pressure drop across it, in live fire situations the pressure drop is an elusive variable. Pressure drop across any valve depends in part on the flow rate of the fluid and the free area of the valve port. Free area is the space between the valve orifice (port), which is stationary, and the valve plug or disc, which is movable. In the case of the pressure reducing valve, free area is varied according to the position of the plug in relation to the seat or port, as the diaphragm operator moves the plug up or down.

The relationship between velocity (V) and pressure drop (PD), is a proportion which changes when either the velocity or pressure drop varies, as follows:

$$\frac{PD_1}{PD_2} = \left(\frac{V_1}{V_2}\right)^2$$

where PD_1 is the original pressure drop across the valve, and PD_2 is the pressure drop after a change in flow rate. V_1 is the original fluid velocity, and V_2 is the velocity after altering the pressure drop across the valve. Thus we say that the pressure drop across a valve or orifice, or through a flow tube, varies as the square of the velocity.

Example problem: From a manufacturer's specification sheet we see that a given motorized gas valve is rated to pass 6095 cfh of natural gas with a 1–inch pressure drop. How much gas will the valve pass when the pressure drop due to increased flow is 3 in. WC?

Solution:

$$\frac{PD_1}{PD_2} = \left(\frac{V_1}{V_2}\right)^2$$

$$\frac{1}{3} = \left(\frac{6095}{V_2}\right)^2$$

$$\sqrt{\frac{1}{3}} = \frac{6095}{V_2}$$

$$.5773 = \frac{6095}{V_2}$$

$$V_2 = \frac{6095}{.5773}$$

$$V_2 = 10,558 \text{ cfh}$$

The net regulated pressure required at the entrance to a given gas train is the sum of the friction losses of the hardware and furnace pressure. Generally, the higher the fuel input rate the higher the required gas pressure. Although furnace pressure increases approximately as the square of the firing rate, the resistance of the fuel shutoff valve or valves accounts for most of the pressure loss through the fuel delivery system. For example, a 700–horsepower Cleaver–Brooks packaged boiler requires 41.5 in. wc gas pressure at the entrance to a 4–inch gas train with two model H118 General ITT Hydramotor gas valves.

Figure 4-1 illustrates the relationship between the pressure drop across typical valves for various flow rates and C_V factors. The graph is an abridgement by the author of a flow chart for compressible fluids supplied by General ITT. To illustrate its use, let us calculate the pressure drop through the two fuel valves on the gas train of the boiler described above, where the maximum fuel demand rate is 29,300 cfh of natural gas.

According to Table 4-1, a 4–inch model H118 Hydramotor has a C_V factor of 168, and to determine what the pressure drop would be across it at rated flow, we enter the graph at the right margin at just under 30,000 cfh, move horizontally left to the C_V 168 diagonal line, then vertically to the .70 specific gravity line (natural gas), then horizontally to the low–pressure gas diagonal, and vertically to locate the pressure drop at approximately 10 in. WC. Since the gas train has two main fuel valves, the total friction loss on this account is 20 inches.

Figure 4-2 is a graphical representation of the data offered in the pipe sizing tables of the previous chapter and is useful for quick approximations. For example, if the gas train we are considering is 10 feet long and has three 90–degree elbows, from Table 3-1 in the previous chapter we see that each 4–inch elbow is equivalent to 10 feet of straight pipe, therefore the equivalent length of the train is 40 feet, disregarding the resistance of the

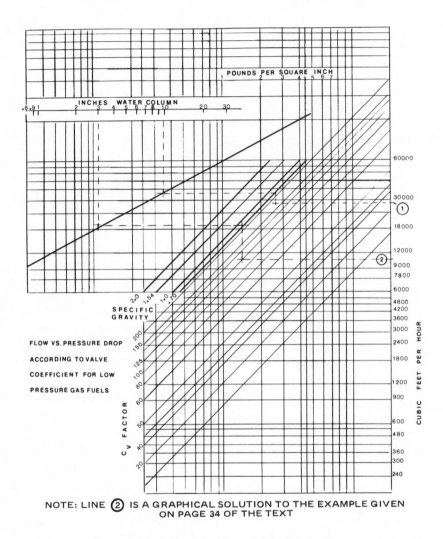

NOTE: LINE ② IS A GRAPHICAL SOLUTION TO THE EXAMPLE GIVEN
ON PAGE 34 OF THE TEXT

Figure 4-1. Flow Chart, Valve Coefficients

gage–tees and butterfly valve (in the open position). Entering
the top of the graph at approximately 30,000 cfh, move vertically to the intersection of the 4–inch pipe diagonal line, then
horizontally to the diagonal representing 40 equivalent feet of
pipe, then vertically to 2.5 inches which is the approximate
friction loss of the gas train pipe and fittings. Adding this figure

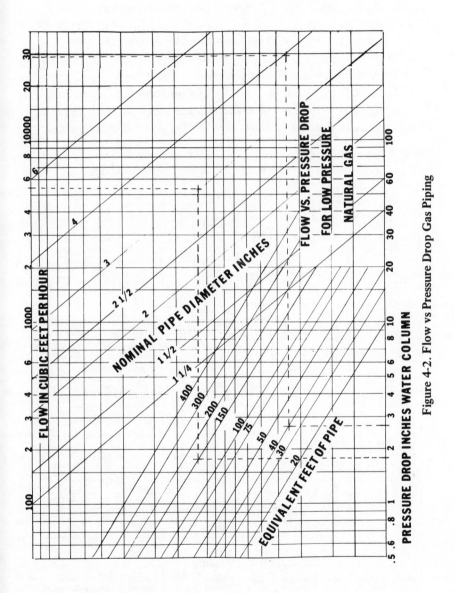

Figure 4-2. Flow vs Pressure Drop Gas Piping

to the 20 inches pressure drop through the shutoff valves, 22.5 in. WC is the total friction loss of the gas train at rated flow. Deducting this from 41.5 in. WC specified by the manufacturer as minimum net regulated pressure at the entrance to the gas train leaves 19 in. WC available to overcome the friction loss of the burner annulus and furnace pressure.

Table 4-2 emphasizes the effect of undersizing and oversizing the gas train on the net regulated gas pressure required for Cleaver–Brooks firetube boilers sizes 50 through 700 horsepower.

Table 4-2. Under- and Oversized FIA Gas Trains *(Pipe Size and Pressure Required in Inches WC)* **Model CB Boilers 50–700 HP.**

	50		60		70		80		100A	
	Pipe Size Inches	Pressure Required	Pipe Size Inches	Pressure Required	Pipe Size Inches	Pressure Required	Pipe Size Inches	Pressure Required	Pipe Size Inches	Pressure Required
	1¼	26.5	1¼	35.5	1¼	48.5	1¼		1½	38.0
	1½	11.5	1½	15.5	1½	21.5	1½	25.5	2	16.0
STD	2	5.5	2	6.5	2	9.5	2	10.5	2½	10.0
	2½	5.0	2½	6.0	2½	9.0	2½	9.5	3	8.5
					3	8.0	3	8.5		

	100S		100		125A		125		150	
	Pipe Size Inches	Pressure Required	Pipe Size Inches	Pressure Required	Pipe Size Inches	Pressure Required	Pipe Size Inches	Pressure Required	Pipe Size Inches	Pressure Required
	1½	38.5	1½	37.0	1½	50.5	1½	49.0	1½	
	2	16.5	2	16.0	2	18.5	2	17.0	2	22.0
STD	2½	10.5	2½	10.0	2½	12.0	2½	10.5	3+	12.0
	3	9.0	3	8.5	3	10.0	3	8.0	3	9.0

	150S		175S		200		250		300	
	Pipe Size Inches	Pressure Required	Pipe Size Inches	Pressure Required	Pipe Size Inches	Pressure Required	Pipe Size Inches	Pressure Required	Pipe Size Inches	Pressure Required
	1½		1½		2	39.0	2	50.0	2	
	2	25.0	2	29.0	2½	27.0	2½	31.0	2½	44.5
STD	3+	15.0	3+	19.0	3	17.5	3	17.0	4‡	18.5
	3	12.0	3	16.0	4	14.0	4	12.0	4	14.0

	350		400		500		600		700	
	Pipe Size Inches	Pressure Required	Pipe Size Inches	Pressure Required	Pipe Size Inches	Pressure Required	Pipe Size Inches	Pressure Required	Pipe Size Inches	Pressure Required
	2½		2½							
	3	33.5	3	35.5	3	56.0	3			
STD	4	18.0	4	14.0	4	22.5	4	29.5	4	41.5
	5	14.5	5	10.5	5	15.5	5	20.5	5	34.5

+ 3" Pipe & Plug valve with 2-1/2" Hydramotor   ‡ 4" Pipe & Plug valve with 3" Hydramotor

5

PRV Selection and Performance

Checking the flow performance of a PRV is a matter of measuring the static pressure drop across the valve. Although some PRVs have gage ports in the body of the valve for this purpose, readings taken in test tees if they have been installed several pipe diameters upstream and downstream of the valve, will be more accurate. A test run of the burner should indicate whether the PRV is maintaining the desired outlet pressure. The downstream gage reading should not vary more than a few tenths of an inch WC from design pressure as the burner goes from minimum to maximum input and vice versa. On the other hand, the upstream gage pressure reading might vary significantly depending on the friction loss factor of the house line and the pressure drop allowance built into it (as previously discussed). As long as the lowest upstream pressure observed at maximum fuel–input rate is twice the net regulated gas pressure there should be no flow problem on account of the house line. However if the downstream pressure falls off as the burner goes to maximum input a problem with the PRV is indicated. It is not maintaining the static pressure required for the gas train. If the upstream pressure falls so that there is less than a two–to–one differential across the PRV and the downstream pressure falls also, it may well be that the PRV has been improperly selected or misapplied. By that is meant the valve is being expected to perform at other than design conditions; actual operating conditions are beyond the range of satisfactory valve performance.

The range of reduced pressures of which a PRV is capable is determined by inlet pressure, flow rate, and the pressure required at the burner gas train. On a given application, only a narrow segment is used of the outlet pressure range of the PRV. A typical PRV, for example, has a total outlet or reduced pressure range of 2–30 in. WC selectable in six increments made possible by the substitution of as many springs of different stiffness and length, as follows:

Table 5-1. Pressure Regulating Valve Spring Selection
(courtesy Maxitrol)

Spring Number	Range (in. wc)	Color Code
Standard	2 to 5	Cadmium plated
SO 1	3 to 8	Orange
SO 2	5 to 15	Tagged
HO 1	4 to 12	Blue
HO 2	10 to 22	Red
HO 3	15 to 30	Yellow

The length of the spring and its stiffness determines the position of the plug or valve relative to the valve seat. The mechanical movement or stroke of the valve from full open to closed is quite small. In the case of brands and sizes of PRVs commonly encountered in the field, the stroke is less than an inch.

Adjusting the outlet pressure within the range of the spring is done by turning in or out on the adjusting screw at the top of the spring stack. (See Figure 2-3, page 19.)

Referring to the valve depicted in Table 5-1, let us assume that an SO 1 spring with a range of 3 to 8 in. WC is installed in the PRV and set to maintain 5 in. WC outlet pressure. For the sake of illustration, let us say we can see through the valve body and observe the valve functioning at the one–quarter open position. Substituting an HO 2 spring, which has a range of 10 to 22 in. WC, and setting the adjusting screw with the same number of turns into the spring stack, might cause the valve to function approximately three–quarters open. Valve movement and spring tension are directly related to diaphragm action, because all three parts (valve plug, diaphragm, and spring) are mechanically

linked. Since the diaphragm inflates and deflates in direct relationship to downstream pressure, valve position is directly related to regulated or outlet pressure. The spring tension works
to open the valve and the downstream pressure on the under-
side of the diaphragm works to close the valve. The downstream
pressure, therefore, balances the spring tension. A weaker
spring results in a lower outlet pressure, and a stronger spring a
higher pressure. Similarly, turning clockwise on the spring adjusting screw compresses the spring, increasing the tension on
the diaphragm, raising the outlet pressure. Counterclockwise
adjustment on the screw relaxes spring tension, allowing the
valve to operate more closed,
lowering the outlet pressure.

Table 5-2 represents the
pressure drop/capacity of three
sizes Maxitrol 210D series PR
valves (Figure 5-1). The left column of Table 5-2 is the capacity in cfh of the various valves.
Horizontally are given the pressure drops across the 1–, 1¼–,
and 1½–inch size valves for each
flow rate. These pressure drops
occur with the valves fully
open (ported). A properly sized
and installed PRV seldom operates fully ported. If it did it
wouldn't be regulating. Recall
that at the beginning of the
chapter it was stated that it is
the function of the PRV to reduce and regulate pressure.

The first step in sizing a
PRV is to consider the pressure
reduction it must perform.
When the reduction must be
made from pounds to inches,
convert psi to in. WC. If a given

Table 5-2

PRESSURE DROP CAPACITY CFH – 0.64 sp. gr. gas			
CAPACITY	PRESSURE DROP (IN. W.C.)		
	1"	1-1/4"	1-1/2"
500	0.31	0.21	0.17
1,000	1.24	0.83	0.70
1,500	2.78	1.86	1.56
2,000	4.93	3.30	2.78
2,500	7.70	5.17	4.35
3,000	11.10	7.42	6.25
3,500	15.10	10.10	8.50
4,000	19.70	13.20	11.10
4,500	24.90	16.80	14.10
5,000	30.80	20.70	17.40
5,500	37.00	25.00	21.00
6,000	44.20	29.70	25.00
6,500	52.00	35.00	29.40
7,000	60.20	40.60	34.00
7,500	69.00	46.60	39.00
8,000	78.50	53.00	44.50
8,500	88.80	59.80	50.20
9,000	99.50	67.00	56.30
9,500		74.80	62.80
10,000		82.80	69.50
11,000		100.00	84.00
12,000			100.00

Figure 5-1. Maxitrol 210 Series PRV (courtesy Maxitrol)

installation requires 12 in. WC at the entrance to the gas train and the service pressure is one psi, for instance, the differential pressure (inlet pressure minus outlet pressure) is 15.71 in. WC. (One psi equals 27.71 in. WC, from Table 2-1, minus 12 inches equals 15.71 in. WC.)

The next consideration is the fuel flow rate at full burner input. Let us state it as 3,000 cfh for this example. Entering Table 5-2 at 3,000 cfh, we must select the one valve best suited for the application. Not only from a cost standpoint, but from a control standpoint oversizing is to be avoided. An oversized valve will not control smoothly under low flow conditions (it has a tendency to hunt). An undersized valve, of course, cannot pass sufficient gas to satisfy maximum burner demand and will not hold design static pressure at the gas train entrance.

Of the total desired pressure differential, it is good practice to take 70% of the drop through reduction and 30% through regulation, especially when the differential pressure is more than 1 psi. By that is meant that the inherent characteristics of the particular valve which have to do with its natural resistance to flow, should be made to account for more than half of the pressure drop required at rated flow. Example: In the problem under discussion, 70% of the differential pressure is 10.99, call it 11 in. WC, and we should choose a PRV with a fully ported pressure drop close to this value. The remainder of the pressure drop will be accomplished by the throttling action of the valve plug, in response to downstream pressure and will account for the other 30% without loss of control.

Table 5-2 indicates that the model 210D 1-inch PRV has a pressure drop of 11.10 in. WC at 3,000 cfh, and is the better choice of the three valves shown. Double checking our selection in Table 5-3 confirms we have the right valve for the job.

In an application where the differential pressure is less than one psi, the main function of the PRV is pressure regulation. Our concern here is to be sure that the inherent characteristics of the valve that offer resistance to flow *do not* jeopardize burner performance, especially at high input rates. It is not unusual that the gas service pressure available is one psi or less. Whether it be due to utility company policy, or just the unavail-

Table 5-3. Maxitrol 210D PRV Pressure Drop Capacities
(courtesy Maxitrol)

CAPACITIES: Capacity in CFH expressed in 0.64 sp. gr. gas;

INLET PRESSURE	OUTLET PRESSURE — Inches W.C.								
	2	4	6	9	12	16	20	24	28
MODEL 210-D-1"									
8.0" w.c.	2,200	1,800	1,250						
0.5 psi	3,100	2,800	2,500	2,000					
0.75 psi	3,500	3,700	3,500	3,100	2,700	2,000			
1.0 psi	3,500	4,000	4,000	3,900	3,600	3,100	2,500	1,700	
1.5 psi	3,500	4,000	4,000	5,000	4,900	4,600	4,200	3,800	3,300
2.0 psi	3,500	4,000	4,000	5,000	5,000	5,700	5,400	5,100	4,700
3.0 psi	3,500	4,000	4,000	5,000	5,000	6,500	6,500	6,900	6,600
5.0 psi	3,500	4,000	4,000	5,000	5,000	6,500	6,500	8,000	8,000
7.5 psi			4,000	5,000	5,000	6,500	6,500	8,000	8,000
10.0 psi			4,000	5,000	5,000	6,500	6,500	8,000	8,000
MODEL 210-D-1-1/4"									
8.0" w.c.	2,700	2,200	1,550						
0.5 psi	3,800	3,500	3,100	2,400					
0.75 psi	4,000	4,500	4,200	3,800	3,300	2,400			
1.0 psi	4,000	5,000	5,000	4,800	4,400	3,800	3,000	2,100	
1.5 psi	4,000	5,000	5,000	6,000	6,000	5,600	5,100	4,600	4,100
2.0 psi	4,000	5,000	5,000	6,000	6,000	6,900	6,600	6,200	5,800
3.0 psi	4,000	5,000	5,000	6,000	6,000	7,500	7,500	8,500	8,200
5.0 psi	4,000	5,000	5,000	6,000	6,000	7,500	7,500	9,000	9,000
7.5 psi			5,000	6,000	6,000	7,500	7,500	9,000	9,000
10.0 psi			5,000	6,000	6,000	7,500	7,500	9,000	9,000
MODEL 210-D-1-1/2"									
8.0" w.c.	2,900	2,400	1,700						
0.5 psi	4,000	3,700	3,400	2,600					
0.75 psi	4,000	4,900	4,600	4,100	3,500	2,600			
1.0 psi	4,000	5,000	5,000	5,200	4,700	4,100	3,300	2,300	
1.5 psi	4,000	5,000	5,000	6,000	6,000	6,100	5,600	5,000	4,400
2.0 psi	4,000	5,000	5,000	6,000	6,000	7,500	7,200	6,800	6,300
3.0 psi	4,000	5,000	5,000	6,000	6,000	8,000	8,000	9,100	8,800
5.0 psi	4,000	5,000	5,000	6,000	6,000	8,000	8,000	10,000	10,000
7.5 psi			5,000	6,000	6,000	8,000	8,000	10,000	10,000
10.0 psi			5,000	6,000	6,000	8,000	8,000	10,000	10,000

ability of higher pressure, or some defect in the design or installation of a particular main or house line, the troubleshooter should be able to cope with ultra–low pressure applications. The object now becomes one of selecting a PRV that will pass the required quantity of gas at low differential pressure. Example: A 200–bhp Cleaver-Brooks boiler with a standard gas train has a gas input rate of 8,370 cfh. The net regulated gas pressure required at the entrance to the gas train is 14 in. WC. Assume that the available gas pressure in the boiler room, after allowance for pipe loss in the house line, is .75 psi (approximately 20.5 in. WC). Differential pressure, therefore, is 6.5 in. WC. In low differential pressure applications (less than 1 psi) it is recommended that we take only half of the differential as inherent friction loss through the valve and regulate with the balance; therefore we should select a valve with a pressure drop capacity of 3.25 in. WC at rated flow (in this case 8,370 cfh, call it 8,500). Table 5-2 indicates the three valves shown have pressure drop characteristics that exceed the available gas pressure. Table 5-3 confirms that the largest of these three valves, the 210D 1½-inch valve will pass only 4,100 to 4,700 cfh at 14 in. WC outlet pressure. Obviously we have got to use a larger or different type valve. The Maxitrol RV series PRVs (shown in Figure 5-2), a pressure drop/capacity chart for which is represented in Table 5-4, offers another solution to low pressure situations like this.

Entering the chart at 8,500 cfh, and moving to the right to the regulator which offers a pressure drop equal to or less than 3.25 in. WC, the RV 110 2½-inch valve has a pressure drop of .96 in. WC and is the correct choice. Note that maximum capacity limitation is at 4 in. WC on the chart. This is not a full shut-off type regulator; under static conditions with no gas flowing, outlet pressure will rise to line pressure.

Even when the inlet pressure to the PRV is twice the required outlet pressure there is a flow capacity loss inherent in all regulating valves because of the throttling action of the valve plug. In order to maintain a low outlet pressure the valve floats near the closed end of the valve stroke. In so doing it is restricting the volume of gas by reducing the effective free area of the valve port. The resistance of the safety shutoff valves, pipe, and other fittings, together with the throttling action of the butterfly valve downstream of the PRV impose a backpressure against the PRV to which the diaphragm action responds. There is a maximum flow capacity for each reduced pressure setting, as can be seen by studying the tables. For example, the Maxitrol 210D 1½-inch PRV considered in the last example will pass 1,700 cfh of gas at 6 in. WC when the inlet pressure is 8 in. WC.

Figure 5-2. Maxitrol Straight–Through Series PRV
(courtesy Maxitrol)

At this inlet pressure there is no way it can satisfy a burner demand rate of 2000 cfh, should that be necessary, and still maintain 6 in. WC outlet pressure. Table 5-3 indicates the reason: at 2000 cfh the pressure drop inherent in the 1½–inch valve is 2.78 in. WC fully ported. Deducting this from the available gas service pressure leaves 5.22 in. WC. All is not lost, however. Perhaps, as is often the case, the burner manufacturer has been conservative in arriving at the 6 in. WC figure he states he requires

Table 5-4

PRESSURE DROP and CAPACITY CHART

This chart shows pressure drop values for each model with regulator in full open position. Differential pressure (inlet pressure minus outlet pressure) must be at least twice pressure drop value for practical use. Maximum capacity limitation is at 4.0" pressure drop on chart.

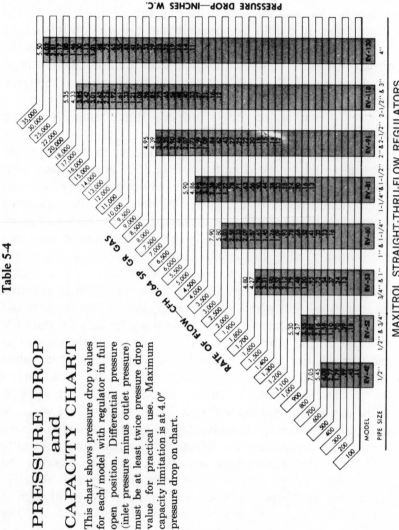

PRESSURE DROP—INCHES W.C.

RATE OF FLOW—CFH 0.64 SP GR GAS

MAXITROL STRAIGHT-THRU-FLOW REGULATORS

| MODEL | RV-42 | RV-52 | RV-53 | RV-60 | RV-81 | RV-91 | RV-110 | RV-130 |
| PIPE SIZE | 1/2" | 1/2" & 3/4" | 3/4" & 1" | 1" & 1-1/4" | 1-1/4" & 1-1/2" | 2" & 2-1/2" | 2-1/2" & 3" | 4" |

at the entrance to his gas train. We can soon determine this by installing a heavier spring and screwing down on the adjusting screw of the PRV so that it is fully ported. If burner operation indicates that we are now delivering the required cfm to the flame zone, it should be apparent that the friction loss of the valves and fittings in the gas train, the butterfly valve, and the furnace pressure combined are less than the available net regulated pressure (5.22 in. WC). It should also be apparent, hopefully, that we no longer have a regulator as such. Earlier in this chapter it was stated that a properly functioning PRV never operates in the full–open position.

A possible solution that would allow us to regain pressure control would be the alteration of the PRV *in accordance with the manufacturer's instructions,* for remote control by means of a pilot line. Instead of using the built–in sensing tube, a sensing (pilot) line is connected to a special port on the PRV and piped to a point on the gas train between the last shutoff valve and the butterfly valve. In the case under consideration, the appropriate spring is installed to maintain either two or four inches water column as required, and a three–way electric solenoid valve is piped and wired in the sensing line so that it opens and closes when the shutoff valves do. This is necessary for the PRV to close on the burner off cycle and to prevent the leakage of gas through the sensing line past the main fuel shutoff valves (see Figure 5-3). Looking again at the rating table for the Maxitrol 210D 1½–inch PRV, we see that at 2 in. WC it will pass 2900 cfh and at 4 in. it will pass 2400 cfh. In effect what we have done is allowed the plug to float more toward the open position by minimizing the effect of the regulated gas pressure under the diaphragm. This allows the spring to position the valve wider open without being inflexible. As the butterfly closes, the backpressure thus created inflates the diaphragm in the PRV as before and moves the valve plug toward closed. The pressure at the immediate outlet of the PRV will seek its own level, so to speak, at whatever value is necessary to overcome the combined resistance or friction loss of the gas train components between it and the sensing line.

In summary, when we say that a PRV will pass a specific

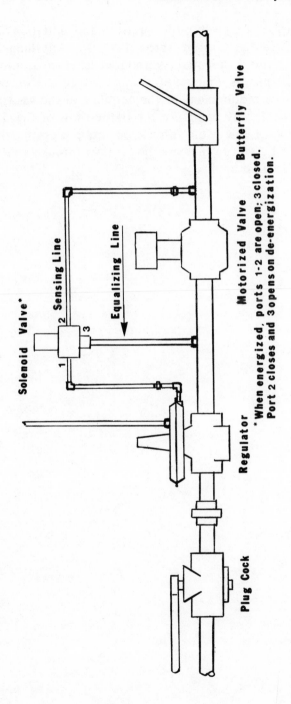

Figure 5-3. External Sensing Line

amount of gas at a given outlet pressure, the limitation is based on the differential pressure across the valve. Anything we can do to widen this differential (symbolized ΔP) increases the flow capacity. If there is a measure of conservatism in the net regulated pressure requirement at the entrance to the gas train, or if there is some way to reduce the friction loss of the gas train components, or lower the furnace operating pressure (through draft control), we can increase the gas flow through a PRV that may have been misapplied.

6

Flow Valve Characteristics

In the introduction to the combination burner at the beginning of Chapter 1, the complex action of jack shaft, air damper, and dual fuel valves was discussed. Where fuel input varies according to the load demand made on the burner, fuel–air ratio and, hence, the fuel and air linkage must remain locked in a fixed relationship and move simultaneously throughout the firing range of the burner. The relative inflexibility of the air volume, which is common to both fuels, is emphasized by what the text refers to now as The Cardinal Rule of Combination Burners: *Since the air flow rate is common to both fuels, adjust the air-handling parts of the burner only as a last resort; and then only after consulting the alternate fuel supplier. Adjust fuel rate to match air rate, not vice versa.*

Harmonizing the independent fuel and air delivery rates so that a correct fuel–air ratio is maintained throughout the firing range of the burner is particularly important where the burner has the capability of switching from one fuel to the other automatically. In many cases, fuel changeover is accomplished with no one in attendance. The switching mechanism is usually an outdoor–air sensor set at some predetermined temperature below which the burner firing mode is changed from gas to oil. Obviously, the fuel–oil firing rate must have been preadjusted to be compatible with the air flow rate being developed by the burner blower, because the changeover merely substitutes one fuel for another.

Since the gas burner has fewer adjusting points than the oil burner, there is somewhat more difficulty in making fine adjustments with the gas fuel. Compounding the problem in certain instances, can be a fluctuating pressure at the entrance to the gas train. When the butterfly valve begins to open and the gas flow rate goes up sharply—faster than the opening rate of the valve—it is extremely difficult to make any compensation in the drive linkage that would prevent the fuel–air ratio from getting grossly out of proportion. Smoke, soot, and potentially harmful gases are some of the results of this kind of problem which stems from poor fuel–flow control. A properly sized and functioning pressure reducing and regulating valve upstream of the butterfly valve is absolutely necessary, for although the butterfly valve can be made to throttle under extremely wide fluctuations in inlet pressure, the resulting flow to the burner ports will not be uniform for each increment of butterfly valve opening.

The performance of any valve is expressed by the industry in terms of its flow characteristics as it operates through its stroke. Valves are categorized according to three basic flow patterns: *quick opening,* which approaches maximum flow rapidly upon opening; *linear,* which maintains a direct proportion between opening angle and flow; and *equal percentage,* which increases flow by an equal percentage over the previous value for each equal increment of opening. Figure 6-1 shows the typical curves of these valve characteristics.

Theoretically the linear flow characteristic is the most desirable valve performance curve since it offers a one–to–one relationship between flow rate and stroke. In practice, however, the equal percentage flow pattern is probably the more commonly used valve characteristic in control valve technology today because it makes it possible to utilize the valve over the widest possible range of flow rates. The quick–opening valve characteristic is least desirable since it is an unpredictable pattern which is difficult to harmonize with the pattern of a parallel flow device such as the air damper.

Air dampers are customarily designed to produce linear or equal percentage flow patterns. If the fuel–air ratio is to remain constant throughout the firing range of the burner, the air–rate curve and the fuel–rate curve must parallel one another at all

Typical Flow Characteristics

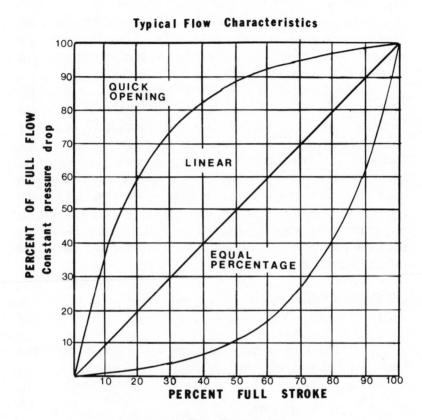

Figure 6-1. Flow Characteristics

times. Obviously, coordinating a fuel valve which has a quick-opening performance curve with an air damper whose flow pattern may be linear could be very difficult, but not impossible. It is a matter of controlling the opening and closing rates of the flow devices with respect to their performance curves.

The relationship between flow through the valve and percent opening of the valve is referred to as the *inherent flow characteristic* of the valve. In order to determine and plot this performance curve graphically, the flow through the valve is measured experimentally at various degrees of opening while the pressure drop across the valve is maintained constant. The data is then tabulated by the manufacturer and published for use in the selection and application of the particular valve or family of valves.

In field application, actually, the pressure drop across the valve is not a constant. As a matter of fact, in order to maintain a near–linear performance curve the valve is often *characterized* in order to deliberately alter its regular flow characteristic.

A *characterized valve* is one which has been designed for or is maniuplated to produce a special flow characteristic; usually different from the inherent flow characteristic of the generic family of valves to which it belongs. For example, a characterized gate valve might produce an equal–percentage performance curve whereas an ordinary gate valve could be expected to produce the quick–opening flow pattern. Characterizing can be accomplished aerodynamically by fabricating special geometric relationships between the internal parts of the valve. Characterizing can also be done *mechanically* by opening and closing the valve at a nonuniform rate.

COMMON TYPES OF
FLOW CONTROL VALVES

The term *flow control* embraces one or more of the following functions:

1. Pressure reduction
2. Pressure regulation
3. Volume control
4. Metering

It has been pointed out here, for example, that the gas pressure regulating valve (PRV) is used to *reduce* upstream pressure and to *regulate* the pressure downstream of itself. However, the PRV must be selected according to which of these functions is the more crucial consideration for the particular job the valve must do. In one case, a globe–type regulating valve might be a better choice than a gate–type regulating valve; and the reverse may also be true under different circumstances.

Volume control and metering accomplish essentially the same objective but, as we will see later in the text when discussing fuel–oil viscosity compensation and control, there is an important distinction between the two. The differences among gate, globe and butterfly valves is in their plug and seat configurations and are irrespective of the type of actuator or valve positioning mechanism.

Gate Valves

A typical gate valve throttles flow by means of a gate moving at a right angle to the path of the fluid, which flows *straight through* the valve body, from inlet to outlet. The gate may be a disc or more streamlined: spherical, even conical. The *lubricated plug cock,* which is commonly used as a manual shut-off valve on the gas train is an example of a type of gate valve which is intended to function either fully open or fully closed. The gate mechanism of this valve is a cylindrical slotted plug which is rotated 90 degrees by a lever or handle.

Most gate valves fall into the quick-opening category as regards their flow characteristics. They also have higher flow capacity per unit of cross-sectional area or pipe diameter than do most other valve types. This is an important consideration in their application. They do not throttle well, unless in nearly closed position and then, due to high fluid velocity, noise and vibration often occur. On the other hand, the straight-through type pressure regulating valve previously discussed is an example of a characterized gate valve that provides sensitive control in special applications where the pressure drop across the PRV must be kept to a minimum and the main function of the valve is to regulate downstream pressure.

Butterfly Valves

The butterfly valve is another straight-through type of throttling valve. Its gate is hinged or pivoted in the center of the fluid passage so that it can rotate 90 degrees. It is used typically in conjunction with the PRV on the gas train for throttling flow and is classed as a *linear* flow device. However, when misapplied or maladjusted it often performs like a quick-opening valve. Not intended for tight shut-off duty, the butterfly valve is the simplest of valves in construction and has the highest flow capacity rating per unit area. It is easily characterized in the field by altering the position of its drive link and/or the control arm. For example, the valve's opening speed can be slowed in order to let the combustion air flow rate catch up with the fuel flow rate when flue gas analysis or other observed condition indicates a too-rich fuel condition.

Globe Valves

Globe valve construction causes the fluid to change direction as it passes through the valve body, creating considerable resistance to flow, even in the wide-open position. Instead of a gate, it has a plug or poppet which closes into a fitted seat. Usually classed as a linear-flow device, it can be characterized to produce other flow profiles. Where the major function of a flow control valve is to reduce incoming line pressure, the globe-type regulating valve is the correct choice because of the high friction loss (pressure drop) inherent in its design. Reducing service pressure from 5 psi to 10 in. WC is a common application where the globe valve works well. Figure 2-3, page 19, is a cut-away view of a globe-type PRV where the gas flow changes direction 90 degrees four times enroute through the valve body.

The function of the PRV is twofold: to *reduce* and *regulate* the gas service pressure. Whether one prefers to call the PRV a pressure-regulating valve or a pressure-reducing valve is of little consequence; manufacturers call them regulators. In any event, the valve must reduce the incoming service pressure to the value specified by the manufacturer of the particular burner to which it is connected, and regulate or maintain this outlet pressure over a wide range of burner demand rates.

7

Coordinating Fuel and

Air Input Rates

It has been seen that, although classed as a linear–flow device, all too often the butterfly's actual flow profile turns out to be more like that of a quick–opening valve. Therefore, it is necessary to be able to control its opening rate to compensate for this inherent characteristic; to literally straighten out its flow rate curve so that it parallels the air–flow rate curve. In this way, the combination fuel burner will exhibit a uniform fuel/air ratio throughout its firing range. The same applies to whatever metering device is used in the oil firing mode, so that there can be automatic fuel changeover.

THE DRIVE TRAIN

Operation of the fuel–flow control valve through its system of rods, levers, and cams is not as primitive as it looks at first glance. On some boilers, for example, it is not unusual to find the butterfly valve at some distance from the drive motor. Interconnecting linkage may well total some 10 linear feet of rod, four or five crank arms, plus swivel joints, pillow blocks, and over–travel (strain release) mechanisms. When added to the linkage system of the secondary air damper and modulating oil valve, the result is a rather complex motion system.

The motive force used to drive the dampers and valves is usually supplied by the crank arm of a *slow*-speed, reversible gear–reduction motor. The arc of rotation (or stroke, as it is also called) of these high torque motors is fixed by internal limit switches. Although in some instances the limits of the arc of rotation are field adjustable, the 90–degree stroke is typical. The 160–degree stroke is also commonly used on some makes of burners.

There are two basic types of motion involved in the drive train; straight line and rotational. Straight–line movement results from a device which pushes or pulls the linkage system. Rotational motion is circular, caused by a device which essentially has a drive shaft which turns like an axle. Both kinds of motion work together in the dual fuel burner, not unlike the piston of an automobile engine, which moves in a straight line but is connected to a crank shaft which revolves.

Figure 7-1A illustrates the elementary physics involved. Gear A has 12 teeth and is enmeshed with gear B which is twice as large and has 24 identical teeth. Each time a tooth of gear A passes arrow a, a tooth of gear B passes arrow b. Obviously, one complete revolution of gear A results in one–half revolution of gear B. If the whole operation took one minute, for example, shaft A would turn 360 degrees per minute and shaft B, 180 degrees per minute. Converting to seconds, shaft A would turn 6 degrees per second and shaft B, 3 degrees per second (in the opposite direction).

In Figure 7-1B, a crank has been substituted on shaft A for gear A and lever B has been substituted for gear B. A rod (called a link) has been connected by swivel joints at points (a) and (b) respectively. Obviously the system cannot be made to turn 360 degrees because of interference between the link and drive shaft, but more important, shaft B turns in the same direction as shaft A. It can be seen that the respective lengths of crank A, lever B and the link are crucial. By applying the principles of gear ratios as used in power transmission problems, it might be concluded that, to turn the stem of a butterfly valve, for example, at one–half the speed of the drive motor, all that would be necessary would be to attach the link so that the driven arm (lever) is twice as long as the driving arm (crank). Unfortunately, although an average speed reduction of 50 percent would be

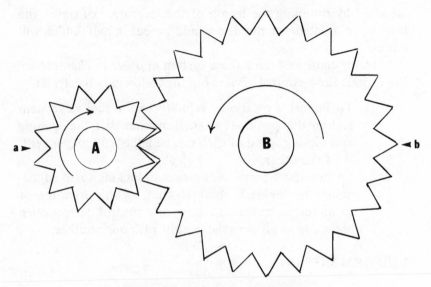

Figure 7-1A. Principle of Gear Ratio

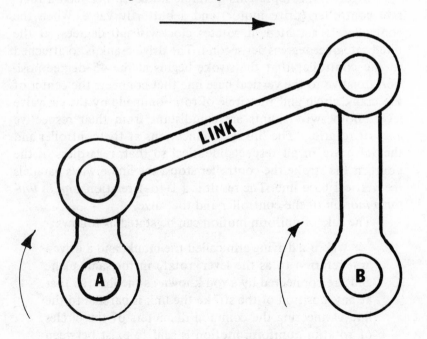

Figure 7-1B. Principle of Crank and Lever

achieved by doubling the length of the lever's arc of travel, the total opening angle of the disc would be cut in half, which will not do.

Manipulation of the linkage system in order to *characterize* the various flow–control devices has the following objectives:

1. To impart a rotational velocity to the fuel valve stem and air damper shaft in such manner that the opening and closing speed of each can be adjusted independently of the other.
2. To provide a permanent means of locking these adjustments to the jack shaft so that, as the drive motor turns the jack shaft, all flow–rate control devices open and close in proper relationship with one another.

UNIFORM MOTION

Figure 7-1C represents a simple hook–up between a fuel–rate controller (drive motor) and a butterfly valve. When the controller is actuated, it rotates clockwise 90 degrees, at the fixed rate of 3 degrees per second. The drive crank is so attached to the controller that the stroke begins at the 45–degree position, relative to the vertical base line that connects the center of the crank circle and the circle of rotation made by the gas valve lever. Both swivel joints are equidistant from their respective axes of rotation. The linkage connections at the controller and the valve are in all respects identical so that, regardless of the point in the stroke the controller stops, the link always parallels the vertical base line. The result is a 1–to–1 relationship, or *uniform motion* of the controller and the valve.

The rule of uniform motion can be stated as follows:

Where a driving arm called the crank, and a driven arm referred to as the lever, rotate in the same plane and are connected by a rod known as the link; so that at any position of the stroke the link is parallel to the line connecting the common diameters of the circles of rotation, uniform motion is said to exist between the crank and lever.

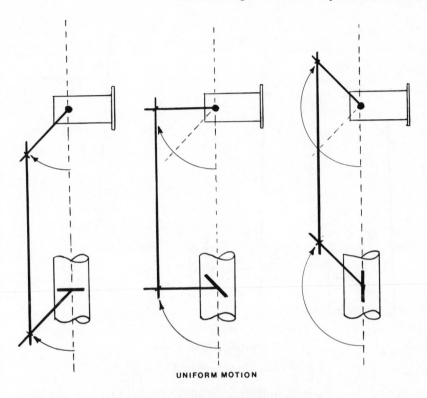

UNIFORM MOTION

Figure 7-1C. Principle of Uniform Motion

Figure 7-1D is the same as Figure 7-1C, except the starting position of the lever is changed to 60 degrees, leaving the crank set as it was at 45 degrees from the base line, the valve closed, and the link adjusted accordingly. There is no longer uniform motion between crank and lever. The link is not parallel to the base line at the start of rotation. If the controller stops after 45 degrees of rotation, the lever will have moved only 40 degrees in the same length of time—nearly one-half degree per second slower than the crank. If rotation continues for the balance of the 90-degree stroke, the lever will make an arc of slightly more than 90 degrees. Total travel time for the arc is 30 seconds, therefore for the first half of the time interval the lever traveled at 2.6 degrees per second (40° ÷ 15 sec.), and for the remainder of the rotation, traveled at 3.46 degrees per second (52° ÷ 15 sec.). The average speed was approximately 3 degrees (3.06) per

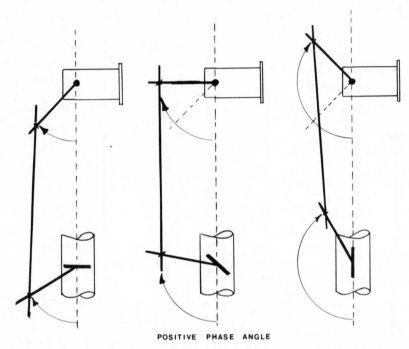

POSITIVE   PHASE   ANGLE

Figure 7-1D. Characterizing/Phase Angle

second, but was not uniform. At some point in the arc the link paralled the base line, and until then, the lever was traveling slower than the crank. After that point, the lever was traveling faster than the crank.

The difference in angular degrees between the crank and the lever, relative to the base line, is called the phase angle, and where uniform motion exists, the phase angle is zero. In the example of Figure 7-1D, we manipulated the lever on the butterfly valve while keeping the crank angle and swivel joint connection on the crank constant. Under actual conditions, this would also be the practice, since the crank usually drives the jack shaft to which the oil valve and air damper linkage are also connected and, in compliance with the Cardinal Rule (chapter 6) that setting must not be altered. Therefore, when setting the lever at 60 degrees from the base line as in Figure 7-1D, we say the phase angle is in the positive direction. A setting at angular degrees less than the crank would be a negative phase angle.

Some experimentation on the part of the reader with scale drawings of various crank–lever arrangements, where the respective lengths of the crank and lever are kept the same and only the phase angle and length of the link are changed, will point up the fact that the degree of the link's divergence from the base line, creates a corresponding difference in the angular speeds of the crank and lever. The law that applies here states:

> The angular velocity ratio for any position of two rotating arms (crank and lever), connected by a movable link (connecting rod) may be determined by scaling the length of the perpendiculars drawn from the axes of rotation to the centerline of the movable link (Figure 7-2). The angular velocity ratio is *inversely* proportional to the length of these perpendicular lines.

The fuel–rate controller or drive motor can reverse direction in response to load demand, alternately increasing and decreasing the fuel/air flow as directed. Throughout this movement, the gas valve and air damper, which are mutually connected to the jack shaft, are turning at rates different from the motor, and different from one another, by virtue of their different leverage ratios and phase angles.

If, as a result of visual observation of the flame, or flue gas analysis, it is determined that it is necessary to change the opening rate of the fuel–metering valve while maintaining the same air–flow rate, consider the following recommendations:

Case 1: Setting the crank arm and lever at the same length, and the lever at about a 15–degree negative phase angle will result in a valve action that opens quickly, then slows, with stroke approximately 90 degrees. With greater than 15 degrees negative phase angle, the opening speed does not increase appreciably, but the stroke will exceed 90 degrees.

Case 2: Setting the crank arm and valve lever at the same length and the lever at a 15–degree positive phase angle will result in a valve action that starts slowly and then speeds up with stroke approximately 90 degrees. Excessive positive phase angles are impractical.

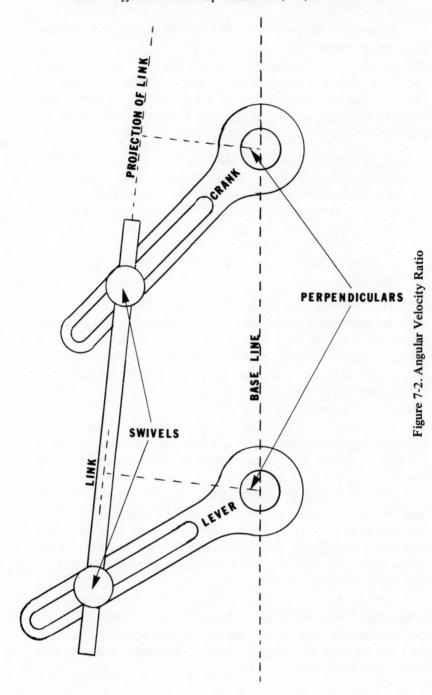

Figure 7-2. Angular Velocity Ratio

Case 3: Lengthening the lever while holding the crank length constant slows the speed and shortens the stroke of the valve.

Whenever the length of the lever or its phase angle is changed, the connecting rod or link will have to be lengthened or shortened accordingly. By application of the phase–angle principle and by varying the arc of rotation of the metering valve stem as necessary, a reasonably close fuel/air ratio can be established. The final trimming is done by flue gas analysis, and will be discussed in a subsequent chapter.

OVERTRAVEL LINKAGE

The discussion of valve control linkage systems, up to this point, has dealt only with cranks, links, and levers that move in direct relationship with one another. Our concern has been with relative opening and closing speeds. For each motion of the driving arm there has been motion of the driven arm. In a great many cases, however, the opening *angle* of the valve is also crucial. Or the free area of the valve port (especially in the case of the oil metering valve) must be maintained between narrow limits and is, therefore, mechanically restricted in its travel or stroke. In other words, the metering valve is not permitted to travel as far as the crank is capable of moving it. Inasmuch as the crank action is essentially nonadjustable, some provision must be made in the linkage system to allow for the excess motion of the drive link after the valve has reached its set stop screw, so that the lever does not bind the system and overload the drive motor.

Where valve travel must be limited, manufacturers provide strain release or overtravel devices which are comprised of specially selected springs used in conjunction with cams and levers. The effect of these devices is that jamming of a driven shaft does not cause the connecting rod, crank arm and drive motor to bind also. Instead, the crank and rod are allowed to complete their stroke while the springs at the lever absorb what would have been the motion of the driven shaft, had it not been restricted; it is a soft, flexible connection.

The overtravel device (Figure 7-3) can also be used to compensate for the tendency of a valve to open too quickly, and thereby function as a kind of time–delay mechanism. By using an overtravel link at the lever of a gas butterfly valve, for instance, we have an alternate method of slowing down or characterizing its performance curve to parallel the combustion air. We can delay its opening even though the air control damper system is moving, by adjusting the butterfly lever into overtravel condition in low–fire mode. In other words, the butterfly is adjusted full against the low–fire stop screw and the lever, with strain release provision, is brought farther toward low position, stretching the overtravel springs. In this way, the first few degrees of rotation of the lever do not rotate the butterfly shaft; they merely relax the spring tension. The amount of tension applied determines how much delay there will be before rotation of the butterfly begins. The delayed opening allows the air damper to get far enough ahead of the butterfly valve to compensate for the quick–opening effect of the latter.

A defect in this arrangement, however, is the difficulty in coordinating the action of the air damper and the spring tension on the valve. Occasionally, low fire gets so small and lean before the butterfly begins to open that noise problems and, sometimes, flame–outs occur. At best, this is a less satisfactory and cruder technique than the speed–control methods previously described.

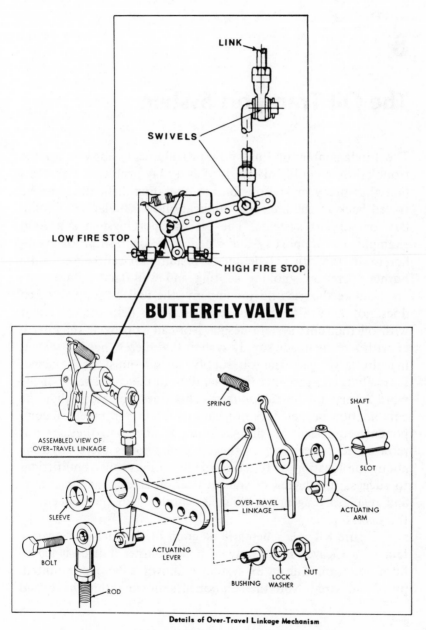

Figure 7-3. Overtravel Linkage (courtesy Cleaver-Brooks)

8

The Oil Transport System

The fundamentals of fluid flow provide ready answers for the troubleshooter in the diagnosis of everyday problems. For it is a fact that many mysterious burner operating difficulties can be traced back to the improper application or installation of auxiliary or support systems. The oil transport system is a good example of a support system where unrecognized problems inherent in the original design or installation can cause erratic burner operation, smoking, sooting, and even flame failure.

Unlike the gas utility company, the fuel–oil supplier often does not have a field engineering staff to help the consumer with oil transport system design. Nor can he provide the installer with a ready–made supply system that merely needs connecting. In large part the oil supply system must be designed, fabricated, and installed from scratch. In the truest sense of the word, every job is *customized.* This does not mean that the combination burner does not have its factory–installed oil components equivalent to the gas train. It does, but they are not referred to collectively as the oil train; nor is there anything about the location or function of the various valves and fittings to suggest the degree of standardization among manufacturers and regulatory agencies which is embodied in the concept of the gas train.

Figure 8-1 is a schematic diagram of the fuel–oil flow system of a Cleaver–Brooks steam boiler–burner unit designed to burn heavy oil. The entire system as shown is factory–mounted, piped and wired. Note the components shown within the dotted

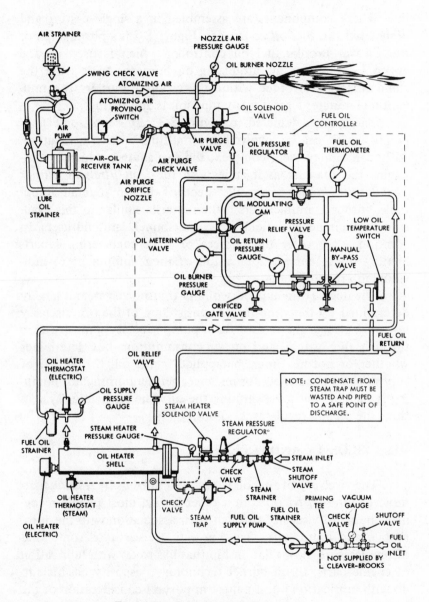

**Figure 8-1. Fuel Oil Flow Schematic
(courtesy Cleaver–Brooks)**

line. These components are assembled in a single casting and designated the *fuel oil controller*. Figure 8-2 is a photograph of the Cleaver–Brooks fuel oil controller which is used on the entire C–B line of air atomizing oil burners. Aside from the standardization afforded within this group of burners, the innovation eliminates a great many pipe joints and fittings.

The system depicted in Figure 8-3 represents some *field piping* which can be involved in a multiple burner installation. Although it may seem complex, the explanation which accompanies the drawing as it appears in the *Iron Fireman Burner Installation Manual* covers all aspects of the job in detail. Reputable burner manufacturers make manuals similar to this available to their dealers, field service personnel, and end users. In addition, they offer the services of their engineering departments for the correct application of their equipment to individual job requirements.

The degree of complexity of any transport system is largely determined by the viscosity or consistency of the oil. Viscosity not only affects the rate of flow, pump capacity, pressure drop through the system, and power consumption, but determines whether or not heat must be applied to the oil. In the case of very thick or viscous oil, for instance, neither burning nor pumping is possible without warming the oil. The oil–heating system thins the oil and regulates its viscosity.

OIL VISCOSITY AND ITS EFFECT

The viscosity of fuel oil is best described as its *resistance to flow,* or *internal friction.* In a general way, most people recognize the word viscosity through their association with the automobile and motor oils. They know that viscosity is some kind of temperature–flow relationship that has to do with lubrication of engine parts. In oil–burner technology, viscosity has little to do with lubrication but is a most important consideration of the engineer and service man. It is a measure of the number of seconds a given volume of oil takes to flow through a certain fixed orifice at a specific temperature. *Seconds Saybolt Universal* (SSU) at 100°F and *Seconds Saybolt Furol* (SSF) at 122°F are the two widely used units of measure.

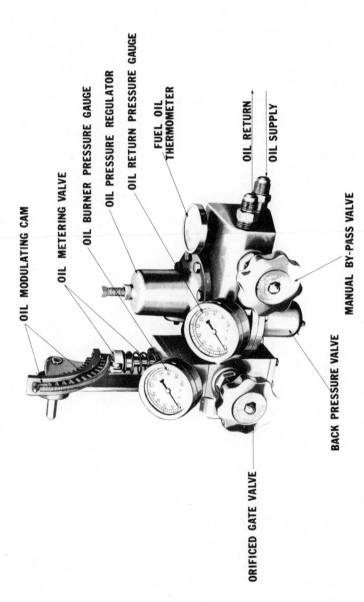

Figure 8-2. Fuel Oil Controller (courtesy Cleaver-Brooks)

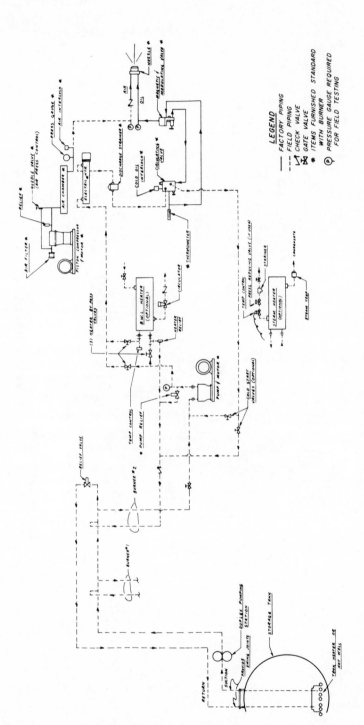

Figure 8-3. Field Piping, Typical (courtesy Iron Fireman)

Technicians usually describe heating oils as either being *light* or *heavy*. Light oils are among the first by–products to come from the fractioning tower in the crude–oil refining process. These transparent colorless–to–amber oils are also referred to as *distillates*. Before the government's clean–air campaign and subsequent energy crunch, these fuels were marketed almost exclusively as home heating oils, jet engine and diesel fuels. Now they are also used extensively as industrial fuel oils because of their low sulfur content, especially where a favorable price differential exists over imported residual oils. Heavy oils are composed of the residue still rich in the black color of the crude oil after the light oils have been extracted. Hence the term *residual oils*. There also are available *blends* of distillates and residuals which are carefully combined at the bulk plant, not to mention the *truck mixes* the processing of which is a short ride over a rough road.

Fuel oils are marketed in five numbered grades and are generally recognized by several commercial standards as follows: Grade No. 1 is a distillate oil originally intended for vaporizing pot–type burners and often sold as kerosene. Grade No. 2 is also a distillate for domestic and commercial use in burners requiring moderately volatile oil. Its maximum viscosity is 40 SSU at 100°F. There no longer is a No. 3 oil. Grade No. 4 is available as a distillate or as a blended oil of proportions of No. 2 and up to 15% residual stock. The maximum viscosity of No. 4 oil is 125 SSU. Number 5 oil can be a residual or heavy distillate and can be used only in burners equipped with oil preheaters. This grade is often marketed as "cold No. 5" since it requires heating for atomization but not for storage or pumping. It may consist of as much as 40% residual stock and has a maximum viscosity of 750 SSU. Finally, grade No. 6 is 100% residual stock for use with burners equipped with elaborate oil preheating systems. It must be heated while in storage and for pumping and atomizing. Also referred to as *Bunker C oil*, its viscosity ranges from 800 to 8000 SSU!

Of the other fuel–oil characteristics which determine their grade classification in the commercial standards, such as flash point, water and sediment content, carbon residue, ash, distillation characteristics, and pour point, only the latter is of real significance to the troubleshooter. The *pour point* is the temperature at which fuel oil ceases to flow and, to a large extent, is a function of its wax content. It determines the minimum temperature at which oil must be kept while in storage, and the extent to which heat and insulation must be applied to the piping interconnecting the storage tank and the burner.

As a general rule, residual oils are heated and circulated continuously, especially in cold climates where a combination of weather conditions and exposed piping could cool the oil perilously near its pour point. At the same time, the maintenance of heat on storaged oil reduces its internal friction and permits the use of smaller, more economical pumping systems. In any case, No. 6 oil at viscosities over 4000 SSU are generally considered impractical to pump. Pumping temperature, also referred to as transport temperature, ranges from 80 to 150 degrees depending upon pour point and the oil viscosity desired. It is somewhat enigmatic that with low sulfur content fuel oils the viscosity is quite low, requiring minimum heat for pumping, but the pour point is higher than the old conventional residual oils. The boiler operator in the typical plant is confronted with the possibility, therefore, of the oil congealing if let get too cold, or of vapor binding the pumps if overheated. The heating range exists between the pour point of the oil and its flash point and is sometimes a matter of only 10 or 20 degrees. The fuel supplier, through the facilities of the testing laboratories available to him, should be made to bear full responsibility for the recommendation of proper storage and atomizing temperatures required by the oil he delivers as they relate to the requirements of the burner equipment of the consumer.

Oil atomizing temperatures are governed by the viscosity specifications of the particular type of oil burner. For example, horizontal rotary burners perform satisfactorily with oil viscosities between 150 and 450 SSU. High–pressure steam or air atomizing burners perform better if the oil viscosity is less than 250 SSU whereas low–pressure atomizers require that the oil viscosity not exceed 100 SSU. We will discuss the various oil atomizing methods in greater detail later in the text.

In order to see specifically what effect temperature has on oil viscosity, refer now to Figure 8-4, which is a graphical representation of the temperature/viscosity relationship of the various grades of fuel oils. Let us consider a typical No. 6 oil with a viscosity of 2000 SSU and a pour point of 45 degrees to determine the proper storage, pumping, and atomizing temperature for a low-pressure air atomizing burner. Proceeding with the selection of the storage temperature first, find 2000 SSU in the appropriate column at the left and move along that line horizontally to the right to a point where it intersects with the 100-degree vertical line. At this point a line representing this specific oil was drawn parallel to reference line **AB** and labeled **CD**. Line **CD** is a graphical representation of the viscosity–temperature relationship of this 2000 SSU oil. Where line **CD** crosses the 4000 SSU horizontal line is found the temperature below which it is impractical to attempt pumping this oil (85 degrees). Regardless of the pour point which was given as 45 degrees, 85 degrees is minimum transport or pumping temperature. Storage temperature might be somewhat lower but in all cases higher than the pour point. Seldom can we tell what the average temperature of the oil in the tank actually is. We can only assume that it would approach the temperature of its surroundings if no heat were added. Traditionally, tank heating equipment has been designed to heat the oil in the immediate vicinity of the suction stub only, and thermometers were located so as to measure the temperature of the *moving oil*.

If the burner in question is to burn this oil at a viscosity of 80 to 90 SSU, a temperature of 215 degrees would be necessary as indicated by the intersection of line **CD**, the SSU and the temperature lines. The same burner, using No. 4 oil with a viscosity of 100 SSU at 100 degrees presents quite a different picture. Proceeding as above, except working from the point where the 100–SSU and 100–degree lines intersect, another line labeled **EF** was drawn. Looking to the left along line **EF** it is obvious that pumpability is no problem. Nor is any heat required for storage. Moving to the right along **EF** to intersection with the 80–90 SSU line and then vertically to the temperature scale it is indicated that 110 degrees is the proper atomizing temperature for this oil. From the foregoing it can be seen that the heavier grades of fuel oil require more sophisticated heating systems for viscosity control. Heaters are part of the oil circulating system of the combination fuel burner.

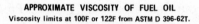

APPROXIMATE VISCOSITY OF FUEL OIL
Viscosity limits at 100F or 122F from ASTM D 396-62T.

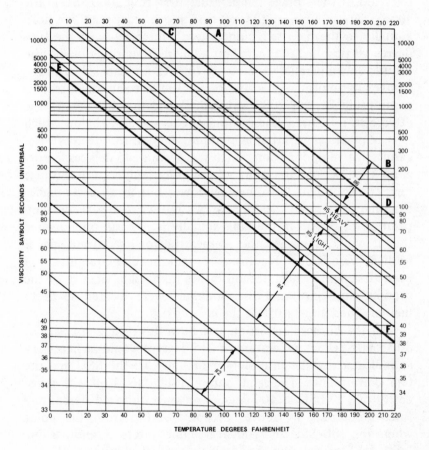

Figure 8-4. Viscosity/Temperature Relationship

9

The Oil Circuit

In the language of the troubleshooter, the oil circulating system has two sides, a suction side and a pressure side. Some may split a hair here and say there is no such thing as a *suction* or *vacuum,* only subatmospheric pressure. They are no doubt right, but the words suction and vacuum are well established in the engineering idiom and the author uses them freely and interchangeably.

The suction side of the system begins at the shaft seal on the oil pump. It includes the oil pump casing and gears and all the pipe and fittings to the bottom of the suction pipe in the tank. It also includes the vent pipe connected to the storage tank. The fact that the tank's vent pipe figures in the circuit is not so surprising when you realize that it is atmospheric pressure which moves the oil up through the suction pipe. The very same atmosphere that exerts 14.7 pounds of pressure per square inch on everything and everybody at sea level also applies its weight to the surface of the oil in the tank. When atmospheric pressure forces the oil out of the underground tank and puts it to work, we say the pump has overcome a *suction lift.* Suction lift is another of those well–used terms which float around in our jargon and make the perfectionists twinge. Nevertheless, suction lift is a convenient way to describe the static head that exists between a fuel–oil pump and the storage–tank bottom by virtue of their physical distance apart vertically. It is measured from the highest point in the suction line to the bottom of the suction pipe in the tank. There is a definite amount of work required by the pump per unit of suction lift, simply because the vertical column of oil weighs more the longer it gets. The conventional unit of measure is inches of mercury (in. Hg). The higher reading indicates a deeper vacuum; or for the purist, a greater difference between atmospheric pressure and the subatmospheric or negative pressure inside the system being measured. There is a thumbrule that says an inch of vacuum is required to raise oil one foot; meaning an eight-foot lift would produce a vacuum gauge reading of 8 in. Hg. Technically, this generalization does not take into consideration such factors as the viscosity of the oil or the friction loss due to the pipe and fittings. But it will not get you into any trouble when used to approximate what a normal vacuum gauge reading might be when the height of the vertical lift is known. An exception, where the thumbrule would not apply, would be when a positive head or syphon exists.

Whenever the burner pump is at a level below the surface of the oil in the tank, a syphon or gravity head can exist when the suction line is full of oil. Actually, a syphon always exists in the suction line, in one direction or the other. For when the burner pump is higher than the surface of the oil in the tank, opening the suction line at the pump without closing the inlet valve would cause the oil to flow by gravity back to the tank. *Check valves* are used in suction lines to prevent this from happening; otherwise the pump would have to reprime itself every time a suction-line strainer was opened for cleaning. By the same token, when the pump is below the surface of the oil and a positive syphon exists, opening the strainer cover without first closing the inlet valve would result in an overflow of oil from the tank. An accidental rupture of this inlet line could result in a flood of oil also, and this is why antisyphon valves are required by fire codes in many cities. An antisyphon valve in a suction line is preset to open only when the pump has developed several inches of vacuum in the line. When the pump stops, or in the event the suction line ruptures on the downstream side of the valve, it closes tightly and prevents a gravity flow. By mounting the valve as close as possible to the point where the suction line enters the building, maximum protection is afforded against emptying the contents of the tank on the boiler room floor. Where a burner operates with a positive head at the inlet to the pump, and there is no antisyphon valve, a compound gauge at the pump inlet would indicate a pressure rather than a vacuum when the pump is in operation. A situation like this could be dangerous if the main electric fuel valve does not hold tightly, even when the pump is not running. The head of oil in the tank may exert sufficient pressure to slide right past the gears of the pump and a flooded combustion chamber or worse could result.

SUCTION PROBLEMS

It almost goes without saying that the suction side of the oil transport system must be absolutely perfect, since we are not going to move oil anywhere if we cannot get it out of the tank. It must be sized properly and constructed absolutely airtight. A pump that has a positive head at its inlet, on the other hand, can push oil nearly anywhere we can pipe it—uphill, downhill, crosswise, several directions at once—and at virtually any pressure within the limitations of the hardware. We can even have some leaks in the inlet piping and not hurt anything but the decor. In the case of a pump that must lift or draft oil, it is another story.

Aside from airtightness, the most important requirement for dependable oil pumping is that the suction line be full at all times. It must be full of *solid* oil, as the jargon goes; no air, no vapor, *no voids*. Taking the last point first, a suction line that runs from the pump and then up and over a wall or some other obstruction higher than the pump, before dropping down to the level of the oil tank, is a constant source of trouble. *The pump should be located at the highest point in the suction line.* Loops in the suction line are almost impossible to keep full of oil, especially if the running vacuum is perilously close to the vapor pressure of the oil. Oil, like water, will flash from a liquid to a gas at reduced pressures. Oil vapors have a tendency to accumulate at high points in piping systems and act to reduce the effective diameter of the pipe, increasing friction loss. *When the pump stops, the vapor bubble collapses and the oil runs both ways from the high point.* When this situation is encountered, sometimes the only solution is to install a tee at the high point and fill the loop by hand. The proper solution to the problem is to relocate the pump to the tank side of the obstruction, so that the loop is in the discharge side of the system.

A good strong fuel-oil pump should be able to develop between 22 and 26 inches of vacuum in a test run with a closed valve in the suction line. This is with fully wetted gears and vented discharge line. But there is a practical limit as to how much of this lifting capacity we can use; we cannot expect to lift oil 22 to 26 feet. The reason is simple enough; oil does not exist as a liquid at these deep vacuums, particularly when its temperature has been elevated in order to thin it. In fact fuel oil begins to change state or vaporize at approximately 15 in. Hg. The recommended maximum suction lift for light oil is 12 feet and for heavy oil is 17 feet, according to Cleaver-Brooks. This allows for lower than anticipated pumping temperatures, pump wear and tear, and some dirtying up of the suction-line strainers. The vapor that boils out under deep vacuum conditions can be just as troublesome as air in the system. It produces some of the same symptoms; erratic pressure regulation, noise, loss of prime at the pump, and loss of volume. In the case of a worn but otherwise airtight pump capable of developing a 10-inch vacuum and required to lift oil 8 feet, it might be reasonable to assume that it would be able to do the job, providing we make sure the suction-line strainer is kept clean. But such a worn pump may not deliver the required gallons of oil per hour to keep up with the demand for the same reason it could not develop a deep vacuum; *slippage.* Slippage is due to excessive clearance between the gears and stationary parts of the gear case or gear plate.

Virtually all the pumps with which we deal are gear-type, positive-displacement pumps. A positive-displacement pump moves exactly the same amount of oil per revolution, regardless of the viscosity of the oil—an important thing to remember. The speed at which the pump turns, however, depends very much on a consideration for the consistency of the oil it is to handle. Heavy-oil pumps have large volumetric displacements but turn at slow speeds—on the order of 300 to 1100 RPM. Light-oil pumps are small-volume, higher-speed pumps that work at speeds of 1100 to 3600 RPM.

A pump that will not deliver oil due to excessive internal wear behaves much like a pump with an air leak on the suction side. Both will indicate little or no running vacuum on the gauge. The *difference* is that, even with a leak in the suction line, a good pump will discharge air when the pressure side of the system is vented, whereas a worn–out pump will not. Finding the air leak can be done by valving off both ends of the section of piping to be tested, and placing it under 5 pounds of air pressure. **CAUTION: NEVER USE PURE OXYGEN!!** Then all joints, including the pump itself, are painted with a soapy solution, and checked for bubbles. The large casting surfaces of strainers and valve bodies should not be overlooked for the presence of sand holes. Obviously, packing glands and gaskets should be thoroughly checked before going to a lot of extra trouble. The drain port on the strainer housing, which is usually ½– or ¾–inch pipe size, is a convenient place to attach the air-pressure line, where no gauge port is available, and can also be used to mount a vacuum test gauge when necessary.

The level of oil in the tank, whether it is low or nearly full, changes the suction requirement of the pump, since atmospheric pressure works upon the surface of the oil to *push* the oil up the suction stub. The end of the suction stub could be 2 feet or 20 feet below the surface of the oil, and the running vacuum would be the same in either case. However, as the level of the oil goes lower, more work is required to raise the oil out of the tank, and the vacuum will go deeper accordingly. Needless to say, the designer must consider the lift from the bottom of the suction stub, and base his calculations for the maximum lifting requirement of the pump as being that which occurs just before the tank runs empty. Where a pump is known to be worn, and its capacity thereby reduced, keeping the level of oil higher in the tank by reordering fuel sooner, would compensate. Occasionally a case is found on an old installation where a pinhole develops in the suction stub. The symptom is one where the pump completely runs out of oil, as though the tank has run empty, when actually it has not. No amount of priming will draft oil; the pump develops a good vacuum against a closed valve, but will not pump oil. Topping the tank off with more oil, and starting the pump, reverts everything back to normal. There is no way the suction stub can be checked for leaks, so in a case like this, the operator has the options of replacing the suction stub, living with the situation, or switching to an alternate line. An alternate line is the best insurance short of having two complete pumping systems. By leaving the alternate suction stub several inches higher than the primary line, it can be used also when sludge or condensation causes problems and cannot be remedied immediately by cleaning the tank.

When boiler rooms (Figure 9-1) are updated and expanded, with new steam generators installed and connected to existing tanks and piping, problems occasionally crop up involving restrictions in the suction line, caused by sludge accumulation. Years ago it was standard practice to install a check valve at the bottom of the suction stub. These foot valves, as they are called, are a continuous source of trouble. Located near the bottom of the tank, they can be fouled by the dirt and sludge that accumulates there, so that they stick open, or worse, stick closed. Good installation practice has made the foot valve taboo

Figure 9-1. Modern Dual-Fuel Boiler Room (courtesy Cleaver-Brooks)

and, hopefully, a relic of the past. Check valves should be located in an area where they can be serviced; either in a manhole above the tank, or at the wall inside the building. When confronted with an abnormally deep vacuum, the most common cause of the problem is a clogged filter or strainer. When a pump is starved for oil, it is in a state known as *cavitation,* which is usually accompanied by a pulsing, squeeling, grinding noise. The phenomenon consists of creation of vapor pockets (cavities) in the oil stream due to low vapor pressure, and the sudden collapse of the bubbles as they pass over into the pressure side of the pump. Cavitation can also exist within a pump that is turning too fast for the viscosity of the oil, or is connected to an undersized suction line. In any case, the pump will not be delivering its rated capacity, and its useful life will be shortened.

Locating the restriction, other than at strainers, is a matter of opening and examining the various valves in the suction line for sludge, particularly globe-type valves. Antisyphon valves are a potential source of trouble because of their construction, but this is something that must be lived with. The check valve should be opened and cleaned if necessary. A swing-check is preferred to a globe-type poppet, or vertical check valve. All of this done, it only remains to check the low points in the suction line, including the area of the suction stub, for dirt accumulation.

In troubleshooting suction-line difficulties, it is necessary to be able to isolate portions of the piping system from one another. The strainer that protects the pump should have a valve upstream of it, so that it can be valved off from the rest of the suction line. In that way, one of the most common causes of air leaks, the strainer cover gasket, can be checked for tightness. If running the pump against the closed valve indicates a satisfactory vacuum, the strainer assembly can be ruled out as a source of trouble. In the same way, a valve in the manhole above the tank, just before the suction line drops into the tank, and **on the tank side of the last union** allows for checking the tightness of the line from that point back to the pump. A word about these valves: they are separate from, and in addition to whatever fire valves may be required by law. They should be free-ported gate valves, not globe valves; with good, tight packing glands around the stems, that can be loosened for opening and closing, and retightened afterward. [Where lever–operated valves are used (with fusable links and weighted cables) for fire valves, care should be exercised to keep the packing nuts around the stems air tight, but not so tight they prevent automatic closing in an emergency.]

HOW TO CHECK THE SUCTION LINE SIZE

1. Determine the suction lift and convert it to In. Hg Vac.
2. This is the vertical distance from the bottom of the suction line in the tank to the center line of the pump.
3. Find the Equivalent Length of the pipe and fittings. Use Table 9-1.
4. Find the Friction Value of the pipe. Use Table 9-2.
5. Determine the pumping rate. From the pump manufacturer's data. In lieu of same, double the burner firing rate for light oil, and triple it for heavy oil. If the system was designed to pump heavier oil but has been converted to light oil, use the 3 multiplier.
6. Determine the friction loss of the suction line. Friction loss = Friction factor X Equivalent Length X Circulating rate. The diameter of the suction line is one of the factors which determines the friction loss. The other factors are: the viscosity of the oil, the quantity of the oil being pumped, and the length of the suction line.

Table 9-1. Equivalent Feet of Oil Valves and Fittings
(courtesy Iron Fireman)

FRICTION LOSS IN STANDARD VALVES AND FITTINGS
(Equivalent Lengths of Straight Pipe in Feet)

TYPE OF FITTING	PIPE SIZE · INCHES						
	3/4	1	1·1/4	1·1/2	2	2·1/2	3
GATE VALVE·(OPEN)	.5	.6	.8	1.0	1.2	1.4	1.7
GLOBE VALVE·(OPEN)	22.	27.	38.	44.	53.	68.	80.
ANGLE VALVE·(OPEN)	12.	14.	18.	22.	28.	33.	42.
STANDARD ELBOW	2.2	2.7	3.6	4.5	5.2	6.5	8.0
TEE (STRAIGHT THRU)	1.3	1.7	2.3	2.8	3.5	4.3	5.2
TEE (RT. ANGLE FLOW)	4.5	5.7	7.5	9.0	12.0	14.0	16.0

Table 9-2. Oil Pressure Loss Standard Pipe (courtesy Iron Fireman)

PRESSURE LOSS IN STANDARD PIPE
(Inches of Mercury Per 100   Feet of Pipe For 100 GPH Circulating Rate)

VISCOSITY SSU AT PUMPING TEMPERATURE		PIPE SIZE - INCHES						
		3/4	1	1-1/4	1-1/2	2	2-1/2	3
No. 6	5000			27.0	15.0	5.6	2.8	1.20
No. 6	3000		50.0	16.0	8.6	3.3	1.7	.70
No. 5	1000	44.0	16.0	5.5	2.9	1.1	.55	.23
No. 4	500	22.0	8.2	2.6	1.4	.54	.27	.11
No. 2	50	2.2	.82	.26	.14	.054	.027	.011

One Inch Mercury   = 0.49 Lbs. Per Sq. In.   One Lb. Per Sq In. = 2.016 In. of Mercury

As in the case of gas main sizing, it is convenient to convert the standard pipe fittings to equivalent length of straight pipe. For example, a standard elbow for 2–inch pipe will have the same pressure loss as 5.2 feet of straight 2–inch pipe.

The available vacuum is the difference between the maximum recommended running vacuum and the suction lift. The friction loss should not exceed the available vacuum. The following example is taken from data supplied by Dunham–Bush and illustrates the pipe–sizing method outlined above.

Table 9-1 shows the friction loss in oil piping for several viscosities and common pipe diameters. With No. 5 oil, a burner circulating rate of 124 gph, bottom of the tank 12 feet below the pump, 80 feet of 2½–inch suction line with 5 elbows and 3 angle tees.

Assuming an oil with a specific gravity of 1.0, the lift would be 0.9 in. Hg per foot, or for the example: 12 × 0.9, or 10.8 inches. Subtracting this from the total recommended running vacuum (in this case 15 inches) leaves 4.2 inches remaining for pipe friction. The total equivalent length of pipe, using Table 9-2 works out as follows:

Pipe length	80 ft
Five 2½–inch L's @ 6.5	33 ft
Three 2½–inch T's @ 14	42 ft
Equivalent Length	155 ft

For heavy oils, a pumping viscosity of 3000 SSU is generally assumed. From Table 9-2, 3000 SSU and 1½-inch pipe, the friction factor is 1.7 inches per hundred feet of pipe length. The friction loss in the example would then be:

$$1.7 \times \frac{155}{100} \text{ (length)} \times \frac{124}{100} \text{ (circulating rate)} = 3.3 \text{ inches}$$

Since the available vacuum is 4.2 inches, the 2½-inch pipe is satisfactory.

OIL PRESSURE REGULATION

When confined within the piping of the discharge or pressure side of the transport system, the most important of the physical aspects of liquid oil to be considered is its incompressibility. Since it has mass, occupies space, and possesses internal resistance to flow, its control involves pressure regulation, pressure relief, flow metering, and viscosity compensation and control.

The text of material covered in chapter 3 which discusses the components of total pressure as it is related to gas flow, is well worth review at this time, since the fundamentals of fluid flow outlined there find ready application to the problems of oil delivery.

In order to induce flow, oil must of necessity be subjected to the effects of pressure, but at the same time provision must be made in the design to relieve or limit the pressure build-up at some value well before the rupture point of the system components. In addition, costs associated with pump operation are in direct proportion to system pressure. Initial installation costs, or first costs, on the other hand, are inversely proportional. That is to say that, although increased design pressures permit the use of smaller diameter piping systems, pump-horsepower requirements will be greater. The original selection of the design pressure for a given transport system takes all of this into consideration, in relation to the function it is to perform; whether it is a single-stage or two-stage system.

Stages refer to the number of times the oil is pumped before actually reaching the burner atomizer. For instance, Figure 9-2 shows a transport system which might be designed to supply a battery of burners, each of which contains its own individual, secondary oil pump. Oil, under pressure from a large primary pump would circulate in a piping arrangement, called a *circulating loop system,* past each burner where their respective secondry pumps would connect. This type of two-stage system is characterized by low-pressure, high-volume flow on the primary side, and relatively high-pressure, low-volume flow on the secondary side. In fact, primary side pressure must be kept low, usually five pounds per square inch or less, to protect the seals of the secondary pumps from rupture. When discussing the suction side of pumping systems, it was pointed out that the shaft seal is located in the low-pressure section of the pump, and therefore is capable of withstanding little more than atmospheric pressure differentials. The primary pressure is maintained by a *back-pressure valve* installed in the supply piping just downstream of the branch-off to the last burner.

The back-pressure valve is in reality a relief valve set to open at 5 psig, in this case. Its physical size may be smaller than the actual pipe size of the system it is regulating, however it is extremely important that it have sufficient capacity to relieve the total flow (gallons per minute) of the primary pump *or pumps.* This guards against the possibility of excessive pressure build-up when one or more of the burners are isolated from the primary flow of oil, and/or more than one primary pump is inadvertently put on the line. From the location of the back-pressure regulating valve in the primary-loop system, the oil piping continues back to the oil storage tank, and from this point on, is referred to as *the return line.* Since it terminates just inside the top of the tank which is under atmospheric pressure, the pressure within the return line will be nominal. Any and all return lines from the secondary system or burner pumps, tee into this line forming a so-called *common return line.* It is good practice to size the return-line diameter the same as the suction line.

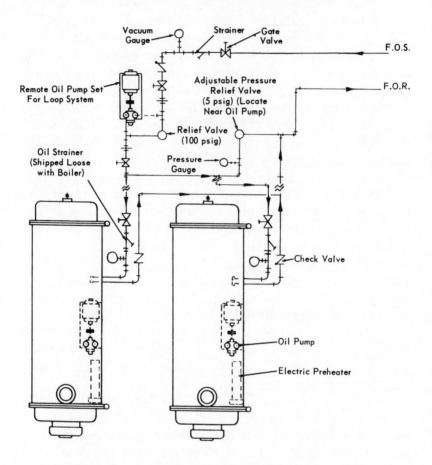

Figure 9-2. Battery of Boilers (courtesy Cleaver–Brooks)

PRESSURE RELIEF

In addition to back–pressure regulation, relief valves are installed at strategic points in the discharge piping of oil pumps to prevent structural damage to the system. Several fundamentals are involved in their application as follows:

The Ten Commandments of Pressure Relief

1.   A relief valve regulates pressure *upstream* of itself only.

2. A regulating valve regulates pressure *downstream* of itself only.
3. A relief valve used as a back–pressure valve should have a manual bypass around it.
4. A relief valve should be set to relieve at or below the maximum working pressure of the system.
5. It should be sized to handle the capacity of the pump(s) in gallons per minute.
6. It should be located so as to relieve locked–up pressure caused when a pump is operated with a closed discharge valve.
7. There should be no valve in the line between it and the piping it is to relieve.
8. There should be no valve in the line or lines between it and the oil storage tank, other than a properly positioned check valve. Where stop valves are found in such lines, they should be left open and have their wheels or handles removed.
9. Where it is not possible to discharge pressure back to the tank, the relief valve should be piped so as to relieve into the suction line as close to the pump as possible, in accordance with rule 8 above.
10. Gauge connections should be provided to aid in the setting and adjusting of relief and regulating valves.

OIL FLOW METERING AND VISCOSITY COMPENSATION

At this point in our discussion of combination burners, the fact that natural gas and fuel oil are both hydrocarbons whose burning characteristics are compatible enough to share the same combustion system, might tend to overshadow the radical difference in the complexity of their respective delivery and metering systems.

Firing–rate control, in the case of fuel oil, essentially involves all the fundamentals of fluid flow applicable to the gaseous fuels. However, where the consistency or density varies only slightly from end to end of the spectrum of gas fuels available commercially, the opposite is true of heating oils. Even within the Commercial Standard used to grade fuel oils, there is wide latitude as regards oil viscosity. To be able to apply the fundamentals of fluid flow to the liquid fuels, then, is to understand the significance of viscosity compensation and control.

10

Oil Viscosity and Its Effect

VISCOSITY COMPENSATION AND CONTROL

Bunker C or C.S. No. 6 oil is usually delivered by large tanker truck. At the refinery or tank farm, it is kept warm in storage and loaded into the tanker hot, so that it is still well above the pour point on arrival at its destination. Unlike the lighter grades of fuel oil, it is not generally metered but sold by the tank load, by weight, or by the barrel (1 Bbl equals 42 U.S. gallons). It is *dropped* from the tanker into the underground storage tank by gravity instead of being pumped and, customarily, the boiler-plant engineer orders oil when he can take a full tanker load. Upon its arrival, he climbs aboard the tanker, opens the hatch and verifies that he has indeed received a full load; a reference *pin* inside the hatch having been set by a sealer of weights and measures, to indicate a certain number of barrels or gallons capacity for each tanker when filled to that point. Similarly, he again inspects to verify that all the load has been emptied. The ticket that the transport driver leaves, indicates the quantity, API gravity number, and temperature of the oil that was loaded on his truck at the terminal. A competent engineer will note this information in the boiler room logbook. The cursory examination of such a log will indicate a wide range of API gravity numbers over the course of a year's fuel consumption. This is the nature of the product, and underlies the fact that factors other than viscosity which go into the classification of fuel oils can vary widely too.

Viscosity, as we have seen, is an extremely important element of the classification, and, unfortunately, is one of the variables that must be contended with. From the technician's standpoint, it involves the knowledge of the function of certain mechanical devices designed to compensate for these variations. Viscosity is not indicated on each delivery ticket, nor is it easily measured in the field. The only indicator or comparison we have as to the consistency of the product is the *API gravity number* of the fuel.

Many years ago, before the adoption of the Commercial Standard, the petroleum and oil–burner industries based the ultimate classification of fuel oils entirely on *specific gravity*. In physics, the term specific gravity expresses the ratio of the density of a body or substance to that of some other substance which is considered the standard. In the case of solids and liquids, *water is taken as the standard, 1.* Most other liquids, including all petroleum crudes and derivatives, except for very viscous residuals and coke, are lighter than water, and their specific gravities are decimal fractions which are cumbersome to work with: alcohol, 0.806; hexane, 0.655; octane, 0.699; benzene, 0.8724; etc. As a result, a method was adopted by the petroleum industry, while still in its infancy, for more conveniently expressing this value, based on a purely arbitrary scale first devised many years before for work with hydrometers. Anyone who has witnessed an automobile mechanic test a radiator for antifreeze, has seen a hydrometer in action. When he withdrew a sample of the coolant into the tester, he had to adjust an attached scale according to its temperature, in order to read–out the relative strength of the antifreeze. Similarly, the method adopted by the *American Petroleum Institute* ties gravity readings into a temperature base.

With the API gravity of water taken as 10 at 60°F, a fuel oil having a density of 55.755 lb per cu ft and a specific gravity of 0.8927, on the specially calibrated hydrometer would show a reading of *27 degrees API*. The relationship between the API gravity of fuel oils and their calorific value is shown in Table 10-1. You will note that there is some overlapping between domestic, commercial, and industrial grades of fuel oil, which is

Table 10-1. Gravity/Density/Heating Value by Oil Grades
(courtesy Iron Fireman)

DEG. AP I	SPECIFIC @ 60/60 F	LB PER GALLON	BTU * PER LB	BTU PER GALLON
0	1.0760	8.962	17,690	158,540
1	1.0679	8.895	17,750	157,870
2	1.0599	8.828	17,810	157,190
3	1.0520	8.762	17,860	156,520
4	1.0443	8.698	17,920	155,890
5	1.0366	8.634	17,980	155,240
6	1.0291	8.571	18,040	154,600
7	1.0217	8.509	18,100	153,980
8	1.0143	8.448	18,150	153,370
9	1.0071	8.388	18,210	152,760
10	1.0000	8.328	18,270	152,150
11	.9930	8.270	18,330	151,570
12	.9861	8.212	18,390	150,990
13	.9792	8.155	18,440	150,410
14	.9725	8.099	18,500	149,850
15	.9659	8.044	18,560	149,300
16	.9593	7.983	18,620	148,630
17	.9529	7.935	18,680	148,190
18	.9465	7.882	18,730	147,660
19	.9402	7.830	18,790	147,140
20	.9340	7.778	18,850	146,620
21	.9279	7.727	18,910	146,100
22	.9218	7.676	18,970	145,580
23	.9159	7.627	19,020	145,100
24	.9100	7.587	19,190	145,600
25	.9042	7.538	19,230	145,000
26	.8984	7.490	19,270	144,300
27	.8927	7.443	19,310	143,700
28	.8871	7.396	19,350	143,100
29	.8816	7.350	19,380	142,500
30	.8762	7.305	19,420	141,800
31	.8708	7.260	19,450	141,200
32	.8654	7.215	19,490	140,600
33	.8602	7.171	19,520	140,000
34	.8550	7.128	19,560	139,400
35	.8498	7.085	19,590	138,800
36	.8448	7.043	19,620	138,200
37	.8398	7.011	19,650	137,600
38	.8348	6.960	19,680	137,000
39	.8299	6.920	19,720	136,400
40	.8251	6.879	19,750	135,800
41	.8203	6.893	19,780	135,200
42	.8155	6.799	19,810	134,700

GRADE (left margin): 6, 5, 4, 2

due to variations in the constituents of different fuel oils and the different refining methods used.

VISCOSITY AS A
FUNCTION OF FLOW

Burner technicians recognize that there is a gradual *dirtying-up* process that takes place over several months' operation, as air–handling parts of the burner accumulate dirt and lint that reduces air volume to the flame. Another factor that can cause a burner flame to *go to smoke* is the increase in oil–flow rate due to reduced pressure drop through the atomizer caused by imperfect viscosity compensation. Decreased oil viscosity results in increased flow through orifices where operating pressures upstream remain constant. Stated in terms of resistance to flow, the viscosity of a particular fuel oil determines the number of gallons per hour that will flow through the atomizer at a given pressure. A decrease in viscosity is a decrease in resistance to flow, so that pumping pressures must be decreased accordingly in order to maintain the same firing rate. As we have seen, changes in viscosity are deliberately caused by altering temperature. As oil is heated it thins and flows better—we say its viscosity has been lowered. Conversely, cooling results in increased resistance to flow, and requires increased pressure to maintain the same flow rate.

It has been stated previously that rotary–cup–atomizing burners function best when the oil viscosity is between 150 and 450 SSU at 100°. At first glance this might be regarded as a wide latitude that would not appear to be crucial. However, when you think for a minute what these numbers mean in terms of the flow rate of the oil through the atomizer, just the opposite is true. The only thing these numbers indicate is that, if the oil reaches the rotary cup within the limits they represent, it will atomize satisfactorily, *and that is all*—operating efficiency not withstanding.

Referring again to Fig. 8-4 (p. 76) and line CD, which represents a typical No. 6 oil, 150 SSU is equivalent to 170° and 450 SSU is equivalent to 135° respectively. Realizing that viscosity is a function of time, these limits mean that a change in temperature of a mere 35° can result in a 300 percent difference in the time it takes a given volume of oil to pass through an orifice. Applying this to a burner with a fixed firing rate of 25 gallons per hour burning 450 SSU oil at 135°, lowering the viscosity to 150 SSU by heating it to 170°, means that 25 gallons will pass the orifice in one–third of the former time. This is a readjusted hourly rate of 75 gph! On the other hand, a 25–gallon rate at 170° (150 SSU) will be lowered to a 8 gph, if the oil is allowed to cool to 135°. Since it is conventional to lock the air- and oil–flow rates together mechanically, the burner in question would have no way to readjust the air to the varying oil rate, unless specifically provided for.

Viscosity compensation systems take one of two general forms: Either the air and oil rates are driven independently of one another, and are balanced in response to the signal from a flue gas analyzer; or special pressure–volume compensating mechanisms are built into the oil–metering section of the secondary–pumping system. The latter involves hydraulic principles used in variations of one another by some rotary–burner manufacturers for many years. The former is not commonly seen except in large steam–generating stations and, therefore, is omitted from discussion here.

The objective of viscosity compensation, of course, is to pass the same number of gallons of fuel through the atomizer per hour when the oil viscosity is 150 SSU as when it is 450 SSU, or any other value for that matter. Obviously, to do this several factors must be considered. As we have seen, oil pressure must be variable, not fixed, and it must readjust itself automatically as viscosities change. One manufacturer who offers burners with built–in viscosity compensation systems is The Ray Burner Co. The system depends for its operation on a positive–displacement pump, whose uniform and unvarying delivery is unaffected by the fuel oil's viscosity or temperature. The burner employs an oil reservoir as an integral part of the design, in which the pumps are submerged and which contains balancing and relief valves. Here's how it works (Figure 10-1):

A primary and secondary oil pump, coupled to a common shaft, are driven by the burner motor. The primary pump delivers oil from the storage tank or pressurized loop system to the reservoir in excess of the pumping rate of the secondary pump, returning the surplus oil back to the tank, so that the reservoir is always full. The nonvariable flow of the secondary pump is drawn from the reservoir and delivered to the inlet of the patented *viscosity valve.* The oil passes through the externally-adjustable valve in two paths, the flow through each of which is controlled by positioning the eccentric regulating disc in the viscosity valve assembly. Since the flow is viscous, the rate through each side remains constant for a given position, regardless of oil viscosity, the pressure automatically varying to compensate for changes in flow resistance.

The oil from each path enters opposite ends of a pressure-balancing valve in which a free–floating piston proportions the area of the outlet ports from the cylinder, maintaining equalized pressures at both ends. This assures a viscous flow rate to the burner unaffected by changes in pressure in the return line to the tank or in the line to the burner nozzle. The metered oil from one path is delivered to the burner and the remainder, from the other path, back to the reservoir.

Two pressure–relief valves, one at the discharge of the secondary pump and one on the balancing–valve outlet to the burner nozzle, operate only to relieve excessive pressure when operating against a closed valve or in case of incorrect adjustment. For an adjusted position of the eccentric regulating disc, therefore, the flow rate to the burner remains constant, independent of oil temperature changes or line pressure variations.

In summary then viscosity compensation is in fact *oil pressure* compensation, flexibility being the only parameter. The Ray Burner Co., for instance, lists no suggested operating pressure range for their system, stating that it is wholly dependent on the temperature and viscosity of the fuel.

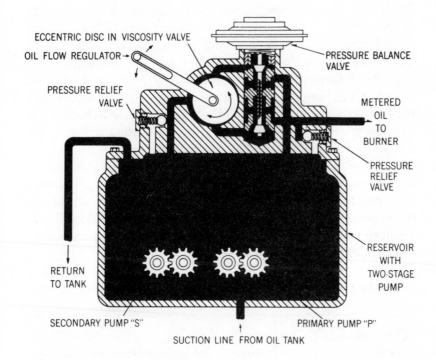

ECCENTRIC DISC IN VISCOSITY VALVE

OIL FLOW REGULATOR →

PRESSURE BALANCE VALVE

PRESSURE RELIEF VALVE

METERED OIL TO BURNER

PRESSURE RELIEF VALVE

RESERVOIR WITH TWO-STAGE PUMP

RETURN TO TANK

SECONDARY PUMP "S"

PRIMARY PUMP "P"

SUCTION LINE FROM OIL TANK

Figure 10-1. Ray Viscosity Valve (courtesy Ray Burner Company)

The fuel–oil systems of pressure–atomizing burners contrast with those of rotary burners of the type like Ray and others, in that oil pressure is not allowed to seek its own level, so to speak. Nor is the oil temperature allowed to wander far afield, for the relationship of these two elements is crucial to the maintenance of a proper fuel/air ratio.

VISCOSITY CONTROL

Viscosity control, rather than compensation, is the underlying principle of pressure–atomizing burners. There is little or no viscosity compensation designed into these burner systems. In fact, very little is made of the atomizing problems associated with changes in viscosity in the engineering manuals of most pressure–burner manufacturers. Cleaver–Brooks and Orr and

Sembower, for example, point with pride to their V-ported, sliding-stem metering valves; and the fact that each is really a variable orifice which, compared to other types of control valves are less susceptible to changes in flow rate due to variations in viscosity. Rightly so, but this is only one factor of several involved. Some natural factors appear to mitigate in their favor, for two fluid atomizers (air and oil) can be made to handle oils that range over C.S. Grades 4 to 6 by readjusting the temperature of the oil only.

Oil temperatures and viscosities are related to one another in an inverse way—a temperature increase results in a viscosity decrease. However, this relationship is not a simple arithmetic or proportional one, but in fact a geometric progression. For as we have seen, a 50 percent change in temperature does not result in a 50 percent change in viscosity.

Table 10-2. Gravity/Temperature Relationship (courtesy Iron Fireman)

API Gravity at 60°F	*SSU at 100°F*	*SSU at 210°F*
11.8	563	56
11.6	780	64.1
14.8	1225	100

Three typical No. 6 oils are arranged above according to viscosities. It is obvious when comparing the 100 and 210 degree columns that the viscosity range compresses rapidly as the temperature goes up; at 210 degrees the spread is only 44.1 seconds.

Figure 8-4 is useful because the so-called curves of the graph appear as straight lines which, as we have seen, are easily drawn from one known point parallel to a given base line. It assumed all oils have parallel characteristics, which is not true, of course, but is used where hair-splitting is not necessary. The graph of Figure 10-2 also represents the viscosities of these oils, and the vertical and horizontal scales of the graph contain basically the same data as does Figure 8-4. However, the coordinates

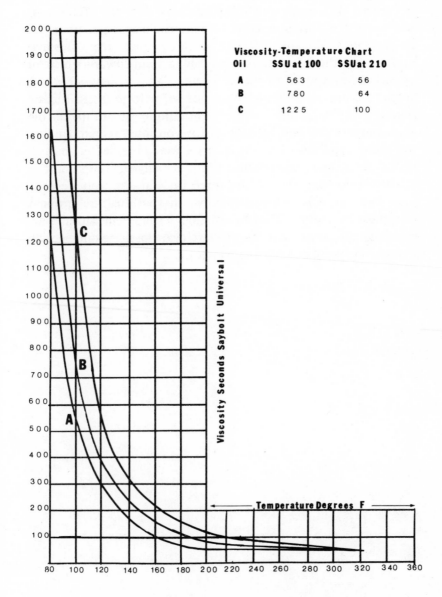

Figure 10-2. Viscosity/Temperature Relationship

are spaced differently (arithmetically), so that the effect is to emphasize the time/temperature relationship as it acts upon the oil. The most valuable information to be gained from this diagram is that there is a kind of vanishing point toward which all oil viscosities appear to move. There is a point beyond which heating of the viscous fuel does not seem to result in further thinning. Actually the merger is not quite so abrupt as the graph might lead one to believe, for you must remember that the values represented by these curves were obtained in an open viscosimeter, and the vanishing point is really the flash point or average vapor pressure of the three fuels at atmospheric pressure. Even so, it is well to remember that residual fuel brought to a pressure atomizer hot (above 200°F) and held within 5 degrees of that point, with its pressure also closely regulated, will atomize properly and burn satisfactorily.

11

Oil Heating Methods

Heat is applied to oil in several ways: electric–immersion heater, heat exchanger or combinations with the first method, electric–cable heating sets, and electric–impedance system.

The electric–immersion heater principle is used with virtually all residual oil burners that require heated oil for atomization. In addition, it is used in the transport system as a back–up, where a heat exchanger is the primary oil heater.

When large volumes of oil must be kept heated and in continuous circulation, and steam or hot water is constantly available from the boiler, the heat exchanger is very practical. Packaged boilers usually have such heaters mounted on the structural support system of the boiler. With integrated piping and control systems, they do double duty by raising the oil temperature sufficiently high for good atomization, while at the same time bypassing hot oil to the storage tank. In a case like this, no other heat is used for transport. If the supply of the heating medium is anticipated to be intermittent, the heat exchanger is piped in tandem with an electric–immersion heater, or a *combination heater* is used. The combination heater (Figure 11-1) typically takes the form of the steam–in–tube, oil–in–shell type, combined with rod–type electric–immersion unit *in one shell.* Ordinarily the electric heater functions for cold start–ups only, or when the steam heater cannot keep up. It is a relatively low-wattage heater that in an emergency may be used alone to heat a modulated, very low quantity of oil for combustion.

On hot–water boilers, or low–pressure steam boilers using so–called below–the–waterline heaters, a special heat–exchanger

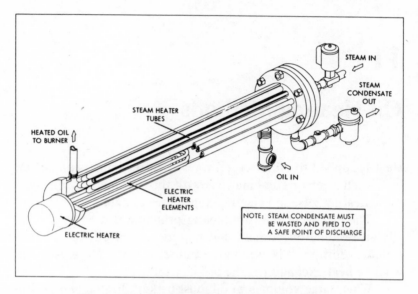

**Figure 11-1. Combination Steam/Electric Heater
(courtesy Cleaver-Brooks)**

design is used. Called the *safety heater* (Figure 11-2), double-tube elements (one tube inside another with a heat–transfer liquid between tubes), completely isolate fuel oil and water systems. This eliminates the possibility of boiler water contamination by fuel oil in case of rupture. For the same reason, the condensate from steam–oil heaters is generally not returned to the boiler; it is piped to waste. However, thermal pollution of rivers and streams caused by heated effluent from steam generators is a legitimate concern of environmentalists today. Oil-detection systems are available that when properly applied and maintained make it reasonably safe to reuse the condensate from such heaters.

RESISTANCE HEATERS

The electric–cable heating method, used in conjunction with a stub heater in the tank, finds application in many systems of fuel–oil piping where it is necessary to maintain a minimum oil temperature in the pipe lines during shutdown or out-of-

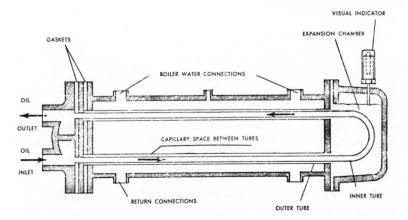

Figure 11-2. Safety Oil Heater (courtesy Cleaver-Brooks)

service periods. Indoor and outdoor exposed piping is literally wrapped with a special rubber or lead–covered electric–heating cable that is thermostatically controlled to maintain a 120–degree oil temperature under 20–degree ambient conditions. The stub heater, also containing its own thermostat, is a bayonet-shaped electric–immersion heater which is installed through the top of a tee of and extending into the suction pipe. Accessible in the manhole above the tank, it is connected by underground wiring to the same power source as (but independent of) the cable system. The total wattage of this system is ultra–low since it is not designed to heat moving oil, but merely maintain it in pumpable condition during standby.

The electric–impedance system performs a similar function to the cable system, in that it allows the oil pump to be shut down for long periods when necessary. In addition, it is capable of holding transport temperatures when the oil *is flowing*. This system works on the principle that electrical resistance can generate heat. All the components of the transport system are electrically transformed low–voltage, high–amperage electricity so that the metal surfaces become warm. The impedance system itself can even be turned off if desired, and the transport oil let congeal, if a sufficiently long time is allowed for warm–up on reactivation before the oil pump is energized.

IN-TANK HEATERS

Instead of, or sometimes in addition to, oil heater sets inside the boiler room, a heater is installed within the oil tank itself. One such type is called a suction-bell heater, and may be electric or a steam/water heat exchanger. Mounted at the bottom of and surrounding the suction pipe, it generally is not sized to heat all the oil in the tank, merely the volume of oil that the pump is moving. Optionally, these heaters may not be used unless a primary heater has failed or fallen behind; or in the case of a seasonal start-up, where the tank has been let go cold. On large, multiple-tank installations, for instance, it is not unusual to allow the reserve tank to stand-by without heat. The suction-bell heater, in addition to conventional pump-and-heater sets, makes this possible. (See Figure 11-3.)

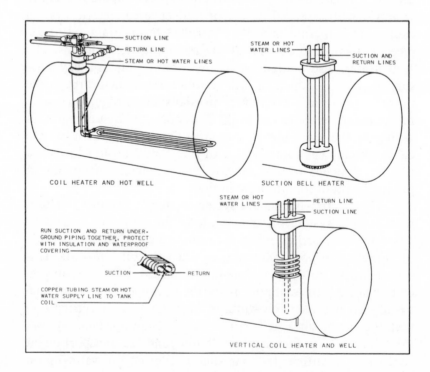

Figure 11-3. Tank Heater (courtesy Iron Fireman)

Another in-tank type heater is the serpentine coil, that winds back and forth over the length of the tank bottom. Its purpose is to heat all the oil in the tank uniformly, which is one of the requirements dictated by the use of high-paraffin-content oil. It too might be electric or steam/water.

BURNER-MOUNTED HEATERS

The intermittent operation of an oil burner that utilizes heated oil presents a special problem, for it is a characteristic of all types of burners that the atomizer, whether cup or nozzle, is invariably some distance from the main fuel cut-off valve. In a sense it is out on a limb, isolated from the heated, circulating oil. Therefore, it cools down during periods when the burner is off, as does the oil in the pipe interconnecting it and the valve. The problem is one not only concerned with pour point—with which we became involved when dealing with oil in storage—but also one of droplet formation and flame propagation. When the burner comes on and congealed oil must be displaced through the atomizer in less than satisfactory condition, hesitation, puffing, and even flame-out can occur.

Designers have attacked the problem in a number of ways. Either the fuel tube (as the pipe between the atomizer and the solenoid valve is called) is: (1) drained dry during post-purge; (2) the trapped oil is kept heated; or (3) the reduced viscosity of the cold oil is compensated for by turning down the air-handling system during light-off. The approach depends on the grade of oil; C.S. No. 6 requires that some provisions be made regardless of burner form, whereas C. S. No. 4 oil presents no problem for rotary and air-atomizing burners. Burners using high-pressure nozzles on No. 4 oil, however, require heat during atomization *and* standby.

THE ROTARY BURNER

The fuel tips of rotary burners are designed to reduce drooling of oil from the fuel tube after the main valve has closed, in addition to their function of distributing the oil on the inner surface of the whirling cup. Where the fuel tube has been kept from draining, and this slug of cold oil must be contended with on each light–off, the technique of *low–fire start* is customarily employed. By means of levers, links, and chains, a slow–speed gear motor closes the primary and secondary air dampers to some preset position relative to the firing rate of the oil metering valve, which is also turned down. The reduced flow rate of the cold oil with its high viscosity is thereby compensated for during the first few shaky seconds after ignition, basically by reducing air volume. An electrical interlock prevents the burner from starting in any but low–fire position, and to say that a smooth, smokeless, light–off with No. 6 oil is difficult to coordinate and maintain is an understatement regarding most rotary burners.

AIR ATOMIZERS

The Cleaver–Brooks air–atomizing burner using No. 6 oil, empties the fuel tube during the post–purge stage of the burner running cycle. As the fuel cut–off valve closes, a normally–closed solenoid valve in the atomizing air line opens, pressurizing the fuel oil in the fuel tube, so that it is literally blown out into the flame. As a matter of fact, it is an operating design feature of these burners that the flow rate of the purging air is metered. The precise pressure is delivered that is required to evacuate the oil from the tube, while maintaining the flow rate of the oil the same as it was before the fuel valve closed. In other words, when load demand ceases and the fuel valve closes, the flame does not go out immediately, because the oil under the influence of the purging air pressure continues a uniform flow until the fuel tube empties during the post–purge stage. Correspondingly, on light–off the flame is not established immediately upon the opening of the fuel valve, since it takes a few seconds for the fuel tube to refill with hot oil from the circulating supply.

The Orr & Sembower Powermaster does not purge the fuel tube. Instead, the oil temperature is monitored thermostatically, and the air pump is cycled as required to warm the fuel tube with hot atomizing air. The fuel tube, which has a relatively small diameter, runs within the air tube to the nozzle, forming a heat exchanger. As a result, the oil absorbs the heat of compression from the primary air stream, which is delivered at approximately 200 degrees.

OIL HEATER TROUBLES

Loss of capacity from an electric–immersion oil heater can usually be traced to the settling of sludge and sediment or water around the elements, requiring routine maintenance. The build-up causes channeling of the oil, which in effect is a bypassing of heating surface. Excessive accumulation of solids around the elements can also cause hot spots that eventually break down the insulating sheathing so that they short–circuit.

It is characteristic of electric heaters that they should not be operated *unless surrounded by oil*. Like the filament of a light bulb, the elements will burn up when exposed. For applications where higher than 140 degrees is required, the unit is generally interlocked to the burner or pump–control electrical circuit, so that oil will be flowing across the elements at times that electricity is on in the heater.

Depending on the number of electrical phases, the operation of the heater is done by a two– or three–pole relay, the coil of which is energized by a thermostat or aquastat. If the heater is the type with its own built–in thermostat, adjustment is made inside the junction–box cover on the heater head, by turning a screw or knurled nut. When an external aquastat is used, its well is located in the discharge line close to the heater.

Heat exchangers are controlled by regulating the steam or water supply from the boiler. This might be a simple solenoid valve in the piping to the steam–oil heater, wired through an aquastat; a pilot–operated valve; or, in the case of a water-to-oil heater, a thermostatically–controlled circulator.

Steam heaters are also subject to the effects of channeling. Since it is a basic shell–and–tube design, like the boiler it is also vulnerable to some of the problems associated with poor steam quality: the carry–over of suspended solids; corrosion and pitting of the tubes caused by the dissolved oxygen and carbon dioxide in the condensate. Steam heaters which are part of the packaged–boiler accessories and take their steam supply directly from the boiler shell, are particularly susceptible to the accumulation of suspended solids carried in with the steam. The solids often end up in the trap on the discharge line of the heater, resulting in obstruction of its valve mechanism and preventing the discharge of condensate and air. The heater then waterlogs and stops heating. If the oil temperature drops far enough the electric heater will come on, but will not be able to maintain the oil temperature required for high fire and the burner may go off on low oil temperature cut–out.

Steam–trap maintenance involves the periodic cleaning and inspection and, when necessary, the repair or replacement of the valves or seats. Control of corrosion requires the use of a good brand of steam–and–return–line treatment which carries over with the steam. Basically a liquid, when mixed with the boiler water it results in a volatile gas of the ammonia family. Referred to as a *foaming amine*, it mixes with the condensate and neutralizes the harmful acids dissolved there.

Bearing in mind that shell–and–tube heaters are pressure vessels of a sort, consideration must be given to the prevention and control of destructive pressures resulting from the loss of oil circulation. The rapid overheating and expansion of the oil trapped in the heater can be prevented in a number of ways. An oil pressure switch, which would open the control circuit to the oil heater upon loss of oil pump pressure, is advisable, particularly where the oil–heater thermostat is external to the heater. The pressure switch should be mounted on the oil inlet line to the heater, *after all shut–off valves* so that their deliberate or accidental closing will not isolate the heater from its control but, instead, assures prompt action upon loss of pressure.

In the case of a steam heater with other than electrical control, expansion can be controlled through the proper application of a relief valve or valves. Where low–design–pressure steam heaters are used on high–pressure–steam systems by means of pressure reducing valves at their steam inlets, a steam relief valve should be provided downstream of the regulator in case the regulator *runs away*. The relief valve should be sized to exhaust the total steam-carrying capacity of the high-pressure supply line to the heater, in case the regulator fails open. The outlet of the relief valve in turn should be piped to a safe point of discharge. The reduced pressure setting of the regulating valve should correspond to the recommended operating pressure of the heater, the steam trap selected accordingly, and the relief valve set to relieve well below the maximum safe operating pressure.

12

Principles of Oil Atomization

The term atomization, as used in oil-burner technology, refers to the physical preparation of fuel oil into a fine mist, each of whose droplets is on the order of 50 to 200 microns in diameter, and mixing it thoroughly with air. The process involves injecting the oil into the flame zone of the burner in a vapor-like conical spray. Actually the modern burner does not vaporize the oil, although years ago there were such burners used in residential space heaters. They gasified the oil by raising it to the boiling point prior to the introduction of air. These so-called *pot-type* burners are largely outlawed today for safety reasons.

In modern practice, vaporization or gasification of the fuel takes place in the combustion chamber as a physicochemical process. The ignition system of the burner starts the process by raising the temperature of the air-oil mixture to its boiling point and setting the resulting gas afire. Once the flame is established, it is said to *propagate*. That is, the environment sustains it as long as the burner system continues to supply fuel and air properly atomized and mixed.

There are several methods used to spray fuel oil into the combustion space, and the mechanics of oil droplet formation determine the group classification of the burner. Thus we have the following types of oil burners: horizontal rotary cup, pressure atomizer, air atomizer, and steam atomizer. Not included in this group are the highly-sophisticated ultrasonic atomizers, or the catalytic-process atomizers, which are largely experimental and have not gained wide acceptance at this writing.

The picture of an oil burner taking in oil on one side and precisely the right amount of air on the other, whipping the mixture into a beautifully homogenized stream which issues forth into perfect combustion, has tantalized original thinkers in the industry for years. The problem, however, has been that although air and oil could be made to mix by breaking down the oil into tiny droplets and spraying them into the air, or by *beating* air into the oil so as to form oil bubbles, uniform proportioning of the ingredients (oxygen, hydrogen, and carbon) could not be achieved. Regardless of the mechanical method used to aerate the oil, no new compound of air and oil resulted; each emerged from the process relatively unaffected by the presence of the other. What the early experimenters hoped to do, of course, was to produce the ideal *chemical solution* of air and oil.

A true chemical solution exists among two or more substances, called *elements,* when the smallest quantity of the compound which can be obtained possesses exactly the same proportion of the ingredients as any other random sample, regardless of the size of the sample. The elements are *chemically bonded* together in the compound, and the smallest quantity of the compound which contains all the elements is called a *molecule.* Air, for example, is a solution of the elements oxygen, nitrogen, and other gases, bonded together by their own molecular movement. Any volume we select at the same atmospheric pressure will contain 20.9 percent oxygen and 79.1 percent nitrogen and other gases.

Mixtures like air–and–oil differ from solutions in that the substances are visibly contrasted from one another like the grains of sand on a beach. They can be separated by physical manipulation such as distillation, filtration, and precipitation because there is no chemical attraction holding them together. In the case of the air–oil mixture, the oil eventually precipitates or drops out of the air stream due to the natural tendency of the oil droplets to recombine. When oil droplets come together to form larger and heavier droplets we say the oil has *coalesced.* That is the specific problem early burner designers encountered when they attempted to homogenize air and oil.

The pioneers were not without encouragement, for even sixty years ago researchers in a young physical science, known as Colloid Chemistry, had discovered that in addition to solids, liquids, and gases, there was a kind of fourth state in which matter could be made to coexist in suspended animation, as if held there by some electromagnetic force field rather than chemical attraction. The phenomenon, called *colloidal dispersion,* produced results not unlike chemical solutions, in that the mixture *could not* be easily separated by conventional means. However, unlike the result of a chemical union, no new compound or substance emerged. It was not like burning hydrogen in the presence of oxygen wherein water vapor is the end result, for this kind of *reaction* takes place at the *atomic level* and in accordance with certain fundamental laws. The hydrogen and oxygen atoms have a known affinity for each other and rearrange themselves in a totally predictable way during the combustion reaction. Colloidal dispersion takes place at the next higher plane of activity—the *molecular level*—and between chemically or physically incompatible substances. Although it would seem that the energy of the elements involved in a colloidal dispersion plays a role, the molecules of the substances do not lose their identities or change state. The participants in the dispersion are held together in intimate *surface* contact only, as though magnetized.

Experimenters found that a colloidal dispersion could be made to exist in all three states of matter by creating and then arresting submicroscopic particles of one substance in another. Submicroscopic gas bubbles in a liquid produced a foam; miniature droplets of liquid in a gas produced mists or aerosols. Droplets of one liquid in another were called emulsions. Invisible solid particles in air were recognized as soot or smoke, and those in liquids were called sols and are jelly–like. It is worthwhile to note that smog, in some instances, is the result of the photochemical reaction of sunlight with the colloidal dispersion of smoke and other solids in air.

Solutions are known to be the best media for chemical change, because they offer the most molecular freedom. But a chemical reaction (which combustion actually is) cannot begin unless the *reactants,* as the participating substances are called, are in intimate contact. Combustion engineers reason, therefore, that in the colloidal condition, the submicroscopic size of the oil droplets would ensure their rapid gasification by the heat energy of the ignition source, and their intimate contact with the combustion air would facilitate the oxidation of the hydrocarbon molecule once gasification of the droplets is completed. Current research and development of the more elaborate atomizing methods are aimed at achieving this ideal droplet size and condition.

Atomizing methods in past and present use, represented by the burner types listed at the beginning of this chapter, are not capable of producing submicroscopic–sized oil droplets. Nevertheless, to produce droplets even 50 microns in diameter requires finely–constructed and properly–maintained equipment.

Whether colloidal conditions can be approached by present burner systems is questionable in view of the limitations of the atomizing methods. But then our knowledge of the mechanism of colloidal dispersion itself is not complete enough to draw firm conclusions. We do know, however, that the smaller the oil droplet the better it disperses in the combustion air stream.

Colloid chemistry has emerged as a whole new field of science devoted to the nonchemical behavior of tiny molecules. An industry was born based on the technology of Surface Chemistry, as it is now known. From this beginning has come catalytically–cracked oils, electronic air cleaners, and transistorized radio and television, to mention but a few of the more obvious and commonplace benefits. Of more compelling importance will be the control of air and water pollution that a better understanding of colloidal dispersion will bring.

13

Atomizer Types

THE HORIZONTAL ROTARY CUP

Probably the simplest oil atomizer in appearance and construction is the rotary cup, shown in Figure 13-1. It derives its name from its water–glass or drinking–cup appearance. The cup has a fuel inlet port drilled in the bottom and attaches to a motor-driven shaft so that it revolves while lying horizontally. The drive shaft is actually a tube, inside of which the oil flows from the fuel–metering valve to the cup. The manner in which this is done is a design peculiarity of each individual make of burner, essentially involving a fuel pipe that passes through the hollow drive shaft and terminates inside the cup in a special orifice or tip, also called a *distributor*.

The design of the distributor is usually patterned after one or two basic types. The first and simplest is an orifice aimed to discharge the oil vertically upwards into the cup, which prevents the emptying of the horizontal fuel tube by gravity when the burner is idle. (See Figure 13-1.) The second design is a variation of the first method, that additionally involves bringing the oil up to cup speed more quickly by dividing the incoming oil into fine streams. In this case a spring–loaded valve in the distributor prevents oil dribble when the burner is not running.

When fuel oil is directed onto the revolving inner surface of the rotary cup, several things happen in quick succession. First, the oil slides around on itself as it comes up to the three- to five–thousand revolutions per minute at which the cup is spinning. Then it begins to move two ways from the point of

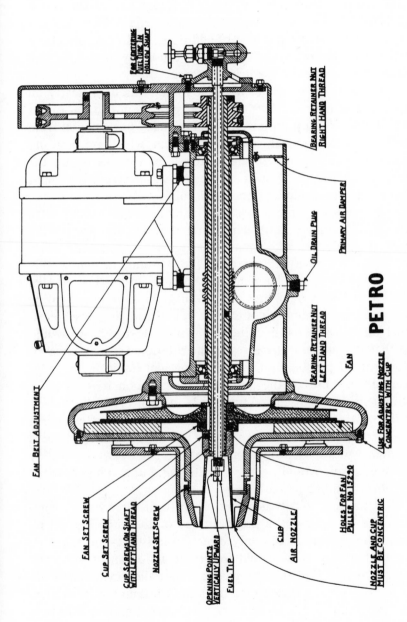

PETRO

FAN CENTERING
WELL TUBE IN
HOLLOW SHAFT

BEARING RETAINER NUT
RIGHT HAND THREAD

OIL DRAIN PLUG

PRIMARY AIR DAMPER

BEARING RETAINER NUT
LEFT HAND THREAD

FAN

USE FOR ADJUSTING NOZZLE
CONCENTRIC WITH CUP

HOLES FOR FAN
PULLER NO.15230

CUP

AIR NOZZLE

NOZZLE AND CUP
MUST BE CONCENTRIC

FUEL TIP

OPENING POINTS
VERTICALLY UPWARD

NOZZLE SET SCREW

CUP SCREWS ON SHAFT
WITH LEFT HAND THREAD

CUP SET SCREW

FAN SET SCREW

FAN BELT ADJUSTMENT

Figure 13-1. Petro Rotary Burner (courtesy Iron Fireman)

initial contact with the cup. Since only one end of the cup is open, the oil that flows toward the closed end remains to form a thin dyke resisting the flow of additional oil in that direction. The flow of oil toward the open end is caused by its incompressibility and the effect of centrifugal force.

The way in which centrifugal force is used in nearly all types of atomizers to develop the oil spray is not so obvious as with the rotary–cup atomizer, which actually hurls the oil from itself. Pressure atomizers and air atomizers, which are basically stationary orifices, use special channels or grooves to get the oil spinning. But, as we will see, centrifugal force is a dominant factor in their principle of operation too.

Any mass that is caused to whirl in a circle exercises a force against its restraint. The faster it whirls the greater the force. If we were to take a plastic bag partially filled with water, tied by the neck with a rope, and whirl it around in a circle, one of two things would happen. If we could turn it fast enough either the rope would break or the bag would burst, releasing the water. If by remote control we could read the pressure exerted on the water inside the bag while it revolved, we would see that the pressure increases as the rotational speed increases. Since for all practical purposes we consider liquid incompressible, its response to the pressure exerted upon it is to cause movement, as we discussed previously in regards to relief valves. In the case of the plastic bag, the resistance it can offer against the bursting pressure of the water is less than a metal pail could provide, had we used one instead of the bag. However exactly the same result would occur with the pail, but at a higher speed and corresponding pressure.

In the rotary–cup atomizer, centrifugal force tries to compress the oil against the inner surface of the cup. The oil responds by moving in the only direction left to it—out the open end of the cup. If we could freeze the action and remove the cup, we would find that we have a thin–walled cylinder of oil. As the oil cylinder is extruded from the whirling cup, it shatters into many thousands of tiny droplets, since it no longer has the cup surface to support and direct it. The thinner the wall of the liquid cylinder of oil is when it emerges from the cup, the more fragile it is. And this is the objective of the rotary–cup method; to create the thinnest film of oil possible, so that it will completely disintegrate when it emerges into the combustion air stream.

Again referring to Figure 13-1, it can be seen that the cup is surrounded by a portion of the burner snout called the *air nozzle*. Its relationship to the cup is critical in that it forms the exit for the primary combustion air. On some burners the nozzle has turning vanes that impart a spinning motion to the air as it collides with the oil droplets. Note that the open end of the cup and the open end of the air nozzle are not necessarily flush with one another, again depending on burner design and conditions. By moving the air nozzle backward or forward relative to the cup, or by combinations of cup and air nozzles of different diameters, the flame pattern can be lengthened, shortened, widened or narrowed to accommodate various combustion space limitations. At least one burner manufacturer provides an unvaned air nozzle that controls the flame pattern by adjusting special turning vanes inside the burner–fan housing. By means of an external control lever, this burner flame can be shaped during operation. In any case, the primary air stream must be directed by the air nozzle so as to surround and capture the oil droplets when they emerge from the cup. In order to do this, the velocity of the air at the nozzle is on the order of 10 to 20 *thousand* feet per minute depending on the oil–firing rate of the burner. It is not unusual, therefore, that the primary air–fan system of the rotary burner develop 18 or more inches water column of pressure at high firing rates. Yet only about 15 percent of the total air volume required for combustion is delivered in this way. Most of the combustion air is taken into the combustion space as secondary air, either by natural or mechanical draft, in most cases without ever having passed through the rotary oil burner. This is done by providing special air–inlet passages into the combustion space, either under the flame through openings in the combustion chamber floor, or around the burner snout through a special air register. (See Figure 13-2.)

If there were no high–velocity primary air stream, the oil

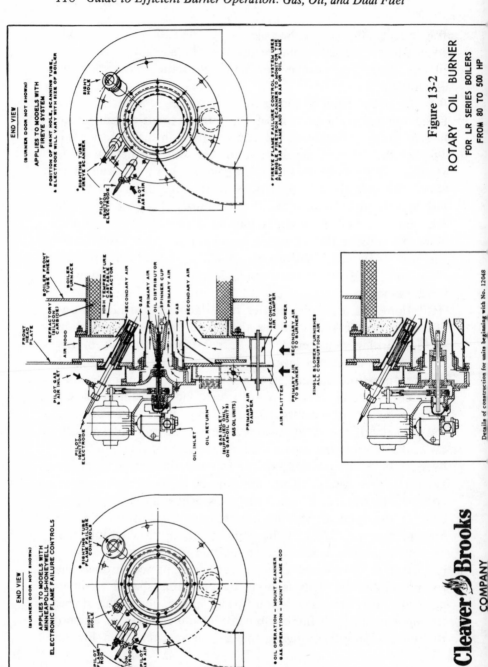

Figure 13-2

ROTARY OIL BURNER

FOR LR SERIES BOILERS
FROM 80 TO 500 HP

droplets would simply fly off the rotary cup at right angles to the fuel delivery tube and either spend themselves or impinge on the nearest surface in their flight path. The primary air stream prevents the escape of the oil droplets by holding them in an *air envelope* while they are brought up to gasification and ignition temperature. The shape of the air envelope is influenced by the nozzle/cup diameter ratio and relative positions as stated, and to a lesser extent by the shape of the cup itself. Not so much the inner shape, because the oil leaves the knife–sharp edge of all rotary cups in the same tangential path as the water bag mentioned in the analogy above would travel if we let go of the rope while spinning it. But the outer configuration of the cup has an aerodynamic effect on the primary air stream.

Generally, a cylindrical cup will produce a longer, narrower flame, whereas the use of a conically–shaped cup will result in a shorter, wider flame shape. This does not mean to imply that experimentation along these lines is advisable, because manufacturers' recommendations are quite explicit for selecting nozzle/cup combinations for just about every burner application.

The rotary–cup burner functions better with heavy oil than with light or distillate type oils. The more viscous the oil is the more resistance it offers against the rotation of the cup. Consequently, the oil comes up to cup speed faster and *slips over itself* less. The result is a more perfect, thinner–walled cylinder of oil emerging from the cup. Conversely, the friction-reducing qualities of most distillates (refer back to page 70) or the application of too much heat to residual oils, work against the thinning effect of centrifugal force in the cup. When the oil cylinder emerges from the cup with relatively thick walls, the droplets formed during disintegration in the primary air stream are correspondingly larger and heavier.

When the primary air and oil mix is imperfect, the appearance of the flame is characterized by brightly burning *fireflies* of oil. Sometimes raw oil drops can be seen striking and smouldering on refractory surfaces. Fireflies, or fireballs, are oil drops that are burning on their surface only, and decompose forming hard carbon deposits, or *coke trees,* where they land. For one of several reasons these drops have passed through the primary air envelope. It might be that the heavy oil droplets are caused by some imperfection in the rotary cup. Damage to the surface of the cup, especially the thin, sharp lip, can cause large drop formation, as can carbon buildup inside the cup.

SPRAY NOZZLES

When all the oil burners in use today are considered in total, the most common mechanism of oil–droplet preparation is the spray nozzle. The great majority of the more than 10 million domestic oil burners in operation in this country, and many thousands operating elsewhere in the world, use this principle of atomization. It is by no means limited to household burners, but finds wide application on commercial and industrial oil burners as well. Because of the enormous popularity of the pressure–atomizing burner for home–heating use, there has come about a certain standardization of spray–nozzle technology among the many burner manufacturers so that for more than 20 years no major domestic burner manufacturer has made his own spray nozzle. He buys his nozzles from a nozzle manufacturer. The same applies to many other burner–system components, such as fuel–oil pumps and electrical controls. But it is not entirely true in the case of air–atomizing burner manufacturers. Here, there is little or no interchangeability of nozzles, for example, among the different makes of air–atomizing burners.

Spray nozzles fall into two main groups: *single–fluid atomizers* and *two–fluid atomizers*. As the categories imply, a nozzle may be designed to spray oil only, which is the single–fluid *pressure atomizer*. Pressure–atomizer burners, such as the domestic burners previously referred to, are commonly called *high–pressure burners* because of the 100 to 300 psi oil pressure at which they operate.

Two–fluid atomizers are designed to spray a mixture of oil and air, or a mixture of oil and steam. Hence we have *air–atomizing burners* and *steam–atomizing burners*. Air atomizers and steam atomizers customarily operate with oil pressures less than 100 psi, and often at oil pressures lower than 30 psi. Therefore, as a subgroup, two–fluid atomizers are referred to as *low– pressure burners.* The purpose of the second fluid, whether it be air or steam, is to spin the oil inside the nozzle. Spinning or swirling the oil is the essential technique of droplet formation common to all mechanical atomizers. The high–pressure nozzle uses the inertia of the oil itself to set up the spinning action of centrifugal force.

THE HIGH-PRESSURE NOZZLE

The high–pressure nozzle (Figure 13-3) consists of two basic sections, comprising one or more parts each. The outer body or tip of the nozzle acts to contain the oil and provide an orifice for its discharge. The inner section (known variously as the core, stem, or swirler) slips or screws precisely into the tip. When the nozzle is assembled, there is an internal space or void between the nose of the core and the tip of the nozzle called the swirl chamber. The swirl chamber is upstream of the orifice through which the oil leaves the nozzle.

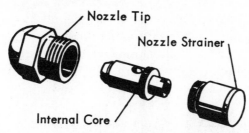

Figure 13-3. High-Pressure Spray Nozzle (courtesy Cleaver-Brooks)

The core contains several channels or slots which meter and divide the oil stream. The slots are machined in the nose of the core at an angle to the inner surface of the tip. The oil flows through the tangential slots, as they are called, under pressure and spins into the swirl chamber at high velocity. The effect is to cause the oil to rotate at high speed before being discharged through the orifice into the combustion space. At the same time, the sudden expansion of the oil into the swirl chamber acts to break its *surface tension,* or natural tendency to hold together.

Centrifugal force, caused by the spinning, spreads the oil evenly over the inner surface of the tip, so that when it emerges from the orifice it literally explodes into a mist.

The oil mist which issues from the orifice takes on certain characteristics as to size and shape depending on the particular configuration of the nose of the core and the inner surface of the tip. However, the symmetrical oil spray is always cone-shaped, with the apex or point of the cone at the nozzle orifice. The spray cone of a specific nozzle may be uniformly filled with oil droplets, and therefore called a *solid spray pattern*. Or the droplets may form a *hollow cone pattern*, which, as the name indicates, would be analogous to an empty ice-cream cone. The type of spray cone the individual nozzle will produce is marked on the side of the nozzle body, usually by the letter 'S' or 'H' accordingly. Nozzles that present combinations of these two basic patterns are also available and especially marked with code letters by the manufacturers. The nozzle body is also stamped with the degrees of the spray angle of the oil cone, ranging from 30 to 90 degrees.

Nozzles are available in assorted spray angles and patterns and offer a distinct advantage over the rotary-cup atomizer which, as we have seen, produces a 180-degree-nonvariable pattern and depends on the capture velocity of the primary air stream to shape the spray pattern. The high-pressure nozzle, on the other hand, can be closely matched to virtually any air pattern of which a particular burner is capable. As we will see in the section of the text on combustion, maximum flexibility in matching the oil mist with the burner's air delivery pattern is the hallmark of good design. As we have seen, satisfactory combustion of the fuel and air mixture depends on intimate surface contact of the oil and air molecules.

Possibly the most important function of the high-pressure nozzle is to meter the oil-flow rate into the combustion space. The size of the orifice in the tip, and to a lesser extent the number and characteristics of the tangential slots, perform this task. Pressure-atomizing nozzles are calibrated and stamped (also on the body) according to the number of gallons of oil per hour they will pass under standard conditions, those being: the oil at

100 degrees and under 100 pounds pressure with a viscosity of 35 SSU.

Table 13-1 lists the flow capacities of conventional oil spray nozzles at other than 100 psi. Note that a nozzle with a nominal rating of 20 gph will deliver 34.6 gph at 300 psi. This phenomenon is used to advantage by a number of burner manufacturers to achieve a smooth, safe ignition when the burner is operating in the oil mode. Referred to as low–fire start, light–off is accomplished at reduced oil pressure and corresponding lowered fuel–input rate. The combustion air volume is generally reduced also according to burner design.

Table 13-1. Simplex Oil Nozzle Delivery Rates
(courtesy Gordon-Piatt Energy Group)

	PUMP PRESSURE IN PSI								
	100	125	150	175	200	225	250	275	300
	2.00	2.24	2.45	2.63	2.87	3.00	3.16	3.30	3.46
	2.50	2.78	3.05	3.30	3.53	3.75	3.96	4.12	4.32
	3.00	3.34	3.65	3.94	4.23	4.50	4.73	4.95	5.18
	3.50	3.90	4.26	4.60	4.95	5.25	5.51	5.78	6.01
	4.00	4.46	4.88	5.27	5.64	6.00	6.32	6.61	6.92
	4.50	5.02	5.48	5.92	6.32	6.75	7.10	7.42	7.78
	5.00	5.58	6.10	6.60	7.06	7.50	7.92	8.28	8.65
5.50	6.15	6.72	7.25	7.80	8.25	8.70	9.11	9.50	
6.00	6.68	7.30	7.88	8.46	9.00	9.46	9.90	10.36	
7.00	7.80	8.52	9.20	9.90	10.50	11.02	11.56	12.02	
8.00	8.92	9.76	10.54	11.28	12.00	12.64	13.22	13.84	
9.00	10.04	10.96	11.84	12.64	13.50	14.20	14.84	15.56	
10.00	11.16	12.20	13.20	14.12	15.00	15.84	16.56	17.30	
11.00	12.30	13.44	14.50	15.60	16.50	17.40	18.22	19.00	
12.00	13.36	14.60	15.76	16.92	18.00	18.92	19.80	20.72	
13.00	14.53	15.98	17.20	18.40	19.54	20.60	21.50	22.50	
14.00	15.60	17.04	18.40	19.80	21.00	22.04	23.12	24.04	
15.00	16.78	18.38	19.82	21.30	22.50	23.60	24.80	25.90	
16.00	17.84	19.52	21.08	22.56	24.00	25.28	26.44	27.68	
17.00	19.00	20.70	22.50	24.05	25.50	26.90	28.00	29.30	
18.00	20.08	21.92	23.68	25.28	27.00	28.40	29.68	31.12	
20.00	22.32	24.40	26.40	28.24	30.00	31.68	33.12	34.60	
22.00	24.60	26.88	29.00	31.20	33.00	34.80	36.44	38.00	

(left axis label: NOMINAL NOZZLE SIZE)

NOTES: Delivery rates are approximate only. Actual rates will vary slightly between different nozzles of same rating.

Delivery also varies with viscosity of fuel. Low gravity, low oil temperature and high viscosity tend to increase delivery. High gravity, high oil temperatures or low viscosity tend to reduce delivery.

The above table is based on No. 2 fuel oil.

Typically, the reduced-pressure starting technique is used on No. 2 and No. 4 oil burners with maximum inputs of about 35 gph. The Gordon-Piatt burner is an example of equipment in the field that uses this low-fire start method.

14

Oil Firing-Rate Control Methods

GORDON-PIATT ENERGY GROUP
STARTING SEQUENCE

The Gordon-Piatt F4 oil supply system is used for low-fire start control of No. 2 oil burners designed for on-off operation and employs a single high–pressure nozzle. The valve and piping arrangement (Figure 14-1) provides a low- and high-pressure oil delivery to the nozzle. The combustion air damper is positioned in response to changes in the fuel pressure by the action of an oil cylinder and piston–drive assembly. The burner air–inlet damper (louver) is connected to the oil piston and spring–loaded in the full–open (high-fire) position. Pressure to operate the piston is generated by the same oil pump which delivers fuel to the nozzle. High–fire oil pressure is adjusted and maintained by a regulating valve built into the fuel–pump unit. Low-fire oil pressure is adjusted and maintained by the bypass oil–pressure regulating valve external to the pump.

When the burner starts, both main and bypass oil solenoid valves remain closed. The oil piston remains in the retracted position allowing high–fire combustion air volume to purge the combustion space before ignition. At the end of the prepurge interval the ignition transformer is energized and the main and bypass oil solenoid valves open, supplying oil to the nozzle at the low–fire pressure setting of the bypass pressure–regulating valve. When the bypass oil solenoid valve opens, the oil piston extends from the cylinder and drives the air damper (louver) closed for low-fire combustion air volume and the burner ig-

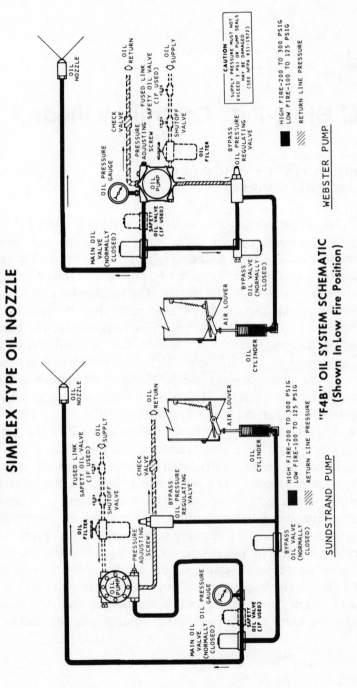

Figure 14-1. Low-Fire Start Schematic (courtesy Gordon-Piatt Energy Group)

nites. After the flame is established and proved by the action of the flame detector, the ignition transformer is deenergized. At the same time, the bypass oil solenoid closes stopping the flow through the bypass pressure-regulating valve thus raising the nozzle pressure to the high-fire setting of the oil pump's integral pressure-regulating valve. When the bypass oil solenoid valve closes the oil cylinder piston retracts, allowing the air louver spring to pull the louver to the full-open position and the burner goes to the high-fire mode.

MULTIPLE NOZZLES

Burners which use multiple nozzles firing No. 2 oil are quite common in the field of commercial-industrial applications. Sometimes referred to as duplex- and triplex-nozzle arrangements, they are offered by manufacturers either to provide finer atomization of the oil or to vary the oil-firing rate.

It has been well established over the years that two nozzles are better than one, especially at firing rates higher than about 10 gallons per hour. Multiple nozzles produce a combined spray cone of finer oil droplets than a single large nozzle could develop. Twin 5 gph nozzles, for example, generate smaller droplets than a single 10 gph nozzle because of the fact that droplet diameter is a function of orifice diameter. Since the orifice in the nozzle tip, which meters the oil, increases in proportion to the firing rate, droplet sizes increase with the firing rate also. Consequently, at a fixed-inlet pressure, large gallonage nozzles do not reach the swirl velocity of their smaller counterparts. Nor does a large orifice permit the degree of expansion needed to completely break the surface tension on the oil as it emerges from the swirl chamber.

The CBH and Model 4 series of Cleaver-Brooks boilers use multiple burner nozzles. The burner operates at two firing rates, high-fire and low-fire, and combustion air is provided by a centrifugal blower located in the front head of the boiler. Combustion air delivery to the burner is regulated by a damper motor. On combination fuel boilers, the same motor regulates the flow of gas fuel through a linkage system connected to a gas butter-

fly valve or by actuating switches that energize multiple oil solenoid valves. The motor is powered electrically to open the air
damper and spring-returned to the closed position when the
power is removed.

The cam switches which are actuated by the rotation of
the damper motor shaft are called *auxiliary switches* and are
wired in series with individual solenoid valves and/or programmer circuits.

METHOD OF OPERATION

The oil-fired Model 4 boiler has a burner-mounted fuel-oil
pump which is belt-driven by the blower motor. The pump has
an integral oil pressure-regulating valve which can be adjusted
to provide the necessary atomizing pressure to the three burner
nozzles (approximately 200 psi).

Oil flow to the burner is controlled by four solenoid valves.
Referring to Figure 14-2, the oil flows through a primary or oil
safety shut-off valve into a manifold block. This valve and the
low-fire oil solenoid valve are energized simultaneously by the
combustion program control and when opened allow oil flow
to the low-fire nozzle.

As the damper motor moves to high-fire position, cam
switches actuated by the damper motor shaft close in sequence
the intermediate solenoid valve and then the high-fire oil valve.
The purpose of the intermediate oil valve and spray nozzle is to
make a smooth transition from low- to high-fire by balancing
the fuel input with the increasing flow of air through the opening air damper, and is called *staging.*

Maximum fuel input to the burner is achieved when all
three nozzles are firing, assuming proper oil pressure is maintained by the fuel delivery system.

CAM ADJUSTMENT

The oil-fired Model 4 boiler uses two switches to energize
the intermediate and high-fire oil valves. According to insurance company requirements, there may be one or two more cam

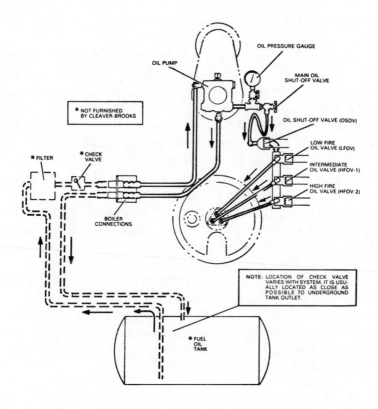

Figure 14-2. Multiple Nozzles (courtesy Cleaver-Brooks)

switches bringing the total to four. One of these additional switches, the low-fire switch (LFS), used on all Model 4 boilers, must be closed to complete programmer circuitry, thus assuring that the air damper is in low-fire position before ignition takes place. The switch opens when the damper motor drives to high-fire air position during prepurge and closes when the damper resumes its low-fire position upon completion of the purge interval. The cam, therefore, must be adjusted so that it actuates this switch just prior to the damper reaching its closed position.

In addition, the high-fire switch (HFS) is used, when required, to prove that the air damper is opened during prepurge. Its contacts should close when the damper is nearly open and just before the timing of the programmer deenergizes the damper motor.

The auxiliary switches which operate the intermediate and high-fire oil valves (AS-1 and AS-2) should be adjusted as follows: As the damper motor moves toward high-fire, the air damper allows an increasing amount of air into the boiler. AS-1 should allow the intermediate oil valve to open at approximately mid-range of the damper movement, but definitely at a point when sufficient air is present so that there is no incomplete combustion or smoke caused by improper air/fuel ratio. The positioning of the cam on the motor shaft should be guided by observing the fire through the inspection port or watching the stack when the valve opens. If smoke other than a slight haze is noticed, the cam should be repositioned so that the valve opens a little later in the damper stroke.

The second oil valve switch (AS-2) should be actuated by its cam just as the damper reaches high-fire position. On the basis of flue gas analysis, damper position or linkage adjustment may be required to increase or decrease air flow at this point, whereupon low and intermediate flame characteristics will have to be rechecked also.

THE RETURN-FLOW NOZZLE

Another device used by some burner manufacturers to vary the fuel input of a high-pressure atomizing-type oil burner is the return-flow or bypass nozzle. Also known as a spill nozzle or variflow nozzle, it is used with a specially designed two-pipe fuel-tube arrangement as shown in Figure 14-3. Essentially a pressure-atomizing nozzle, it has a provision for returning part of the oil delivery from the fuel tube back into the return line to the oil storage tank. The amount of oil available for atomization by the nozzle is regulated by an oil metering valve, or a back-pressure valve, installed in the bypass or return-flow oil line from the nozzle. The bypass return line is closed by the oil metering valve to achieve high-fire input rate and opened for low-fire rate in response to the firing rate modulation system. Also connected to the drive train is the air register or damper,

BYPASS OIL NOZZLE

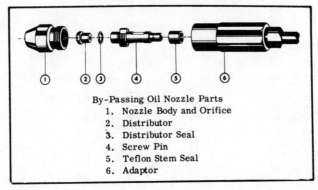

By-Passing Oil Nozzle Parts
1. Nozzle Body and Orifice
2. Distributor
3. Distributor Seal
4. Screw Pin
5. Teflon Stem Seal
6. Adaptor

Figure 14-3. Bypass Nozzle (courtesy Gordon-Piatt Energy Group)

so that combustion air is proportioned to the oil firing rate (see Figure 14-4). Commonly used on burners with firing rates of from 20 to 225 gallons per hour, they will atomize grades 2 through 6 oil satisfactorily as long as the burner's oil–heating equipment is capable of holding the oil viscosity at the nozzle to 100 SSU or less. In the low–fire input mode, approximately 75 percent of the oil is returned to the tank and 25 percent discharged through the nozzle orifice, so we say that typically burners using this fuel–rate–control method have a *turndown ratio* of 4 to 1.

Table 14-1 shows the flexibility of the internal bypass nozzle system.

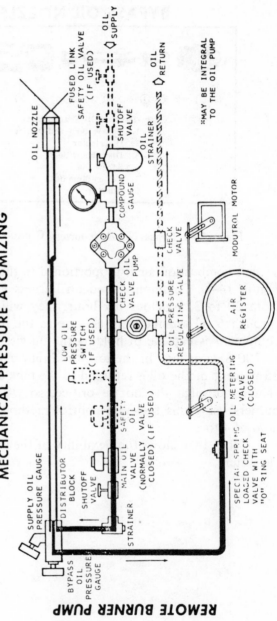

MODULATING OR HIGH-LOW   F7 OIL SYSTEM

- NO. 2 OIL
- PROVEN LOW FIRE START CONTROL
- SINGLE BYPASSING TYPE OIL NOZZLE

MECHANICAL PRESSURE ATOMIZING

REMOTE BURNER PUMP

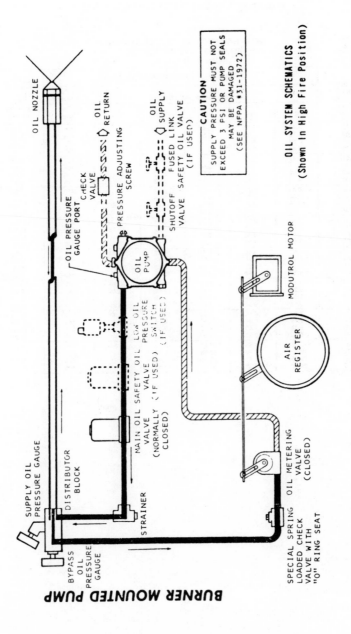

Figure 14-4. Mechanical Pressure Atomizer

Table 14-1. Bypass Nozzle Delivery Rates
(courtesy Gordon-Piatt Energy Group)

INTERNAL BY-PASS NOZZLE SYSTEM
FLOW RATE VS PRESSURE
(MONARCH F-80 BPS)

100 PSIG Nominal Rating GPH By-Pass Closed	U.S. GALLONS PER HOUR No. 2 FUEL OIL BY-PASS PRESSURE PSIG					By-Pass Pressure By-Pass Closed	300 PSIG Nominal Capacity GPH By-Pass Closed
	0	60	120	180	240		
.75	.43	.66	1.07			135	1.30
1.00	.52	.85	1.35			165	1.75
1.50	.87	1.13	2.46			135	2.60
2.00	1.13	1.89	3.10			135	3.45
2.50	1.47	2.41	3.66			150	4.35
3.00	1.47	2.60	3.98			165	5.20
3.50	1.56	2.17	3.55	5.72		195	6.05
4.00	2.34	2.77	4.07	5.93		210	6.95
4.50	2.34	2.77	4.07	6.58		210	7.80
5.00	2.34	2.90	4.16	6.65		210	8.65
5.50	2.34	2.91	4.33	7.96	9.55	240	9.55
6.00	2.86	3.55	4.33	5.54	10.40	240	10.40
6.50	2.86	2.95	3.55	6.24	11.25	240	11.25
7.00	3.03	4.16	5.37	7.62	12.15	240	12.15
7.50	3.03	4.16	5.80	9.70	13.00	240	13.00
8.00	3.03	3.38	4.85	7.97	13.85	240	13.85
9.00	3.47	4.68	5.72	7.97	11.43	270	15.60
9.50	3.73	4.16	5.89	9.18	16.45	240	16.45
10.50	3.98	4.33	6.93	10.48	18.20	240	18.20
12.00	4.33	4.68	6.93	10.57	20.80	240	20.80
13.80	5.20	6.24	9.70	18.00	23.90	225	23.90
15.30	5.20	6.24	9.10	13.51	22.55	255	26.50
17.50	6.50	7.28	11.35	20.60		225	30.30
19.50	6.93	9.18	13.52	20.10	33.80	240	33.80
21.50	7.09	8.49	12.48	19.05	37.30	240	37.20
24.00	7.79	8.84	13.60	22.70	41.60	240	41.60
28.00	9.35	9.53	18.88	29.90		225	48.50
30.00	9.53	12.13	19.92	31.85		225	52.00
35.00	13.85	21.85	31.50	45.00		225	60.70
40.00	16.62	20.80	35.55	61.60		195	69.40
45.(w)	23.95	32.10	49.10	71.60		195	78.00
50.00	29.30	40.80	64.50	86.60		165	86.60

15

Air Atomizing Systems

LOW-PRESSURE AIR ATOMIZERS

The principles of operation of the air–atomizing nozzle found application very early in the evolution of the modern-day oil burner. Firmly rooted in domestic oil–burner development, early burners were fancifully pictured as capable of homogenizing the air and oil. However, it has come to be recognized that the function of the air atomizer is not to blend the air and oil together. Rather, its job is to break down the liquid stream of oil into a mist of tiny droplets. In the process, oil and air streams are brought into the atomizer by separate routes, interact upon one another, and leave through a common orifice. Though there is limited aeration in the mixing process, which aids in the formation of very fine oil droplets through colloidal dispersion, the bulk of the oil is under the primary influence of centrifugal force in a swirl chamber much like its smaller cousin the pressure atomizer.

Physically, the air atomizer is much larger than a pressure-atomizing nozzle of the same gph capacity. The orifice, for example, may be as much as 50 times larger (see Figure 15-1). The relative absence of tiny, easily clogged grooves and openings is one of the built-in advantages claimed for the air atomizer, especially when handling the so-called heavy oils. The oil is delivered to the nozzle at very low pressure, usually on the order of 25 to 30 psi. At low-fire rate, pressures of 5 to 10 psi are not uncommon.

Without the help of compressed air the oil would simply

Nozzle Swirler

Nozzle Tip

Nozzle Body

Spring

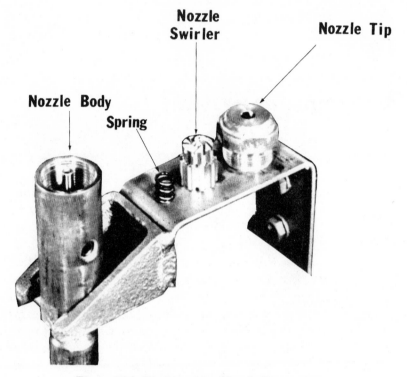

Figure 15-1. Air Atomizing Nozzle Components
(courtesy Cleaver-Brooks)

drool out of the nozzle. Generation of the oil spray is dependent on the interaction of the oil and air within the nozzle. Therefore an integral part of each air–atomizing oil burner is its compressed–air system which develops the *primary air,* as the atomizing air is called.

AIR/OIL INTERACTION

The fact that the oil is so much more dense than the compressed air gives it a dominant role in determining operating pressures not only within the nozzle, but of the primary air system in general. Then, too, the fact that the air is compressible and the oil is not, affects the manner in which the air–oil mix leaves the nozzle through the common orifice.

Figure 15-2 shows schematically the components that make up an air-atomizing oil burner. Like the variflow high-pressure nozzle system previously discussed, this is a two-pipe nozzle system, too, except that one line is for oil and the other

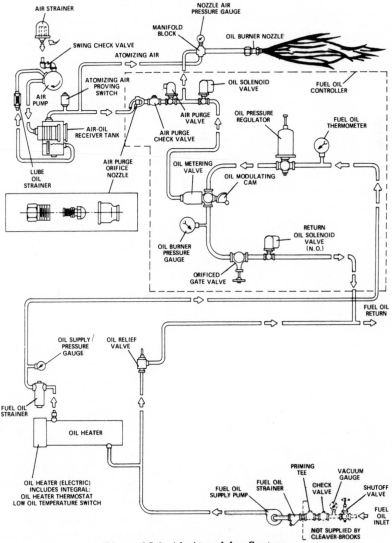

Figure 15-2. Air Atomizing System
(courtesy Cleaver-Brooks)

is for air and there is no return flow from the nozzle. Many air-atomizing burners use the pipe-within-a-pipe nozzle line as illustrated here (Figure 15-2), rather than parallel pipes. As pointed out earlier, the heat absorption possible with this design is an advantage when burning heavy oils.

Notice that there are no valves or regulators in the air line from the compressor to the nozzle, other than a check valve; this is typical of most air-atomizing burners. When no oil is flowing the primary air is free to exit the nozzle unimpeded, and since the air compressor or air pump (as some manufacturers prefer to call it) has a fixed displacement and runs at a constant speed, we would have a relatively high volume, low velocity continuous air flow. The flow might be likened to the water flow from a garden hose without a nozzle attached. Typically, primary air pressure might be 10 to 12 psi.

When the oil solenoid valve is opened, however, the air has a competitor within the nozzle, for the oil too must pass through the nozzle orifice. The dense oil volume tends to fill the passages in the nozzle, swirl chamber, tangential slots, expansion chamber, and so on (Figure 15-3), restricting the air flow so that its pressure goes up, perhaps as much as 4 or 5 psi. Since the air volume is relatively constant, increasing the oil flow rate puts even more back pressure on the air stream so that its pressure goes still higher. The difference in primary air pressure, therefore, from low- to high-fire rate could be on the order of 15 to 20 psi caused from the back pressure acting on it by the oil within the atomizer.

The instant that the oil oozes forth inside the atomizer, the air stream, which enters at a much higher velocity than the oil, literally gobbles up the oil and sweeps it into the mixing chamber where the first stage of droplet formation begins. The air stream provides the energy which propels the oil through the break-up process; an interface of high-velocity air and low-velocity oil producing the finest atomization. The entrainment of the oil by the relatively high-velocity air stream within the nozzle is facilitated by the oblique collision course of the two fluids. From the point of impact of the air upon the oil, each fluid loses its individual identity and takes the form of an oil-

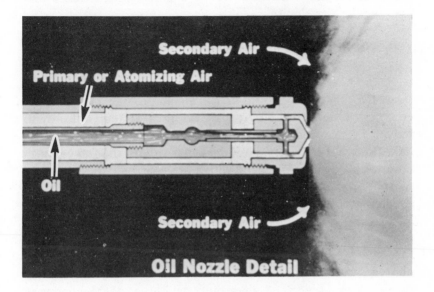

Figure 15-3. Air Atomizer Detail
(courtesy Cleaver-Brooks)

saturated air stream. This turbulent mixture has a density heavier than air but much lighter than the oil alone. When the oil metering valve opens in response to increased load demand the density of the combined air–oil mix becomes even greater because we are putting more oil into a relatively fixed air volume. It is a fact that oil droplet sizes tend to increase in proportion to the increased density of the aerated mixture, which may seem to say that atomizer efficiency drops off as we increase the firing rate or when oil viscosities increase (as sometimes happens). However, there are some other forces at work which tend to offset this potential shortcoming. One is the venturi effect inside the nozzle caused by the squeezing effect the oil has on the air. This results in an increased air velocity and reduced pressure at the interface. It is also a fact that droplet size is inversely proportional to the relative velocities of the two fluids, so that as air velocity goes up droplet size goes down, counteracting to a large extent the effect of increased fuel flow. An increase in oil viscosity which, as outlined in chapter 3, is actually an increase in resistance to flow, causes a similar interaction by increasing the air velocity.

THE AIR PUMP (COMPRESSOR)

The heart of the air–atomizing system is the air pump. In turn, the reliable operation of the air pump, like any other air compressor, depends upon its lubricating oil system, not only to reduce friction, but to provide the 1.5 to 2 thousandths of an inch fluid seal between the moving parts. With the foregoing an indication of the tolerances which are characteristic, it should be no surprise to find that field disassembly and repair is not generally recommended by most manufacturers of air pumps.

Routine maintenance is limited to periodic draining and flushing of the lube oil reservoir or crankcase, cleaning of air filters and screens, and the replacement of worn drive components such as belts and couplings. Methods of lubrication, like many other aspects of air–atomizing burner technique, vary from one burner manufacturer to another. The Cleaver–Brooks system is quite complex, for example, whereas the Orr and Sembower method is not. Though both manufacturers use sliding–vane rotary air pumps, each has a different concept when it comes to lubrication.

Cleaver–Brooks

The Cleaver–Brooks method is to force–feed lubricating oil to the compressor from a large lube–oil reservoir that doubles as an oil separator. With this system, lube oil is in constant circulation when the burner is operating. The pressure that produces the flow is provided by the air pump itself, Figure 15-4.

The air discharge line from the compressor is connected at the center of the lube–oil reservoir (Figure 15-5) and pressurizes the surface of the oil. Beneath the surface of the oil, near the bottom of the reservoir, is where the oil line to the air pump connects. The other end of this line connects with the air pump near the air inlet, so that in effect the air entering the compressor entrains the oil. Since the discharge line of the com-

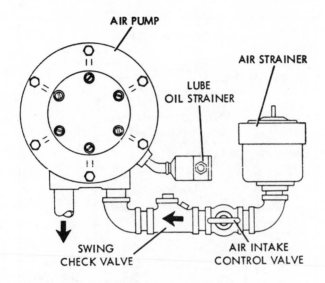

Figure 15-4. Air Pump (courtesy Cleaver-Brooks)

pressor is connected to the center of the reservoir, the entrained lube oil is carried there by the air.

Inside the reservoir, the saturated air stream passes through a bronze–wool, or steel–wool, maze where the oil impinges and drops out of the air stream before it exits to the burner nozzle assembly. The arrangement is less than 100 percent efficient, however, and some lube oil is carried into the combustion process where it is consumed.

Oil is added to Cleaver–Brooks systems with belt–driven compressors by pouring it very slowly into the compressor air inlet while the air filter is removed and the burner operating; or by pouring it directly through the fill cap on the reservoir, with the burner off. A sight glass is provided on the tank for indicating proper level.

Certain sizes of later model Cleaver–Brooks boilers have air–pump modules (Figure 15-6) which are self-contained units comprising air pump, close–coupled to its own electric motor drive; lube–oil tank and cooling system, mounted on the boiler base support, wired and piped into the burner system. These

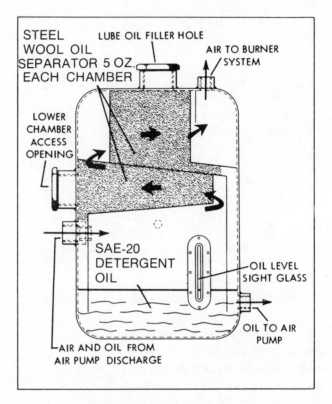

**Figure 15-5. Lube Oil Reservoir, Early
(courtesy Cleaver-Brooks)**

lube–oil reservoirs are considerably more compact and easier to service than the belt–driven compressor systems previously described. Access to the interior of the reservoir is more convenient for cleaning of the metal–wool oil separator (Figure 15-7). Oil separation is considerably more efficient also. SAE 20 *detergent* oil is used in this modular system, whereas SAE 10 *non*detergent motor oil is recommended for use with the belt–drive compressors.

Adding oil to the modular system should be done only while the compressor is running and then only through the oil filler pipe with conical strainer properly in place. The strainer in the filler line serves two purposes, the first of which is to prevent foreign material from entering the pump with the oil, and

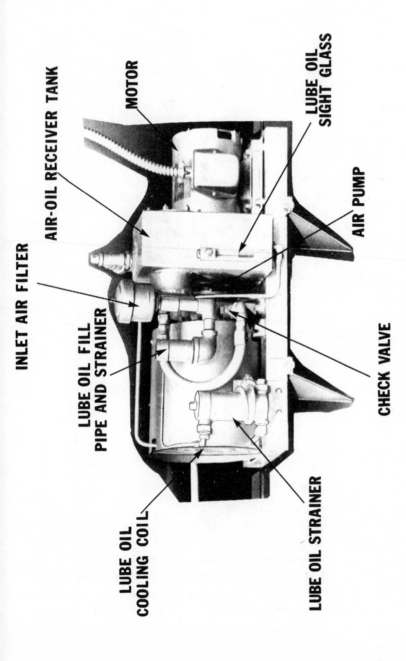

INLET AIR FILTER

AIR-OIL RECEIVER TANK

MOTOR

LUBE OIL
SIGHT GLASS

AIR PUMP

LUBE OIL FILL
PIPE AND STRAINER

CHECK VALVE

LUBE OIL
COOLING COIL

LUBE OIL STRAINER

Figure 15-6. Air Pump Module, Later (courtesy Cleaver–Brooks)

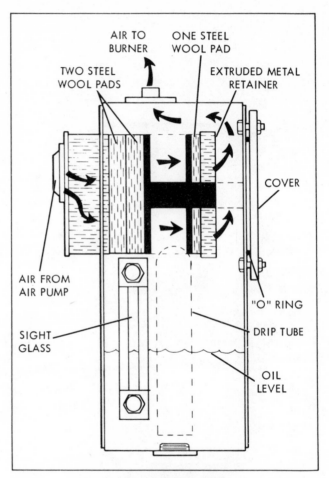

Figure 15-7. Interior of Reservoir
(courtesy Cleaver-Brooks)

the second less obvious reason is to provide a means of restricting the flow rate at which the oil is added. *The manufacturer cautions against bypassing this feature* either by removing the strainer or by adding oil through the air–inlet opening since this may permit the addition of a greater quantity of oil than the pump can normally absorb. Flooding the air pump places a strain on the blades and could cause them to break, as well as overloading the motor.

A final note on lube oil consumption: All other things being equal, lube oil consumption is higher when the burner runs steadily in the low-fire mode than when it modulates or cycles on and off. This is not an argument in favor of intermittent operation, however; merely an observation. The reason the lube oil consumption is higher in low-fire is that primary air volume (cfm) is greater in low-fire position than in high-fire position. As we have seen in our discussion of the dominant effect of the fuel oil inside the nozzle, primary air volume is inversely related to atomizing air pressure. Simply put, more air going to the fire carries with it more entrained lube oil. On Cleaver-Brooks combination burners, with automatic changeover to gas fuel triggered by an outdoor temperature sensor, this could be significant. When the burner is firing gas with the oil gun still in position, atomizing air is allowed to flow through the nozzle to keep it cool. It could be a costly oversight on the part of an operating engineer if he did not maintain a proper lube oil level, *even though the burner is firing gas.* As long as the compressor is operating, lube oil is being consumed. On units where fuel changeover is done manually, and the oil gun is retracted or removed from the firing position, the air pump drive can be disconnected mechanically or electrically, eliminating this concern.

Orr & Sembower (Gast Rotary Air Compressor)

The Orr & Sembower (Gast) air compressor is combined with the fuel oil pump on the same base and shares the same motor drive. Lubrication is provided by either a vacuum or wick-type oiler. The vacuum sight-feed lubricator is used on the larger compressors and is mounted near the air inlet. On some units a solenoid valve arrangement is installed just below the oiler and is wired to open only when the compressor motor runs. When the oiler is functioning properly, two bubbles per minute can be seen escaping from the vent opening into the oil reservoir. A typical lube oil recommended by the factory would be Socony D.T.E. light (SAE 10). Since the main discharge line from the compressor goes directly to the burner nozzle assembly, except for a branch line used to operate an air-piloted re-circulating valve which brings hot oil to the burner during stand-by, no oil separation is provided and all the lube oil is consumed.

Recommended service procedure includes cleaning the oil bath-type air-inlet filter once a month, replacing the lube oil as necessary, keeping the finned housing of the compressor free of lint and dirt which would interfere with proper cooling, and flushing the vanes and cylinder monthly by feeding half a cup of kerosene slowly into the pump inlet while the compressor is running. In addition, the motor manufacturer's recommendations should be followed as regards its lubrication.

16

Flame Volume Dynamics

Millions of barrels of oil yearly are transported, stored, heated, and injected into combustion processes which emerge without contributing a single unit of heat energy. Similarly, thousands of megatherms of natural gas are tapped, processed, metered, pushed and pulled through pipelines thousands of miles long, only to be totally wasted. For it is the testament of contemporary technology that incomplete combustion of hydrocarbon–oxygen mixtures occurs in all internal combustion engines and fired pressure vessels, often amounting to 25 percent or more of the input.

Aside from the utter waste of our precious resources, the additional energy expended in this futile exercise is enormous. Moreover, dealing with unburned hydrocarbons and the oxides of nitrogen, sulfur, and vanadium has become a parasitic technology that has firmly implanted itself in the field of stationary engineering.

In discussing fundamentals of automatic fuel firing in chapter 1, combustion was described as both a physical and chemical reaction. A physicochemical phenomenon, the combustion process involves atomic reaction among the carbon, oxygen, and hydrogen components of the molecules that make up the fuel–air mixture, and therefore the participants were defined as *reactants*. The text also talked briefly about the *products* of combustion and listed carbon dioxide (CO_2) and water vapor (H_2O) as being the products of *perfect combustion* of a hydrocarbon.

The fuel and air are seldom brought to the combustion

zone in exactly the right proportion for perfect combustion. This is not necessarily an indication of a deficiency in burner adjustment or performance, for although perfect combustion is theoretically possible, it is not necessarily desirable. Certain variables over which we as operators have little or no control dictate that a percentage of excess air over and above that which is required for perfect combustion be maintained in the flame zone. With such an adjustment of the burner, therefore, we strive instead for *complete* combustion. Complete combustion is defined as having taken place when all the combustible components of the fuel have been *oxidized* by the oxygen with which they will combine, leaving a surplus of oxygen in the products of combustion. Perfect combustion, on the other hand, occurs when all the fuel and oxygen elements react or rearrange atomically, forming new elements and compounds in accordance with fixed laws, leaving none of the original participants unchanged.

Even under optimum conditions, a practical aspect of the combustion of fuel oil and natural gas is that it is a less than perfect process wherein unburned fuel is always present in the products of combustion, though seldom if ever in its original molecular form. Instead it is found broken down and divided into several gaseous carbon compounds, which as a group are referred to as *intermediates,* as well as free carbon. Intermediates are the products of incomplete or partial oxidation of a hydrocarbon, and the burning process can be shown in a simple line drawing to illustrate the interrelationship of reactants, intermediates, and products as follows:

reactants - - - - → intermediates - - - - → products

Some of the intermediate compounds and their ignition temperatures are listed below:

Acetylene	C_2H_2	900°F
Carbon monoxide	CO	1210°F
Carbon (free)	C	1000°F
Ethane	C_2H_6	1000°F
Ethylene	C_2H_4	1022°F
Methane	CH_4	1202°F

The products of incomplete oxidation of the hydrogen contained in the fuel also show up in the products and are called hydroxyls (OH), hydroxyl radicals, or just oxidants. All of these compounds enter into a chain reaction culminating in carbon dioxide and water vapor, providing the combustion process is not interrupted or the intermediates are not carried out of the high–temperature combustion zone before reaching their ignition temperatures.

THE FUELS

When a combination gas/oil burner is considered purely from the standpoint of the combustion reaction that takes place within its furnace, the similarities in the two fuels are striking. Well they might be, for both belong to the family of hydrocarbons known as the *alkanes.*

Natural gas is found deep in the earth, sometimes coexisting with petroleum, and has a hydrocarbon content of between 60 and 99 percent of the constituency. The hydrocarbon content of petroleum, on the other hand, may vary from as high as 97 to 98 percent in some Pennsylvania crudes, to as low as 50 percent in some Mexican and southern crude oils.

If we arrange the alkanes in ascending order, according to carbon content, the first and simplest compound would be methane (CH_4) which is the principal ingredient of natural gas. In fact, the first five members of the group are gases at ordinary temperatures; butane, propane, etc. The next fifteen heavier hydrocarbons are liquids; heating oils and gasoline fall into this group. Those that have more than 18 carbon atoms are solids at room temperatures, and are white and waxy. The series is therefore also called the *paraffins.*

The carbon and hydrogen atoms are bonded tightly together in all these compounds and, as a result, enter into chemical union with other elements and compounds rather reluctantly; the word paraffin coming from the Latin, *parum affinus,* meaning *of slight activity.* Carbon atoms, the primary source of heat in the hydrocarbon compound, have the ability to form strong bonds with other carbon atoms which are hard to break, while at the same time bonding with hydrogen atoms.

Whether or not a combustion reaction will take place when the hydrocarbon molecules and oxygen molecules come together depends on their relative levels of *activation*. Activation consists of raising the molecules to a high level of energy (exciting them) by thermal collision (heat), absorption of light or otherwise, to what is referred to as their ignition temperature. In the case of the fuel gases under discussion, a chemical reaction such as combustion depends on the exchange of atoms from the hydrocarbon molecule to the oxygen molecule, and vice versa. Whether or not the oxygen can penetrate or break the strong bonds between the carbon–carbon atoms and the carbon–hydrogen atoms, depends on the temperature of the activated fuel–air mixture. The reaction process occurs when the energy of collision of the oxygen molecules with the hydrocarbon molecules equals or exceeds the energy holding the atoms of the individual compounds together. Even when the combustion reaction has been successfully initiated, there is no guarantee that it will continue until all the reactants are consumed to form products. The oxidation of liquid hydrocarbons such as fuel oils involves several individual steps and proceeds at a specific rate. The likelihood of the whole process faltering at some intermediate point and yielding products other than anticipated is a distinct possibility. Even relatively simple gas reactions, where droplet vaporization is not a factor, proceed through several steps.

The combustion process is an extremely rapid reaction involving the successive oxidation of the constituents of the hydrocarbon molecule and their rearrangement to form the products of combustion while liberating heat and light energy.

AUTOIGNITION

In the case of very simple hydrocarbon compounds such as methane, it is theorized that physicochemical reactions leading to autoignition in air mixtures proceed slowly at first, wherein intermediate compounds form as a result of the absorption by the hydrocarbon compound of heat and light energy. Then, once a critical concentration of the intermediates has been formed, very fast chain reactions occur which lead to autoignition and the final products of combustion. In reality, not much is known about the precise manner in which the intermediate products are formed leading to autoignition of fuel gases in air. One of the reasons for the difficulty in determining such information as ignition threshold temperature and other factors affecting flame stability, for example, lies in the lack of exact knowledge of the chemical composition and proportions of the various compounds that go to make up the so-called intermediates. It is known, however, that a given source energy cannot cause ignition of a fuel-air mixture if either the initial temperature of the heat source is below ignition temperature, or the heated volume exceeds a certain critical limit, or if the heating period is too long. No matter how hot an electric spark may be, for instance, if its energy content is less than minimum, it cannot produce a self-propagating *combustion wave,* and the zone of chemical reaction which the spark is capable of generating will only penetrate the combustible mix to small depth.

In fuel-air mixtures, an ignition source such as an electric spark produces a local zone of chemical reaction, which proceeds layer to layer by the transport of heat and the formation of intermediates which are believed to act as chain carriers. This highly concentrated zone of chemical reaction and high temperature constitutes the combustion wave. Its propagation is controlled by heat conduction from the burned to the unburned gases and diffusion into the unburned gases of the various molecular compounds comprising the products, intermediates, and chain carriers.

Once the combustion wave is established, it passes through a series of nonsteady states which lead either to extinction or propagation. The ignition source energy distribution in the combustible mixture is the crucial factor. For, as we have seen, there exists a critical source energy per unit area of the combustion wave below which ignition is not possible, even though the combustible medium adjacent to the source may be made to react chemically. When wave propagation is established, however, the combustion reaction is then independent of the ignition source.

THE OIL FLAME

It has been postulated that the combustion of fuel oil takes place through several steps, namely: vaporization, gasification, autoignition, dissociation, and finally reaching heating temperature.

By means of probes, the temperature at various points in a typical oil flame have been found to vary from 240° to 2200°F, the coolest point being near the atomizer, and the hottest on the periphery near the flame tips. The temperature of vaporization for fuel oil is generally considered to be between 100° and 500°F, depending on grade. Gasification takes place at approximately 800°F, and final flame temperature is two to three thousand degrees.

The combustion reaction takes place over a time span of but a few milliseconds, although the rate of flow of the burning gases through the furnace may be as slow as 15 to 20 feet per second. This is due in part to the fact that, by design, the burning gases revolve in a vortex, rather than move in a straight line. This affords the maximum benefit from the recirculation of the products of combustion in the oil mist, which maintains the high temperatures necessary for gasification and ignition of the droplets, while at the same time preheating the incoming air–oil mixture.

One of the characteristics of an oil flame is its brilliant luminosity, which is due to the oxidation of the carbon molecule during the gasification of the oil droplet. This dissociation of the carbon should not be confused with the term decomposition, which refers to the reduction of the hydrocarbon molecule to various intermediate products other than carbon dioxide and water. Although luminosity is no indication of the total heat in a flame, such a flame gives up more of its heat by *radiation* to the furnace walls than does a blue flame. The blue, or nonluminous flame, gives up most of its heat by conduction, or actual contact with the walls. As discussed in chapter 1, the fact that combination burners reflect the concern for proper oil combustion, often resulting in what at first might be thought to be unnecessarily vigorous flame characteristics when burning natural gas, this is not necessarily a disadvantage. In view of the nonradiant nature of the blue flame, the scrubbing effect of the turbulent vortex aids in the heat conduction function of the pressure vessel.

A TIME ELEMENT
CRUCIAL WITH OIL

A given volume of fuel and air molecules requires a certain minimum time in which to unite, liberate energy, and rearrange to form new compounds. Tests have shown, for example, that in the presence of sufficient oxygen to sustain combustion, ignition of a fuel oil droplet occurs in 0.1 millisecond and its burning lifetime is from 2 to 20 milliseconds, depending on its size. Further laboratory experimentation to determine droplet residence time in the high-temperature flame zone required for complete combustion indicated that ideal propagation velocity was less than 10 feet per second. Yet when comparative tests of actual oil burners were made in the field, air stream velocities of 25 to 30 feet per second were encountered. Droplets were observed being blown downstream faster than they could propagate upstream. By means of high-speed motion pictures and strobe lights, it was possible to record individual drops coming from the atomizer and approaching the flame front. Large drops with high momentum were seen to pass right through a portion of the flame volume without being completely vaporized, leaving the combustion air stream on the far side of the flame.

One of the primary design considerations of any oil burner is that its air delivery pattern have the capability to capture and hold the oil-spray droplets in the turbulent air stream during the mixing, heating, and gasification process. Needless to say, some burners do this better than others, and the extent to which they excel in this department is the hallmark of good design. As a result, more attention has been paid to air delivery patterns in recent years than to fuel atomization, inasmuch as it has come to be universally appreciated that oil droplets which escape the air envelope cannot be satisfactorily mixed and vaporized in the preignition zone.

Air pattern studies made a number of years ago by Esso Research and Engineering Co. revealed some interesting facts about the character of the flame volumes produced by a number of brands of burners then operating in the field. Although the study involved domestic gun–type burners utilizing distillate fuels, the information compiled is relevant to the operation of residual oil burners since the fundamentals of combustion having to do with oil–droplet vaporization, ignition, and flame propagation apply to all liquid fuels and methods of atomization.

Significantly, it was found that the flame volumes of the majority of burners tested were hollow. See Figure 16-1.

LOW TEMPERATURES IN CENTER SHOW IT IS NOT BURNING

83 % EXCESS AIR - 80° NOZZLE

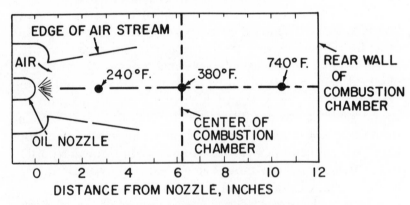

Figure 16-1. Hollow Flame Pattern
(courtesy American Petroleum Institute)

By using probes to measure CO_2, O_2, and smoke, it was determined that although there was an adequate supply of air and oil in the center of the flame, the oil droplets were not burning at that point. A typical burner tested in the laboratory was operated with enough excess air to permit no more than a trace of smoke at the stack. Under these conditions, which would be equal to the best adjustment an experienced operator could attain without the aid of instruments, the excess air in the stack gas was measured to be just under 80 percent. Obviously not all the air that passed through the combustion process took part in the reaction.

Throughout most of the air envelope, the velocity was in the range of 1500 to 1800 hundred feet per minute. Only near the outer edge of the envelope did the velocity drop below 600 feet per minute, which had long been established as ideal flame propagation velocity. Therefore it was not a surprise to find that CO_2 readings taken at various places within the flame volume indicated complete combustion was occurring only around the edge of the high–velocity core. In addition, a considerable number of oil droplets, large enough to be photographed, were observed escaping the air stream into the hot low–oxygen zone around it, accounting for the large amount of excess air required to eliminate smoke. It was theorized that the reason for the hollow flame was that air velocity in the central region was considerably higher than burning speed, which prevented the oil from igniting until it had traveled a considerable distance downstream; here, too, the air was blowing the flame downstream faster than it could propagate upstream. Thus emerged a totally realistic picture of the flame front as a kind of semispherical boundary between a core of atomized fuel and burning gases surrounding it. Regardless of the complex shape it may assume, the principles of energy transmission—radiation, conduction, and convection—still apply to any cross section of the flame volume we may select.

The experimenters discovered that by placing an obstruction in the center of the air stream, the flame could be established throughout the air pattern, permitting a marked reduction in the amount of excess air without producing smoke (Figure 16-2). This suggested that eddy currents of low–velocity air, downstream of the obstruction, permitted the flame front to move farther upstream. A disc of expanded metal, dubbed the Magic Grid, was fashioned slightly larger than the burner end-cone and mounted in a vertical plane about an inch into the firebox. All of the air and fuel passed through the grid, and produced a remarkable transformation of the flame characteristics from a long, lazy flame to a short, hard flame of brilliant yellow-

GRID CREATES STAGNANT ZONES
WHERE FLAME IS STABILIZED

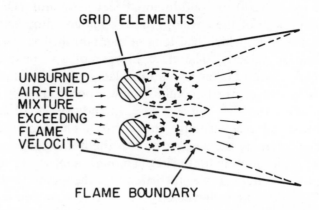

Figure 16-2. Magic Grid (courtesy American Petroleum Institute)

white color. The fuel–air ratio was exactly the same but the flame appeared to be smaller. Actually, it had compacted into a smaller relative volume, and the excess air could be reduced to soften it somewhat without producing smoke. Now the fuel–air ratio showed improvement by the indication of a reading of 10 percent CO_2 in the core region where previously there had been no flame, and a reduction of the excess air in the stack gas to less than 40 percent.

On the basis of the successful performance of this and other prototypes, the program was expanded the following year to include 14 different makes of burners located in 30 homes in New Jersey. The composite result of the tests was almost more than hoped for and is detailed as follows:

*Average of 30 Homes**

Operating Conditions	Original	With Magic Grid
Excess Air, Vol. %	89.7	36.9
Net Stack Temperature, °F	603	390

*Conference Paper CP 62–14, API Research Conference, Chicago, Ill.

Operating Conditions	Original	With Magic Grid
Absorption Efficiency	71.2	83.3
Bacharach Smoke Number	3.7	0
Savings		
Estimated, %	– –	17.6
Measured, % (Based on		
gal./degree day)	– –	21.2

The incredibly simple method of compacting the flame volume by directing the combustion air through a screen–like expanded metal grid mounted on the burner head is now a design feature of at least two large burner manufacturers. Figure 16-3 shows the burner drawer assembly of a 50–million Btu/hr Cleaver–Brooks burner that employs the principle to stabilize the center of the secondary air envelope.

Figure 16-3. Expanded Metal Grid (courtesy Cleaver-Brooks)

Another manufacturer uses a variation of this arrangement, without the turning vanes. The burner nozzle merely protrudes through an expanded metal air diffuser. The resulting flame pattern is short and vigorous but does not rotate.

THE MECHANICS OF COMPACTION

When we make some adjustment to the air–oil interface, other than altering the mass–flow rate, which makes the flame appear smaller, we are not actually changing the volume of the flame itself. Therefore, we cannot say we have reduced the flame volume just because it appears smaller. Nor is it entirely right to say we have *compressed* the flame volume, because the term compression is reserved for a totally different concept in combustion engineering. So, for want of a better term, *compaction* must do.

Compaction, then, involves the bringing together of the fire pattern that characterizes the appearance of the overall flame volume. We have already seen that it is possible to have a hollow flame volume, where the core is filled with unburned fuel and air. Likewise, it is possible to have a hollow pattern where no fuel and only oxygen–starved air is present. Furthermore, it is possible to have overlapping layers of flame, stagnant air, and unburned fuel in the flame volume. Compaction, therefore, refers to the elimination of this incongruency, so that a cubic foot of flame volume then consists of one cubic foot of fire.

For more than two decades the trend in burner design has been toward compacting the flame into the smallest possible volume. There are several advantages to the compact flame, not the least of which is that it makes it possible to use a shorter furnace and consequently a shorter pressure vessel. Another is that compact flames depend less on external influences such as refractory material. In addition, a compact flame tends to be more stable.

THE COMBUSTION CHAMBER

The manner in which the flame is confined is an important element of the general term "environment" peculiar to the oil burner. The temperature of the combustion zone is more critical with oil fuel than with gas fuel, since chemical decomposition is in large measure a function of low flame temperature. At any given time in the course of burning, the heat released in the combustion space serves both to evaporate and to heat the interior of the oil droplet. For this reason the combustion process should be completed before the flame is allowed to cool to the critical point where the reaction becomes more physical than chemical. The combustion chamber aids in the flame–propagation process by radiating heat energy back into the flame volume, hence the general term *refractory* is used to describe particular brickwork shapes and other materials that go into the construction of combustion chambers, baffles, and the like.

In the case of modern burner design where flame temperatures reach very high levels quite quickly, reflected heat from the combustion chamber was found to be of less significance than formerly thought. As a result, refractory material is used primarily to protect structural components of the pressure vessel from the destructive effects of high temperature and secondarily as a combustion noise muffler.

Well–designed and installed combustion chambers are a must, however, with burners that are classed as poor atomizers. The concentration of heat energy improves internal movement of the flame volume and preignition zone that augments the mixing ability of the burner's air–oil delivery system. The emphasis here should be on materials of construction that come up to radiant temperature quickly, and are shaped or installed in a way that, through reflection and refraction, heat energy can be beamed toward the preignition zone. The so–called *throat tile* and *ignition arch* are examples of refractory shapes which concentrate heat energy in this zone.

Target rings, in the case of Scotch-type boilers, and *target walls* installed in firebox boilers, reflect heat back into the reaction zone from the downstream or product side of the flame. The target ring, which as the name implies is doughnut–shaped, also compacts the product volume and increases turbulence in the flame by venturi action.

Corbelling, which is a technique used for years by designers of rectangular combustion chambers, involves letting each of the top several courses of fire brick at the rear of the chamber protrude a third or so of their width toward the center of the chamber, so that the effect is to turn the hot gases back on themselves.

The results of an ineffective or improperly designed combustion chamber are, generally, a low value of temperature which leads to a corresponding loss in gas velocity, and regions of stagnation. The size and shape of the chamber directly affects the diffusion process through which the intermediate products of combustion reach the walls of the pressure vessel. The walls, in turn, have a catalytic effect on the combustion process, initiating and breaking chain reactions by the absorption of reactants on the surface of the wall. It has been well–established, for example, that the combustion process is accelerated by incandescent surfaces.

GAS COMBUSTION

In the combustion of gaseous fuels, we are primarily concerned with the fuel–air ratio of the combustible mix. Once ignition has taken place the actual temperature of the flame zone of a combination fuel burner, as it affects complete combustion or flame propagation, plays a somewhat less significant role in the gas firing mode than when burning oil. With the gas fuels, the activation of the reactants is much less complicated since the preparation of the fuel for ignition does not involve the stirring and heating of liquid droplets. Improper air or fuel velocity into the flame volume can, however, cause instability, incomplete combustion, or at the very least, noisy operation.

Historically, natural gas has been considered an extremely stable fuel. It is a nontoxic and nonpoisonous mixture of methane (CH_4), ethane (C_2H_6), and other gases, mainly nitrogen (N_2), the proportions of which typically are 90–5–5 respectively. It is roughly 35 percent lighter than air and has a heating value, taken for easy calculation, of approximately 1000 Btu/cu ft. Mixtures of 4 to 14 percent natural gas in air can burn with a controlled flame; they also can explode. Whether or not an explosion will occur depends primarily on whether a gas–air mixture is allowed to collect before it is ignited. A mixture of 15 to 100 percent natural gas in air will not explode, for mixtures in this range are outside the upper flammability limit.

The flame propagation rate of natural gas in air depends to some extent upon the amount of air in the mix and its temperature. Methane is an especially slow burning gas. Its highest burning speed is 0.9 foot per second and occurs at about 10 percent concentration in air. This contrasts sharply with hydrogen, for example, that has a burning speed of 9.3 feet per second. Generally speaking, peak burning speed for all fuel gases occurs when the gas-air mix is about 10 percent richer than chemically correct, and increases as the molecular weight of the respective gases. In other words, burning speed is a function of the carbon-hydrogen content of the fuel.

We have already established that the ideal fuel-air mass-flow rate for an oil burner is approximately 10 fps, and if the author may anticipate the reader's question, well you might wonder how a burner whose air delivery system is set for such a high rate can be made to burn natural gas satisfactorily without major adjustments. The fact of the matter is, flammability limits and burning rates are established for relatively placid gas-air mixtures under more or less ambient conditions, and do not take into full account the effects of turbulence and temperature, or the catalytic effects of combustion chamber walls.

COMBUSTION INSTABILITY

We have described ideal or perfect combustion as a steady-state reaction where no trace is left of the reactants and the full amount of products is achieved through chemical union. Even under laboratory conditions, however, combustion reactions are seldom 100 percent efficient due in part to the fact that the products react with one another to regenerate the reactants.

In high-energy reactions that produce heat, such as combustion, there is an inherent incompleteness. But a state of equilibrium is reached in which some quantity—perhaps exceedingly small—of each of the reactants and products is still present. However, the equilibrium is *dynamic* and can be thought of to move—forward toward completion of the reaction, or backward toward reversal of the reaction. In an open system reaction, such as combustion, the chain reaction goes to completion due to the escape of the products.

The intermingling of partially burned and unburned products as well as the catalytic effect of the size, shape, smoothness, and materials of construction of the flame zone has a significant effect on the reactive center of equilibrium. Data obtained from laboratory experiments that simulate the flow processes of industrial combustion systems show that as long as two-thirds of the intermediate compounds which comprise the chain carriers are consumed or neutralized by combining with other intermediates the reaction tends to be stable in the direction of completion. Conversely, it was found that the disproportionate build-up of the intermediate products of combustion leads to a sudden backward thrust of the center of equilibrium producing a phenomenon known as *pulsation.*

PULSATION: THE NON-STEADY STATE

All chemical reactions are theoretically reversible. Often the *activated complex,* which in the case of combustion is the flame volume, hangs in delicate balance. A steady-state reaction depends on the interaction of many factors. Air flow into the furnace, for example, is normally from only one direction. The propagation rate of the reactants and the orderly expansion of the products in turn depend upon this fact.

Pulsation is an unstable combustion condition that results in a two-way or back-and-forth motion of combustion air and products from the combustion space. The action instigates a vibration in and about the boiler and flues, that rattles access plates, clean-out doors, and anything else that is not securely bolted in place. This cyclic phenomenon, which the author has crudely measured in various instances, seems to occur at a rate of some 5 to 20 cycles per second. It results in a rumbling sound, the effect of which is quite frightening. It begins suddenly, usually at the same point of input in the firing range of the burner. Often, when it starts, pulsation can only be stopped by abruptly decreasing the firing rate, or extinguishing the flame altogether.

When a burner begins to pulsate, the flame does not usually go out. But the very rapid thermal expansion of the burning gases tends to discharge backward through the burner and air-intake system, completely destroying the pressure drop across the burner head, fan, damper, and the like, causing a momentary air-flow stoppage. The air-starved flame goes to smoke and the operating overfire draft goes sharply positive, which causes the access plates and relief doors to lift. Once the unbalanced condition is relieved, the air-handling equipment reestablishes air flow to the flame, the smoke clears, and the reaction reverts to its original unstable condition, whereupon it unloads again—repeating many times per second.

Most early boilers were designed to burn coal and later "converted" to burn one or both of the so-called automatic fuels. From an operating standpoint, they burned the liquid and gaseous fuels satisfactorily if not efficiently, for they had wide, direct flue gas passages and ample furnace volume. The subsequent trend toward tightly-gasketed, multipass boilers and pressurized furnaces, heightened the emphasis on good aerodynamic burner design. For it became increasingly apparent that the tendency toward flame instability was more prevalent in a flame volume with an inordinate amount of partially burned and unburned fuel in the products of combustion.

Historically, pulsation was a seldom heard of temporary condition, almost exclusively associated with oil firing, caused by excessive furnace pressure due to clogged flues. Even in the case of residential burners tested in the Esso research project, where combustion was found to be grossly inefficient, the flame volume was considered stable. Incomplete combustion therefore can also be thought of as a steady-state reaction and does not necessarily connote instability. However, soot accumulation was the most obvious result of incomplete combustion in an oil boiler and, where allowed to interfere with the escape of the products of combustion, pulsation was inevitable.

Insufficient draft was the almost universally accepted explanation for pulsation. However, as boiler design evolved from the basic brick-set horizontal-tubular type, with its large masses of firebrick and insulation, to the modern marine-type boiler that has water-cooled furnace walls and little or no refractory, combustion system concepts had to be updated accordingly.

Heavy soot accumulations and frequent soot blowing could no longer be tolerated as a way of life.

Obviously, among the first burners to show the adverse effect of the demand for smaller, more efficient pressure vessels were those whose flame–volume dynamics depended heavily on refractory material. Also, burners whose preheat–and–mixing zone was relatively large, and whose flame volume stabilized considerably far downstream instead of up close to the burner atomizer, often became pulsation prone when required to function in a pressurized furnace. Burners with long, lazy flame patterns could not accommodate a short furnace, and so on. Therefore the onus fell to the burner designers to come up with something better than the heretofore "universal" burner, because no longer was it adaptable to "anybody's" boiler. As borne out by the survivors, the answer lay in the *total package* concept, where the boiler was designed as a combustion system, and the unit was assembled, tested, and rated as a complete energy–conversion package.

17

Flue Gas Analysis

The mathematics of the chemistry of combustion are well established and as a result certain norms or parameters exist with which to compare operating conditions wherein it is possible to account for every molecule of substance contained in a volume of flue gas (see Table 17-1). However, the troubleshooter is primarily interested in only two specifics regarding the composition of the flue gas sample: the oxygen it contains and its temperature.

The oxygen which takes part in the combustion reaction combines with the carbon in the fuel to form carbon dioxide. Some of the oxygen admitted to the process combines with the hydrogen in the fuel to form water vapor. To illustrate:

$$\text{carbon to carbon dioxide} = 2C + 2O_2 = 2CO_2$$
$$\text{hydrogen to water vapor} = 2H_2 + O_2 = 2H_2O$$

Of course, heat and light energy are released in the process.

In flue gas analysis, the term *dry gas* is used to describe the components that make up the products of combustion. For practical reasons, the heat liberated by the combustion of the hydrogen (325 Btu/cf) and the water vapor resulting therefrom are disregarded. However, it is worth knowing that the water vapor content of the flue gas is proportional to the carbon-hydrogen ratio of the fuel. The products of combustion of natural gas, for example, contain a higher proportion of water vapor to carbon dioxide than fuel oil and other fuel gases as follows:

Table 17-1

Cleaver ⚙ Brooks°

BY	DESIGN ENG. CHART #	REV.
ℒ	**E-3**	O
		DATE Feb. 27, 73

STACK EMISSION DATA   Fuel: No. 4, 5, 6 Oil

For CB, Model 4 (mini), and WT's with A-, BR-, & CN-Burner	Line	Column A % of Flue Gas, by Volume (dry basis)	Column B SCF/ Million Btu	Column C Lbs/ Million Btu	Column D For Solids: Grains/SCF For Gasses: PPM (Parts Per Million)	Column E How is this Measured?
Burner Adjusted for	1	20% Excess Air (by volume)				Starting Condition
CO_2	2	13.8%	1520 SCF	175#		Orsat & Calculations
CO	3	0.002%	0.22 SCF	0.016#	20 PPM	Colorimetric
						PPM MEASURED
O_2	4	3.7%	410 SCF	35#		Orsat & Calculations
N_2	5	82.5%	9120 SCF	670#		Orsat & Calculations
H_2O	6	— — —	980 SCF	45#		Calculations
Total	8	100.0%	12,030 SCF	925#		Total
NO_x	9	0.02-0.04%	2¼-4½ SCF	0.27-0.54#	200-400 PPM	Electrochemical
						PPM MEASURED
Particulates	10	— — —	— — —	0.07-0.14#	0.04-0.08 G/SCF	EPA Dry Train
						G/SCF MEASURED
Hydrocarbons as CH_4	11	0.001%	0.12 SCF	0.005#	10 PPM	Flame Ionization
						PPM MEASURED
SO_x per % S in Fuel	12	0.057%	7 SCF/% Sulfur	1#/% Sulfur	570 $\frac{PPM}{\% S}$	Calculated

Conversion Data:

PPM:

$$1 \text{ PPM} = \frac{1 \text{ Part}}{1,000,000 \text{ Part}}$$

$$= 0.000\ 001 = 0.0001\%$$

$$= \frac{1}{10,000} \text{ of 1\%, by volume}$$

7000 Grains = 1# = 1 Pound Avoirdupois

SCF = Standard Cubic Feet
i.e., at 60°F and 14.7 psia.

1 # Mol = 380 SCF

Air (by volume) = 79% N_2 + 21% O_2

Molecular Weights used:
CO	= 28	N_2	= 28
CO_2	= 44	NO_x	= 46 for NO_2
H_2O	= 18	SO_x	= 32 for SO_2
O_2	= 32	CH_4	= 16

The amount of NO_x and of Particulates in the stack gas vary in the same direction, though not proportionately, with the amount of ash and chemically combined Nitrogen in the fuel. The ranges tabled above may be considered typical but do not apply to all commercially available heavy oils.

NO_x, Particulate, and Hydrocarbon data tabulated above are representative of Cleaver-Brooks burners for Firetubes, for Model 4's, for Watertubes equipped with CB burners, and for Industrial burners. While this data is a compilation of the results of several laboratory tests that have been conducted on various sizes of boilers, testing is not yet complete and ALL DATA IN THE CROSSHATCHED AREA MAY BE USED ONLY FOR PREDICTING, BUT NOT FOR GUARANTEEING PERFORMANCE.

BY	DESIGN ENG. CHART #	REV.
ℒ	**E-3**	O
		DATE Feb. 27, 73

C9-5693
Printed in U.S.A.

Methane
(the principal constituent

of natural gas)	CH_4	$CH_4 + 2\,O_2$	$= CO_2 + 2\,H_2\,O$
Propane	$C_3\,H_8$	$C_3\,H_8 + 5\,O_2$	$= 3\,CO_2 + 4\,H_2\,O$
nButane	$C_4\,H_{10}$	$2\,C_4\,H_{10} + 13\,O_2$	$= 8\,CO_2 + 10\,H_2\,O$

The amount of air required to burn a given quantity of fuel is related to the Btu content of the fuel. Therefore:

theoretical air = 1 cu ft/100 Btu

so that one cubic foot of natural gas, whose heat content is approximately 1000 Btu, requires 10 cubic feet of air; and a gallon of fuel oil, with a Btu content of approximately 140,000, would need 1400 cubic feet of air to burn completely. It must be emphasized that this is the theoretical amount of air. Actual air supplied exceeds theoretical air requirements by 10 to 50 percent, depending on the kind of fuel burned, the type of equipment in which it is utilized, and the conditions existing that could adversely affect the cleanliness of burner fans and air intakes. The relationship of actual air and theoretical air can be shown as follows:

$$\text{excess air } \% = \frac{\text{air supplied} - \text{theoretical air}}{\text{theoretical air}} \times 100$$

Air is composed of oxygen, nitrogen, and other inert gases, but here again for practical reasons we assume the mixture is 21 percent oxygen and 79 percent nitrogen by volume. When convenient, we also refer to the excess air in a sample of flue gas products in terms of the oxygen only.

When all the carbon contained in the fuel unites with all the oxygen in the air supplied, we say *perfect* or *stoichiometric* combustion has taken place, and the carbon dioxide formed as a result is called the *ultimate* CO_2. Table 17-2 lists some fuels and their approximate theoretical ultimate CO_2 values and the CO_2 values with different percentages of excess air.

Perfect combustion is only a theoretical condition and cannot be achieved in practice. Instead, we strive for *complete* combustion, which is said to have occurred when the maximum amount of carbon in the fuel has been oxidized by the oxygen

Table 17-2. Ultimate CO₂ Various Fuels
(from *HVAC Guide*, 38th Ed., ASHRAE)

Type of Fuel	Stoichiometric Percent CO₂	Percent CO₂ of Given Excess Air Values		
		20%	*40%*	*60%*
Coke	21.0	17.5	15.0	13.0
Anthracite	20.2	16.8	14.4	12.6
Bituminous Coal	18.2	15.1	12.9	11.3
No. 1 and 2 Fuel Oil	15.0	12.3	10.5	9.1
No. 6 Fuel Oil	16.5	13.6	11.6	10.1
Natural Gas	12.1	9.9	8.4	7.3
Carburetted Water Gas	17.2	14.2	12.1	10.6
Coke Oven Gas	11.2	9.2	7.8	6.8
Mixed Gas (Natural and Carburetted Water Gas)	15.3	12.5	10.5	9.1
Propane Gas (Commercial)	13.9	11.4	9.6	8.4
Butane Gas (Commercial)	14.1	11.6	9.8	8.5

with which it will combine, and a small percentage of unused oxygen remains. Therefore the products of complete combustion contain excess oxygen. They also contain unburned carbon in one form or another, oxides of other elements that may have been present in the fuel—such as sulfur and vanadium in the case of fuel oil—as well as nitrogen. Nitrogen is the major constituent, having entered with the air, and to a small extent with the fuel. Natural gas, for example, typically contains 90 percent methane, 5 percent nitrogen, and 5 percent ethane. All these elements and compounds exist in the flue gas at stack temperature, and are carrying heat away from the boiler.

Traditionally we refer to nitrogen as a nonparticipant in the combustion process because, being chemically neutral, it does not combine with any of the other elements to release energy. Actually, it lowers the temperature of the flame volume, and carries away the largest percentage of the heat input not absorbed by the boiler. For each cubic foot of oxygen admitted to the flame zone approximately four cubic feet of nitrogen enter too. Good practice, therefore, comes down to regulating the amount of air to produce good combustion—complete combustion—while maintaining the stack temperature as low as practicable.

The percentage of nitrogen contained in a sample of dry flue gas is calculated as the balance of the air supplied for combustion after the percent CO_2 and excess oxygen have been deducted. For example, if a sample of products of gas combustion indicates 7.5% CO_2 and 7.5% O_2, 100% minus 7.5% minus 7.5% equals 85% N_2. We have already established that the percentage composition of air is 21 percent oxygen and 79 nitrogen; therefore it is obvious that more than 100 percent of the air required for combustion has been admitted to the reaction.

If 100 cubic feet of flue gas contained 85 cubic feet of N_2 and, for all practical purposes, this nitrogen came from the air which contains only 79 cubic feet of nitrogen per 100 cubic feet of air, it follows that it would require 85/0.79, or 107.6 cubic feet of air to yield 100 cubic feet of flue gas.

In the dry gas sample there is a total of 15 cubic feet of oxygen; 7.5 percent as carbon dioxide, and 7.5 percent as excess oxygen. However, the 107.6 cubic feet of air which formed the 100 cubic feet of flue gas contained 107.6 times 0.21, or 22.6 cubic feet of oxygen. The difference, 7.6 cubic feet (22.6 minus 15) must have combined with the hydrogen in the fuel to form water vapor, which, as stated previously, does not figure into the combustion efficiency test. However, it does figure into the computation of the excess air admitted to the reaction, since obviously 7.6 cubic feet of oxygen are unavailable to combine with the carbon. The necessary oxygen is that which has combined with the carbon and hydrogen, and in this case, is 7.5 plus 7.6, or 15.1 percent. The excess, or unnecessary oxygen, shown by flue gas analysis, is 7.5 percent; therefore the ratio of excess oxygen to actual oxygen is 7.5/15.1 and works out to 49.6 percent. The proportion of excess air to actual air, of course, is the same.

Figure 17-1 offers a graphical method of establishing the relationship between carbon dioxide, oxygen, and excess air for six different fuels when either CO_2 or O_2 has been determined by flue gas analysis. Dotted line number 1 illustrates the example just worked out in the text. Entering the graph at 7.5 percent O_2 and moving vertically to the particular fuel curve (A in this case), then left horizontally read equivalent percent CO_2 at

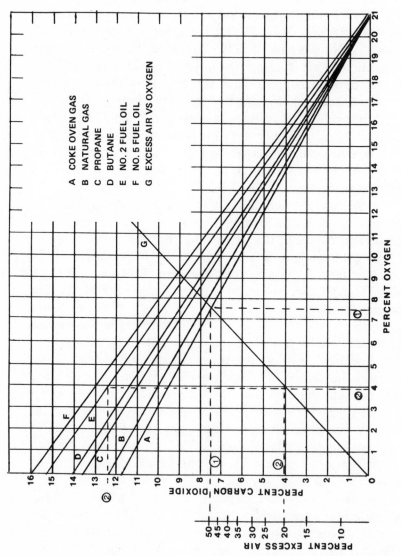

Figure 17-1. CO_2, O_2, Air Relationship

the left-hand scale. Where the vertical line crosses the G curve, read 50 percent excess air in the extreme left-hand column. (It happens that this point coincides with the fuel curve in this example.)

In case No. 2, a flue gas sample from No. 2 oil combustion where we have measured 4 percent oxygen, entering the O_2 scale at the bottom of the graph and moving to curve E and to the left scale we locate 12.5 percent CO_2. Where the vertical line crosses curve G we find the excess air indicated to be 20 percent.

In summary, excess air is introduced to the combustion process to be sure there is enough oxygen to combine with as much of the carbon and hydrogen (and sulfur in the case of fuel oil) in the fuel as possible. Once it enters the flame zone it is physically and chemically rearranged so that we consider it only in terms of the oxygen and nitrogen it contains, and joins the other products of combustion in what is called flue gas. Flue gas analysis and interpretation attempts to establish the proportions of the new compounds formed during combustion and to establish the minimum amount of excess air required for complete combustion.

Stack temperature is, to the technician, the most useful measurement of thermal efficiency of the heating plant. It is probably the one element of those that figure into the calculation of the *energy balance* over which he has the most control. Energy balance computation is the accounting of the disposition of all the heat units available in the quantity of fuel burned. Some of the other factors are:

a. heat lost in the water vapor contained in the stack gas formed by the combustion of the hydrogen in the fuel
b. heat lost in the water vapor of the stack gas brought in with combustion air
c. heat loss from incomplete combustion
d. heat loss from unburned carbon contained in the soot
e. radiation and all other unaccounted for losses.

Assuming complete combustion of the fuel has taken place, stack temperature is a function of excess air and the ratio of boiler heating surface to fuel input. Naturally the cleanliness of the heat exchanger surface area, on the water side as well as the fire side, has a bearing on the ability of the boiler to absorb the heat produced by the burner.

The term *combustion efficiency* characterizes the effectiveness of the combustion reaction and can be expressed like this:

$$\text{combustion efficiency} = \frac{\text{heat released in the combustion process}}{\text{heat energy contained in the fuel input}}$$

Since the ultimate CO_2 represents 100 percent combustion efficiency, we can approximate actual combustion efficiency as follows:

$$E_c = (CO_2/U) \times 100$$

where E_c is combustion efficiency %
CO_2 is the percentage in the flue gas
and U is the ultimate CO_2 for the fuel

Steady-state efficiency takes into consideration the ability of the boiler or other heat exchanger to absorb the heat of combustion, and can be read directly from Table 17-3. The distinction between combustion efficiency and steady-state efficiency is an important one when it comes to troubleshooting such problems as high fuel consumption and inability of a boiler to develop its rated capacity.

According to the table, decreasing excess oxygen or lowering stack temperature will improve steady-state efficiency. Generally, the most dynamic improvement can be made by lowering stack temperature. For example, an oil-fired boiler operating with 10 percent excess oxygen and a 700-degree net stack temperature will be 9 percent more energy efficient if some way can be found to lower the stack temperature to 450 degrees. The relatively simple act of removing the soot and scale accumulation from the flue passages can often accomplish the desired result.

The question sometimes arises as to what constitutes a normal stack temperature. A mechanical draft boiler, designed and constructed in accordance with the best accepted standards

Table 17-3

STEADY-STATE EFFICIENCY PERCENT

Net Stack Temp. (degrees F.)

OIL O_2 %	300°	350°	400°	450°	500°	550°	600°	650°	700°	750°	800°	850°	900°
15	75½	72½	69½	66¼	63	60	56¾	53½	50¼	47	43½	40¼	36¾
14	77¼	74½	72¾	70	68	64¼	61½	58¾	55¾	52¾	49¼	47¼	44½
13	79¾	77¼	75	72½	70	67¾	65¼	62¾	60¼	57½	55	52½	50
12	80¾	78½	76¾	74¾	72½	70¼	68¼	66	63¾	61½	59	56¾	54¼
11	82¼	80¼	78½	76½	74½	72½	70½	68½	65¾	64¼	62¼	60	58
10	83	81	79¾	77¾	76	74¼	72½	70¾	68¾	67	64¾	63	61
9	84	82¼	80¾	79	77¼	75¾	74	72¼	70¾	68¾	67	65¼	63½
8	84¾	83	81¾	80¼	78½	77	75½	73¾	72¼	70½	69	67½	65¾
7	85½	83¾	82½	80¾	79¼	77¾	76¼	74¾	73¼	71½	70	68½	67
6	85¾	84½	83	81½	80¼	78¾	77¼	75¾	74½	73	71½	70	68½
5	86	85	83¾	82¼	81	79½	78¼	77	75½	74	72½	71¼	70
4	86½	85¼	84	83	81½	80¼	79	77¾	76½	75¼	73½	72¾	71
3	87	85¾	84½	83½	82¼	81	79¾	78½	77¼	76	74¾	73¾	72
2	87¼	86	84¾	83¾	82¾	81½	80¼	79	78	76¾	75½	74½	73
1	87½	86½	85	84¼	83¼	82	81	79½	78¾	77½	76¼	75¼	74

GAS O_2 %: 12, 11, 10, 9, 8, 7, 6, 5, 4, 3, 2

and practices, can be expected to operate with a net stack temperature approximately 150 to 200 degrees higher than the heated medium, provided it is clean, in good repair, properly closed and gasketed. In the case of steam boilers, the equivalent temperature of the saturated steam is considered the temperature of the heated medium (see Table 17-4).

A boiler which depends on natural draft to transport the products of combustion through the flues necessarily operates with a higher stack temperature, as will be discussed in chapter 19 under chimneys and draft.

Forced draft boilers, or more accurately pressurized boilers, operate with furnace pressures above atmospheric, so that air dilution of the products of combustion cannot occur. It follows that all the oxygen present in the flue gas can be assumed to have passed through the combustion zone. Whether or not it took part in the combustion reaction is, as we have discussed, another matter. At least the possibility of a diluted gas sample is minimal, defective sampling equipment and carelessness notwithstanding.

Induced draft, whether mechanical or natural, encourages the infiltration of ambient air into the boiler–burner setting through such fissures as may exist between the base of the boiler and the combustion chamber, or between the combustion chamber floor and the boiler room floor. This leakage, most of which is hard to detect and harder to control, allows the passage of unneeded air into the flame zone, lowers the CO_2, and chills the flame. Even though the oxygen in the air might possibly take part in the reaction, and could therefore be regarded as part of the secondary air stream, the fact remains it is uncontrollable and unpredictable. Air leakage into the combustion process which does not take part in combustion, on the other hand, represents a loss in efficiency.

Infiltration of air into the boiler flues (the so–called secondary heat–exchanger areas, as differentiated from the furnace area) which receives the radiant (infrared) energy of the flame, also shows up in the products of combustion. This air can create the erroneous impression that combustion efficiency was lower than it actually was when, in reality, we are contending with a

Table 17-4. Properties of Saturated Steam (courtesy Iron Fireman)

Gage Pressure PSIG	Temperature °F	Heat in Btu/lb.			Specific Volume Cu. ft. per lb.
		Sensible	Latent	Total	
In. (Hg) Vac. 25	134	102	1017	1119	142
20	162	129	1001	1130	73.9
15	179	147	990	1137	51.3
10	192	160	982	1142	39.4
5	203	171	976	1147	31.8
0	212	180	970	1150	26.8
1	215	183	968	1151	25.2
2	219	187	966	1153	23.5
3	222	190	964	1154	22.3
4	224	192	962	1154	21.4
5	227	195	960	1155	20.1
10	239	207	953	1160	16.5
20	259	227	939	1166	11.9
30	274	243	929	1172	9.46
40	286	256	920	1176	7.82
50	298	267	912	1179	6.68
60	307	277	906	1183	5.84
70	316	286	898	1184	5.18
80	324	294	891	1185	4.67
90	331	302	886	1188	4.24
100	338	309	880	1189	3.89
110	344	316	875	1191	3.59
120	350	322	871	1193	3.34
130	356	328	866	1194	3.12
140	361	333	861	1194	2.92
150	366	339	857	1196	2.74
175	377	351	847	1198	2.41
200	388	362	837	1199	2.14
225	397	372	828	1200	1.92
250	406	382	820	1202	1.75
275	414	391	812	1203	1.60
300	421	398	805	1203	1.47
325	429	407	797	1204	1.36
350	435	414	790	1204	1.28
375	442	421	784	1205	1.19
400	448	428	777	1205	1.12
450	460	439	766	1205	1.00
500	470	453	751	1204	.89
550	479	464	740	1204	.82
600	489	475	728	1203	.74

diluted gas sample. At any time the troubleshooter suspects such a condition exists, he should take a new gas sample from as close to the furnace section of the boiler as possible.

The degree to which excess air can be controlled is a measure not only of the fuel/air mixing ability of the burner, but of the overall efficiency of the boiler–burner package. The burner manufacturer is, in a way, at the mercy of certain field conditions which mitigate against the achievement of the high combustion efficiency of which his burner may be capable. The application of a given burner to the many and varied field-erected boilers requires a great degree of expertise over which he seldom has any control. Packaged–boiler manufacturers have no similar excuse for poor burner performance.

Modern boiler–burner units operate day in and day out at steady–state efficiency levels of 80 percent or more. There are a great many older and neglected units, however, incapable of operating without smoke with excess air levels of 50 percent. Therefore the state of complete combustion is relative, and the operating efficiency is set as high as possible without exceeding clean–air standards.

Cleaning the burner regularly, especially the fan and air intakes, can improve combustion performance. Replacing worn and warped burner heads and diffusers is essential also. Similarly, throat tiles and other refractories necessary to maintain high temperature at the flame front, particularly with oil burners, should be inspected and repaired on a regular basis. When oil viscosity control is essential to the vaporization of oil droplets, heater cleaning and regulation must be done routinely. In short, good preventive maintenance pays off in peak performance.

18

Interpreting Flue Gas Data

Flue gas analysis is an indispensable procedure in the adjustment of oil and gas burners. Interpretation of the data collected not only enables the engineer to pinpoint operating losses, but enables the fine adjustment of fuel–air ratios that would be impossible to make by visual observations. It is also a valuable tool in troubleshooting service problems. By means of the traditional "CO_2 kit," and its fraternal twin, the Oxygen Analyzer, flue gas sampling is a quick and easy procedure.

Adjusting the gas flame by visual observation, for example, is virtually impossible, due to the fact that there is nothing "typical" about its appearance. Nor can we say that because we have smokeless combustion, we have good combustion—or even *safe* combustion. For there is an extremely important phenomenon regarding natural gas combustion wherein it differs from oil, which is that it is possible to have carbon monoxide (CO) present in a flue gas sample which might otherwise indicate a satisfactory CO_2 content. Figure 18-1 demonstrates how this is possible.

The graph shows the relationship between the various components that are contained in a flue gas sample, namely carbon dioxide, oxygen (as contained in the excess air), and carbon monoxide. Point M represents the theoretical maximum CO_2 for natural gas, if perfect combustion takes place. The curve shows what would happen if we took a very lean fuel–air mix at point A where the CO_2 indication might be a little over 6 percent, and gradually increased the gas flow rate while holding the air rate constant. At point D the CO_2 will have increased

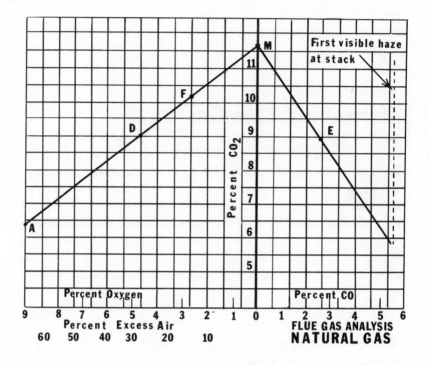

Figure 18-1. CO_2, O_2, Air Relationship
(courtesy Cleaver–Brooks)

to 9 percent and the O_2 will have decreased to 4½ percent. At point M there is nothing in the dry flue gas but CO_2. If we continue increasing the fuel flow, carbon monoxide will appear in the flue gas and the percentage of CO_2 will go down proportionately. At point E the CO_2 will be back down to 9 percent and the CO will be 2½ percent. Increasing the fuel rate still more will lower the CO_2 to less than 6 percent and smoke will become visible at the stack. From the above it can be seen that in order for a flue gas analysis to be valid, it must first be determined on which side of the apex of the graph (point M) the sample is located.

Whether the CO_2 reading obtained by flue gas analysis is over the hump, so to speak, and CO is present in the flue gas, can be verified by taking another sample, this time with an oxygen analyzer. If the sample indicates very little oxygen you can assume you are to the right of point M and monoxide is present. If, on the other hand, a reading of between 4 and 5 percent oxygen is obtained, there is little or no CO present.

If the CO_2 kit is the only service tool available, readjusting the fuel input rate and taking another gas sample will locate point M. Reducing the fuel–input rate while maintaining a constant air–flow rate will lower the CO_2 if there is no CO present. If the CO_2 percentage goes up, on the other hand, we are to the right of point M and the fuel–input rate should be reduced still further until successive flue gas samples indicate we are back in the excess oxygen zone. Leaving a setting of 9.5 to 10 percent CO_2, or 4 percent excess O_2, is recommended good practice.

It is entirely possible to have excess O_2 levels higher than 4 percent and still have a trace of CO present in the flue gas sample, just as it is possible for an oil burner to produce a smokey fire with as much as 6 percent excess oxygen present in the flame zone. Some of the reasons are applicable to gas as well as liquid fuels—inadequate mixing of the fuel and air, insufficient residence time, and so on. The hand–held Bacharach gas sampler, available in two models, is a sure way to check for CO in the flue gas.

The model 19-7016 is a universal gas sampler with components available to measure hydrogen sulfide, carbon dioxide, sulfur dioxide, nitrogen dioxide, and chlorine, in addition to carbon monoxide. The MONOXOR model CDX, is a compact, pocket–size instrument for detecting dangerous CO concentrations; it is not intended for precise measurements of CO percentages for which laboratory–type instruments are required. A CO test is made by drawing a controlled sample of flue gas through a glass indicator tube containing yellow–colored potassium pallado–sulfide which reacts with carbon monoxide to yield a brownish stain of exceptional readability and contrast. Stain length is proportional to the concentration of carbon monoxide.

If after one pump stroke the stain forms only at the edge of the yellow gel, the concentration of CO is approximately 300 parts per million parts of flue gas, but the CO concentration is much higher if the stain extends over the entire length of the gel. If no stain appears after the first pump stroke, but a definite stain develops after the second stroke, it is an indication that the CO concentration in the sample is in the range of 100 to 300 parts per million. If the yellow color of the chemical stays clean and clear after two pump strokes, it is an indication that the concentration of CO is less than 100 parts per million.

The American Gas Association recommends that the concentration of CO in flue gases from vented furnaces and boilers not exceed .04 percent on a *free air basis* (400 parts per million parts of air). This is approximately equivalent to .03 percent (300 PPM) CO as measured in flue gas. However, some utilities have their own standards and it is wise to check with them if there is any question.

SMOKE, SOOT, SLAG, AND SMELL

The effluent from gas and/or oil–fired boiler stacks contains particulate and nonparticulate matter, some of which are combustible and may range from opaque to colorless, odorless to highly offensive, and from relatively harmless to highly toxic. Gases and vapors make up the nonparticulate constituents, while soot, fly–ash, and other carbonaceous material comprise the particulate matter. Those which are photochemically reactive to sunlight form the most obnoxious ingredients of the smog in our urban areas.

The question of air pollution caused by the smoke produced in heating and manufacturing first came under serious consideration at the close of the decade of the 1920s. Cities and towns throughout the country had passed ordinances relative to the quantities of smoke that could be emitted from a stack, and the failure of operators to live up to the requirements of such ordinances brought recrimination and fines. Of the numerous and frequently unsatisfactory definitions of the conditions that constituted a violation, it can be said that the term *visible emission* has survived the test of time and even today is the cornerstone of many air–pollution codes. Ironically, not only do the invisible or practically colorless gases issuing from the stack represent a greater loss in efficiency than do the visible particulate matter, but they also represent the greatest potential threat to the public health and welfare.

The presence of carbon or soot particles in the stack gases results from the incomplete combustion of some of the less volatile hydrocarbon constituents, and it is the wholly or partially incomplete combustion of these so-called *heavy ends* that causes smoke from *all* fuels—solid, liquid, or gaseous. The direct loss from the unconsumed free carbon passing off in this manner is probably rarely in excess of one percent of the total fuel burned, even in the case of the densest smoke. The loss due to unconsumed or partially consumed volatile hydrocarbons, on the other hand, though not indicated by the *appearance* of the gases issuing from the stack may represent an appreciable percentage of the total fuel input.

Noxious odors associated with the products of combustion from gas or oil burners are usually indicative of the presence of so-called aldehydes, which are intermediate products caused by incomplete combustion of the hydrocarbon. Conditions which contribute to the formation of aldehydes also favor the formation of carbon monoxide, which is odorless. The condition should be attended to and corrected immediately.

The rotten-egg odor associated with the incomplete combustion of residual oil, is due to the incomplete oxidation of the sulfur contained in the fuel. Normally, sulfur oxidizes to sulfur trioxide and precipitates as a dry ash. When sulfur dioxide gas condenses with water it forms a corrosive acid which attacks metal surfaces and the mortar in masonry chimneys. Obviously, this is an unsatisfactory combustion condition which needs attention.

SMOKE MONITORING

While the loss represented by visible smoke leaving the stack may be considered negligible, the adherence of the unconsumed carbon and tarry hydrocarbon mixture to flue passages of the boiler acts as an insulator, greatly reducing the heat-absorbing ability of these surfaces. While not a direct combustion loss, the soot accumulation results in a much greater loss than does the visible smoke. It has been said that as little as one-eighth of an inch of soot has an R factor equivalent to 2 inches of insulation.

Smoke density measurement is done by drawing a predetermined volume of stack gas through a standard grade filter paper fitted into a special hand-operated sampling pump. The color of the resultant smoke-stained area of the paper is compared with a graduated smoke scale, typically consisting of color spots ranging from white to dark black, numbered from 0 (representing smokeless combustion) to 9 (which represents the maximum smoke density apt to be produced by a maladjusted burner). Laboratory and field tests have established a correlation between smoke number and degrees of fireside sooting but, more importantly, some regulatory agencies cite the Ringleman or Bacharach smoke scales when establishing limits for visible emission control.

Reliability of smoke readings are predicated on a given ratio of sample volume to filter paper area, and the use of the smoke scale for which the particular sampler was designed. It is essential that the sampling equipment deliver a uniform volume of stack gas from one test to another and that the connection between flue and filter paper be kept at a minimum, yet allow cooling of the combustion products sufficiently to prevent burning or charring of the filter paper. On the other hand, if this connection is excessively long, some soot will drop out in the suction tubing and substantial errors in measurement can result.

Some cities require, and many boiler-plant installations have installed, automatic smoke monitoring equipment that is designed to give an alarm when certain acceptable smoke limits are exceeded. Much of this equipment utilizes a light beam which shines across the diameter of the stack or breeching and is received by a photoelectric cell. As the strength of the light energy is absorbed by the dense, smoke-laden, flue gases, so is the resultant signal from the light-sensitive amplifier. At some preset value an alarm circuit is activated, calling attention to the situation. Needless to say, the equipment must be kept clean and the viewing tubes clear of soot and scale buildup. The amplifier tubes, bulbs, and photo cells, need to be renewed at periodic intervals, in order to function reliably. Unfortunately, the accessibility of these units, located as they often are in the breeching high above the boiler room floor, leaves a lot to be desired, and for that reason do not always receive the routine maintenance they need. Enterprising operators have, in many cases, saved a lot of hazardous climbing by pressurizing the viewing tubes and lenses of the sending and receiving units by running a small air line to each, from the plant's compressed-air system, or from the windbox of the forced draft fan of the burner. In addition, they find it convenient, where available, to use the light meter which is mounted on the face of the wall-mounted amplifier panel, to corroborate a visual observation after having made a burner adjustment. The meter has a scale graduated like a smoke color comparator indicating percent opacity or Ringleman Number and responds promptly to changes in smoke density.

OVERFIRING

Care should be taken to guard against overfiring the burner. Although technically its air-handling ability determines the maximum firing rate, and the requirement for smokeless operation dictates that we stay within this limitation, overfiring of the burner is inadvertently possible. Using a CO_2 kit to set the maximum firing rate has certain built-in pitfalls. If we assume that the high-fire damper position allows the passage of just the right amount of air for the design fuel rate, we could be making a serious mistake; even though manufacturer's operating instructions may assure us that as long as we adjust for smokeless combustion we cannot be overfired. Such recommendations are predicated on the fact that the manufacturer has sized the air-handling equipment according to the maximum fuel input, and that rate is all it is capable of accommodating. However, most forced-draft boilers are designed to run with stub stacks. That is, they need no chimney draft to exhaust the products of combustion, and in fact often run with a positive pressure in the vent stub. If such a boiler is connected to a very high chimney—that is a relic of bygone days—we could be in serious trouble. Such stacks might run with several tenths of inches water column negative pressure that can substantially alter the pressure drop through the boiler, against which the draft fan was calculated to operate. If we adjust the fuel input to yield the design CO_2 with this kind of air flow we will be overfired. The author knows of a case where expensive baffle repairs had to be undertaken in less than a year of operation caused by inadvertent overfiring of a forced–draft oil boiler due to excessive natural draft.

BOILER RATING VS CAPACITY

Occasionally one may hear or read of certain boilers that are being fired at 150 or even 200 percent of capacity. The term *percent of capacity* has to do with the ratio of boiler heating-surface area to fuel input, and is based on standards that have evolved as a result of the efforts made by manufacturers and the American Society of Mechanical Engineers to rate boilers uniformly according to their ability to do work. Many years ago, 10 square feet of surface area was thought to be required per boiler horsepower, and most boilers were rated on this basis. As automatic fuel–burning equipment began replacing hand–firing methods it was found that the large area formerly occupied by the grates offered more than enough space for the installation of oil burner combustion chambers. As a matter of fact, often a third or more of the space behind the refractory had to be filled with insulation and capped off with hearth cement, leaving it unused. Perhaps through insight, or possibly lack of expertise, in the course of conversion from coal to oil there was a tendency to provide more physical heating capacity under these boilers than the original coal fire was rated to produce. This generosity, together with the ease with which the fuel input could be increased to meet the growing demands of manufacturing on the steam–generating facilities of the plant, soon gave rise to the situation where a particular boiler might be operating at more than 100 percent of capacity. Many of these old boilers, rated at 10 square feet per horsepower, are today performing satisfactorily though perhaps less efficiently with input–to–surface ratios equivalent to eight, seven, or even fewer square feet per horsepower, each foot being called upon to absorb more heat as the fuel input was increased.

The amount of heating surface that has been considered by manufacturers as capable of evaporating 34.5 pounds of water at 212 degrees per hour (a condition representing the development of one boiler horsepower) has changed from time to time as the state of the art has progressed. At the present time, five square feet of heating surface is ordinarily considered the equivalent of one boiler–horsepower (1 Bhp) among manufacturers of stationary fire–tube boilers, and the horsepower for which a boiler is sold on such a basis is known as its *nominal rated capacity*. In view of the widely varying rates of evaporation possible per square foot of heating surface with different boilers and different operating conditions, it can be seen that such a basis of rating has in reality no practical bearing on the question of a particular boiler's ability to handle a given load, and should be considered merely as a reference. For this reason the *net rated output in Btu per hour* has become the accepted standard in the selection of boilers according to the jobs they must do, and is the topmost item on the list of specifications published by all manufacturers for their boilers.

TURNDOWN

The relationship between the maximum and minimum fuel input rate is called *turndown ratio*. For example, a burner whose maximum input is 10 million Btu and minimum rate is 2 million has a turndown ratio of 5 to 1. How far the input can be reduced in the low–fire mode depends on several factors:

1. The furnace pressure
2. Minimum gas pressure drop across the gas burner ring
3. The combustion air pressure drop across the burner head or diffuser in low–fire mode
4. Minimum air requirement for the gas pilot burner
5. Viewing angle and sighting characteristics of the flame scanner.

As explained previously, furnace pressure diminishes approximately as the square of the firing rate. Furthermore, the pressure drop across the diffuser diminishes with the air volume. It is not unusual that flame volume dynamics at low fire do not permit the degree of combustion efficiency attainable in the high-fire mode. In low fire as much as 50 percent excess air is needed with some burners to maintain the jet entrainment effect required for proper stirring and mixing of the gas. Since the air setting at low fire is fixed according to pilot burner requirements, the only alternative is to lower the fuel-input rate. Steady-state efficiency does not suffer greatly from the less efficient combustion which results, because the stack temperature is relatively low compared to the high-fire mode, as discussed previously.

Depending on the location of the gas ring or orifices with respect to the air stream, there is a turndown point below which flame symmetry is destroyed and/or the scanner loses sight of the flame because there is insufficient gas to fill the ring.

19

The Chimney and Its Effect on Modern Boilers

In modernizing power plants, the factors that determine what effect an existing tall chimney will have on the operating characteristics of a new boiler which has replaced one for which the chimney was originally designed, are pretty well established though often disregarded. The knowledge of the fundamentals of natural draft is gradually becoming a lost art to modern-day burner technicians. In a way, this is largely due to the fact that mechanical-draft boilers do not require a chimney as such; merely a vent to the atmosphere for the products of combustion. The construction of very large chimneys today is limited almost exclusively to utility company electric-power generating stations. Although modern boilers have air-handling systems specifically designed to establish the correct mass-flow rate against the friction loss of the boiler gas passages, breeching, and the vent stub, without the aid of natural draft, it is no less important to know what adverse effects a tall chimney might have on burner operating conditions. Overfiring is one such condition we have already discussed, resulting from excessive natural draft.

In the case of the single boiler installation, natural draft is not a problem in the traditional sense which requires the addition of a barometric draft regulator to the system. As a matter of fact, stack pressures are sometimes positive rather than sub-atmospheric. Therefore, many manufacturers of forced-draft boilers emphatically recommend the *omission* of draft regulators from their installations, even when the boiler is connected to a fairly high chimney, in order to preclude the possibility that the products of combustion might escape into the boiler room through the draft regulator opening in the breech. The foregoing may seem a contradiction, but it is a fact that under the right conditions a formerly very powerful chimney can *go positive,* with a forced-draft boiler connected to it. Multiple boilers, on the other hand, present some unique problems when they are connected to a single, tall chimney, necessitating some form of natural-draft regulation.

Draft, the term used to describe the movement of gases— usually the products of combustion—through a flue or chimney, is a measurement expressed in inches water column that represents the difference in weight of the column of flue gas and a corresponding column of air of equal dimension outside the flue. *Theoretical natural draft* is directly proportional to the height of the chimney above the boiler's furnace, and is dependent upon the average temperature of the column of gases within the flue. The average temperature of the flue-gas column is affected by the materials of construction of the chimney, air leaks from outside, the velocity of the gases through the chimney, and the temperature of the ambient air which surrounds it. The smoothness of the bore also has a minor effect on chimney performance. However, the coefficient of friction is traditionally taken as a constant for all types of construction since, in time, the inside surface of most chimneys becomes covered with a layer of soot. Ironically, these monuments to the Industrial Revolution, which were so vital to the operation of the power plants of yesteryear, are a liability today. Insurance companies view them apprehensively, ecologists watch them vigilantly, and power engineers cope with them reluctantly. Moreover, when modern forced-draft boilers are coupled to these relics, operating problems result from the fact that the conditions for which they were designed no longer prevail.

Essentially, chimney height was governed by the draft requirements of the mechanism of combustion, and chimney diameter by the number of pounds per minute of stack gas it was to handle. Finally, a height-width relationship, based on the results of the manipulation of these two measurements, was established to arrive at the lowest possible construction cost. Historically, chimney performance has been based on the following design parameters:

Average chimney gas temperature	500°F
Average atmospheric temperature	62°F
Average coefficient of friction	.016
Average chimney gas density,	
0°F at 1 atmosphere	.09 lb per cu ft
Barometer reading, sea level	29.92 in. Hg

The most significant departure from the above criteria is the fact that the average temperature of the stack gas of the modern gas/oil boiler is much lower, perhaps 300°F lower. It is important to recognize that, in the case of the field–erected, coal-fired, natural–draft boiler, typified by the once very popular dry bottom fire–box design and the horizontal return tubular (HRT) boiler, the average inlet temperature to the chimney was well over 500 degrees. It was not that the state of the art could not produce a boiler design capable of wringing more heat from the products of combustion; high gas temperatures were necessary to establish the proper mass–flow rate through the boiler. The flow of combustion air to the burner was related directly to the amount of draft available from the chimney, the draft loss (pressure drop) through the boiler flues, and the pressure required to force the air for combustion through the bed of fuel on the grates. Thus the maximum firing rate of the old boilers originally connected to these monsters was tied inseparably to chimney efficiency.

Modern packaged boilers rarely run with stack temperatures of 500 degrees unless they are in dire need of cleaning. New design concepts have made the difference: totally submerged furnaces and longer gas–travel passages, made possible by carefully integrated mechanical draft and combustion systems; lower mass flow rates per boiler horsepower, resulting from improved burner configurations. No longer is burner performance dependent upon available chimney draft.

Available draft is the theoretical natural draft minus the friction loss of the flue. As the amount of gas flowing increases, the available draft decreases until it becomes zero at maximum gas flow. A steady state is thereby established, wherein the draft loss due to friction equals the theoretical intensity. The point where the gas flow reaches maximum intensity varies as its temperature varies. The lower its inlet temperature, the lower the available draft. Therefore, a chimney designed for use with a natural–draft boiler, and contingent upon an average inlet gas temperature of 500 degrees, will develop less draft when the inlet temperature is 200 degrees. The effect of temperature on the mass–flow rate is very important, because it determines when the chimney ceases to function as a chimney and, instead, becomes a mere exhaust duct. In the old days when this happened, it was called the *wide–open point*—the point of zero draft and maximum flow. The words do not carry the same dramatic connotation today. In fact, with a modern boiler we seldom know that it is happening, for the trend is away from draft gauges and recorder charts, especially on single–boiler installations. When a forced–draft boiler, with its low–temperature, low–volume stack–gas flow characteristics is connected to an old, tall chimney, the draft goes positive when the wide–open point is passed. A draft gauge needle would indicate on the plus or positive side of the scale. Mass flow beyond this point is developed *mechanically,* and the chimney is then just an extension of the breeching. There are few noticeable and no adverse effects, because modern draft systems are customarily designed to operate against an inch or more positive draft at the exhaust stub.

The interpretation of draft–gauge readings is an important consideration, especially where multiple boilers are connected to a single, tall stack. In the case of a battery of boilers, we must assume that the chimney was originally designed to handle the boilers simultaneously, so that if we have three 400–horsepower boilers we have, in effect, a 1200–horsepower chimney. This being the case, what happens to the draft when only one boiler is on the line? A look at Figure 19-1 demonstrates an important relationship between mass flow and available draft that applies to all chimneys, regardless of size or materials of construction. The relationship can be stated axiomatically as follows: There

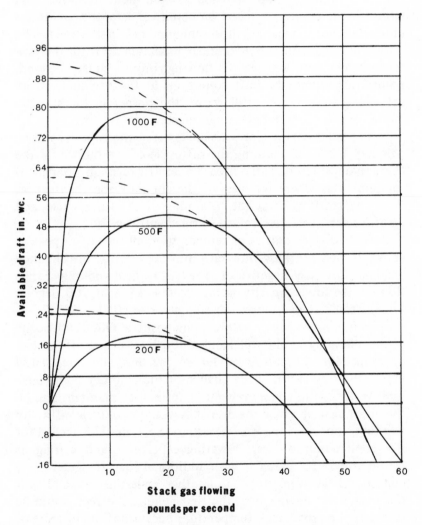

Figure 19-1. Temperature/Draft Curves

is a certain mass-flow rate that produces a maximum available draft for any flue-gas temperature.

Referring to the graph, note that curves representing flue-gas temperatures of 200, 500, and 1,000 degrees are shown, and although the curves are based on empirical data, the conditions illustrated are typical of those encountered in the field. The dotted lines indicate the theoretical maximum draft for the various temperatures, with no gas flowing. From a practical standpoint, this represents draft conditions at the beginning of an off cycle—the chimney still warm, the burner in the standby mode, air inlet or uptake dampers closed.

The solid curves represent cold-start conditions where the chimney has cooled during the off cycle of the burner. In the case of an intermittently-fired boiler, there is an interval of some minutes where the mass of the chimney absorbs the heat from the stack gases at the beginning of the firing cycle, and does not *draw* effectively until warmed sufficiently.

Note that regardless of temperature, all the curves peak at about 25 percent mass-flow rate. In other words, the chimney becomes intensely negative once it has warmed and only a fraction of its total capacity is being used. Even at 200 degrees average stack temperature, the chimney can still handle 65 percent of its total capacity before going positive! Our 1200-horsepower chimney could still handle 800 horsepower. If we had only one 400-horsepower boiler on the line, and even at full input, there would be little chance of the chimney going positive. Instead, the chimney would continue to maintain a negative draft against which the draft fan would have little difficulty working, thus allowing easy access to more air than needed for the combustion process; lowering efficiency, and baiting us treacherously to match it with additional fuel. If, under these conditions, we were to cut in another boiler instead, and split the load between the two, the first beneficial effect would be to lower the gross stack temperature because of the increase of boiler heating surface per unit fuel input (we have doubled it). A second effect would be an increase in the total mass flow to the chimney, due to the increased density of the stack gas (each cubic foot weighs more the cooler it gets). The two effects work together to lower the available draft by increasing the friction loss. As a result the chimney draft will be less intense when more than one boiler is on the line. For this reason, operating fuel rates and excess air settings should not be adjusted with one boiler on line alone.

From the foregoing, it should be evident that some type of draft control would be needed to operate a single boiler of the battery. A balanced gate–type regulator on the common breeching, set to maintain either a neutral or few tenths of an inch negative pressure in the breeching at the low–fire rate would be practical, so long as it closed reasonably tight under positive draft conditions. It should be mounted as close to the chimney as possible, between the chimney and the run–out to the first boiler, so that it is sensing chimney draft unaffected by standby loss through the uptake dampers of the idle boilers.

The effect of draft loss due to the infiltration of room air through idle boilers connected to a common breeching has long been recognized. Years ago, of course, manually–operated and semiautomatic boilers were operated almost continuously, it being most inconvenient to "let out the fire," and a major operation to relight it. Intermittent firing came into vogue with increased sophistication of automatic control. It was then that it was realized how, during the off cycle of the burner, the boiler was a huge air heater radiating to the atmosphere by way of the chimney.

Keeping the chimney warm was, of course, essential to the maintenance of adequate draft in anticipation of the next running cycle. However, it was found that by starting the burner at the minimum firing rate, and gradually increasing the rate as the chimney warmed and more draft became available, the uptake dampers could be left nearly closed during the off cycle. The mass of the chimney, particularly of masonry construction, would retain enough heat so that the next light–off would be reasonably smooth.

Modern packaged boilers have programmed firing cycles that automatically position air dampers prior to light–off, and regulate combustion air continuously during the running cycle. Fuel–air ratios are carefully balanced so that excess air is kept to a minimum. At the completion of the firing cycle, the draft is maintained only long enough to insure that the products of combustion have exited the boiler. The draft fan is then stopped, and the air damper reverts to a standby mode, effectively trapping the heat in the boiler where it can be absorbed by the medium instead of leaked up the chimney.

BOILER ROOM AIR SUPPLY

The size and location of outside–air–intake openings to the boiler room are based on combustion–air requirements and the effect chimney draft has on ventilation air. Obviously the draft intensity of the stack must be taken into account whether boiler room air is drawn into the burner or through a barometric draft regulator. The following recommendations are accepted good practice.

1. Two (2) permanent openings in the outer walls of the boiler room are recommended. Locate one at each end of the boiler room, preferably below a height of 7 feet. This allows air to sweep the length of the boiler.

2. Air supply openings can be louvered for weather protection, but they should not be covered with fine mesh wire as this type of covering has poor air–flow qualities and is subject to clogging by dust and dirt.

3. A vent fan in the boiler room is not recommended as it might create a slight vacuum under certain conditions and cause variations in the quantity of combustion air. This could result in unsatisfactory burner performance.

4. Under no condition should the total area of the air supply openings be less than one (1) square foot.

5. Size the openings by using the formula,

$$\text{Area (square feet)} = \frac{\text{CFM}}{\text{FPM}}$$

6. The amount of air required (CFM)
    Combustion Air = Maximum Bhp $\times$ 8 CFM/Bhp
    Ventilation Air = Maximum Bhp $\times$ 2 CFM/Bhp

or a total of 10 CFM/Bhp up to 1000 feet elevation. Add 3 percent more per 1000 feet of added elevation.

7. Acceptable air velocities in the boiler room are

From floor to 7 foot height	250 FPM
Above 7 foot height	500 FPM
Ducted air supply to boiler	1000 FPM

Example: Determine the area of the boiler room air supply openings for one 300–horsepower boiler at 800–feet altitude. The air openings are to be 5 feet above the boiler room floor.

a. Air required: 300 X 10 = 3000 CFM

b. Air velocity: Up to 7 feet = 250 FPM

c. Area required: Area $=\dfrac{\text{CFM}}{\text{FPM}} = \dfrac{3000}{250} = 12$ sq ft

d. Area/opening: $\dfrac{12}{2} = 6$ sq ft per opening (2 required)

NOTE: Consult local codes which may supersede these requirements.

As a personal observation, the author recommends that in the case of manned boiler rooms in frigid climates extra attention be paid to the location of outside–air intakes relative to the maintenance of minimum comfort conditions. Otherwise an operator may block one or more off to keep from freezing to death, and die of asphyxiation instead.

20

The Realities of Air Pollution

The traditionally held view of nitrogen as a chemically–impotent nonparticipant in the combustion reaction has been modified considerably as a result of research work like that done at the California Institute of Technology in the early 1950s. Findings have demonstrated that, in the presence of sunlight, nitrogen dioxide (NO_2) and certain hydrocarbon compounds react to form a variety of smog–producing oxidants. In power plant operation, energy conversion involves the transport of huge quantities of air through high–temperature reaction zones, providing the potential for the rearrangement of the oxides of nitrogen leading to NO_2 formation.

Oxides of nitrogen are compounds of the two most abundant gases in the atmosphere—oxygen and nitrogen. In total, there are seven known oxides of nitrogen in equilibria with each other, and with ozone. However, only nitric oxide and nitrogen dioxide are of concern in air pollution. From the standpoint of combustion, nitric oxide (NO) can be considered as the intermediate product of a parallel reaction between nitrogen and oxygen in which the final step, the formation of nitrogen dioxide, takes place *outside* the boiler. At ordinary temperatures and at concentrations of 1000 parts per million nitric oxide, about five minutes are necessary to convert one–half of the nitric oxide to nitrogen dioxide in the atmosphere. However, at concentrations of 1 ppm, 100 hours are required for one–half conversion. In the presence of hydrocarbons, and when irradiated by sunlight, the conversion is much faster.

The catalytic action of nitric oxide, which was found to inhibit the thermal decomposition of paraffinic hydrocarbons, has been studied as far back as 1939. In fact, the role that nitrogen dioxide plays in smog formation is not completely understood even today, and a controversy exists over the importance of regulating its emission at all. A report, *The Oxides of Nitrogen in Air Pollution,* prepared in 1964 for the California State Legislature concluded: "In view of the uncertainty of the supporting data and the conflicting opinions of scientists, a standard based on the specific role of the oxides of nitrogen in photochemical air pollution is not recommended at this time." There is no question as to the detrimental effect it has on the environment, however. That is to say, that regardless of its role in smog formation, NO_2 in sufficient concentration in the atmosphere warrants concern by man, for nitrogen dioxide has a phototoxic effect on plant life. There is evidence that long-term exposure to NO_2 concentrations below 1 ppm may lead to growth suppression, blanching, and perhaps premature defoliation. Exposures to 1 ppm NO_2 for eight hours will produce significant growth reduction.

NO_2 has a coloration effect on the atmosphere quite apart from its role in smog formation. It has been estimated, for instance, that at 0.25 ppm on a day when visibility is 20 miles, the color effects on objects 10 miles distant will be objectionable to the public. This is because NO_2 absorbs light in both the ultraviolet and visible spectrum. In sufficient concentrations, it will reduce brightness and the contrast of distant objects and will impart a yellow-brown color to the horizon, sky, and distant white objects. It is believed that a standard of 0.25 ppm would prevent possible plant damage by NO_2. In addition, the data available indicates that 0.25 ppm is lower than the concentrations at which effects on health would be expected from prolonged exposures to the gas.

Chemical equilibrium and reaction rate data have indicated that nitric oxide is the predominant oxide of nitrogen formed in combustion processes, and spectrographic studies have confirmed its presence in post-reaction gases. However, many variables affect the emission rate from the boiler, among them peak combustion temperature and duration, and the availability of free oxygen and nitrogen, as well as the rate of cooling of the gases. Actually, the generation of nitric oxide requires that all these factors be arranged like the tumblers of a combination lock. It has been estimated, for example, that at about 2780°F with 20 percent oxygen present, 4400 ppm nitric oxide is formed at equilibrium and 90 percent of equilibrium value is reached in 12 seconds. Although flame temperatures of approximately 3000°F are entirely feasible in modern boilers, a 12–second *soaking* period is totally unrealistic, when you realize that the mass flow rate of the reactants is on the order of 15 to 20 feet per second. Conversely, at higher temperatures the soaking time required is far less. At 3860°F, 20,000 ppm NO is formed and 90 percent of the maximum concentration is reached in one–half second. To maintain the NO thus formed, however, requires that the gases be cooled to 3140°F in about two–hundredths of a second, or at a rate of approximately 20,000C per second—an impossibility. From this we can see that at temperatures and residence times commonly encountered in conventional combustion processes, we are talking about concentrations amounting to a fraction of those theoretically possible. It is important to remember, however, that the nitric oxide that does form at temperatures of about 3000°F and lower persists in nonequilibrium amounts during the expansion process through the boiler flue passages and breeching, exiting the boiler with the other stack gases.

The *oxidant level* of the atmosphere is directly related to the combined hydrocarbon and oxides of nitrogen content. At a level of .15 ppm oxidant, approximately 50 percent of the population experiences some eye watering. The Department of Health, Education, and Welfare in 1971 set .08 ppm as the federal standard for one–hour exposure level. It is interesting to note that nationally automobiles contribute 59 percent of the hydrocarbons and 32 percent of the oxides of nitrogen to the atmosphere.

Laboratory smog–chamber tests, conducted by state and federal authorities, major automobile manufacturers, and others, have shown that manipulation of hydrocarbon and nitric oxide concentrations often yield unexpected results. For example, reduction of only one constituent may not reduce, and in fact may increase, oxidant formation. There is evidence, however, that the combined reduction of hydrocarbon and nitric oxide in the atmosphere reduces oxidant yield, and in every case a reduction in hydrocarbon concentration reduces the *rate* of smog formation. The manner in which nitric oxide and nitrogen dioxide react is responsible for the complexities of the system and accounts for the unpredictable effects that changes in nitric oxide concentration have in altering the rate of smog formation. In one set of circumstances it is the compound that absorbs sunlight to trigger smog formation, yet in another set of circumstances reacts with the oxyalkyl hydrocarbon to form alkyl-nitrate, which inhibits smog formation. Thus nitrogen oxides both start and stop smog formation.

Hydrocarbons enter the atmosphere primarily in two ways: as the result of incomplete combustion of fossil fuels, and through the evaporation of volatile fuels from storage. Atmospheric hydrocarbons number in the hundreds, and as many as 200 distinct species have been found in the automobile exhaust alone. Not all the hydrocarbon compounds disgorged into the atmosphere figure in smog formation, fortunately. Paraffinic hydrocarbons, the family to which fuel oils and natural gas belong, are strongly bound compounds of little affinity and are relatively inert in the atmosphere. Others, such as the olfins—in which automobile fuels are grouped—are extremely reactive and combine readily with nitrogen dioxide in the presence of sunlight to form oxidants. As power engineers we can take little comfort in our tame hydrocarbons, however, for regardless of the origin of the oxidant that may have precipitated the smog formation, meteorological conditions which often accompany smog development must be taken into account. Air stratification due to a temperature inversion, which concentrates airborne wastes in a tight layer near the ground (often only a thousand feet or so thick) and prevents diffusion and ventilation, is an important consideration. Obviously, on the basis of volume alone, any unnecessary emission into a stagnant situation like that is compounding a felony.

The successful combustion of fuel oil can take place only after atomization and gasification of the oil droplet. It follows therefore that anything that interferes with droplet size or distribution, or with its diffusion into the swirling air stream, could result in their partial combustion. The most common cause of excessive hydrocarbon loss in the stack gas of an oil–burning boiler is incomplete or improper air–oil mixing in the combustion chamber. The mixing area, referred to as the preheat or preignition zone, is located between the burner atomizer and the flame front. All the oil, all of the primary air, and some of the secondary air pass through this zone. The fuel is still in the liquid phase here, undergoing a very rapid heating, expansion, and mixing process. The speed and thoroughness of the mixing determines the physical distance of the flame from the atomizer, because autoignition will not take place unless and until a critical concentration of hydrocarbon and oxygen molecules is reached, regardless of the mass velocity of the fuel–air mixture. A vigorous, stable flame, burning up close to the atomizer, indicates thorough mixing; whereas a lazy, floating flame indicates an unsatisfactory mix.

From the boundary between the liquid phase and the actual flame itself, which we have called the flame front, the mass retains some of its physical character, but is now also undergoing chemical change. New compounds are evolving from the original constituents. The most dramatic aspect is the increase in speed with which the reaction races to completion. Photographic records of laboratory experimentation demonstrate that droplet life after ignition is from 2 to 20 milliseconds, all of which emphasizes an important fact: there is little or no opportunity to compensate for imperfect droplet formation by attempting to manipulate the flame itself. On the other hand, remarkable results have been obtained by the careful attention to factors that affect droplet formation, the most important of which are atomizer geometry and cleanliness.

Geometry in this context refers to such physical aspects as internal and external mating surfaces of nozzles, rotary cups and diffusers. Sharp cut–off surfaces, flared contours, lands and grooves, ports and orifices, should be free from distortion caused by bending, warping, fatigue, crystallization (burning), nicking, chipping, or encrustation. The maintenance of concentricity is extremely important, since it has a direct bearing on the shape of the air–oil interface. Even where slight eccentricity exists, it can be responsible for uneven fuel–droplet distribution in the air stream, and in the extreme can result in the flight of unburned droplets right past the combustion zone.

The relationship of the atomizer and the air nozzle or diffuser is crucial, not only as to concentricity but also with respect to horizontal distance. Of course manufacturer's recommendations should be strictly followed, but in general, moving the atomizer away from the flame front while holding the air nozzle fixed results in a narrowing of the flame pattern. It also, however, increases the possibility of raw oil impingement on the air nozzle or diffuser. In any case, careful flame observation should be made after each adjustment. Any judgment as to improvement of a given condition is facilitated by having as few variables at work at one time as possible; so avoid simultaneous adjustments. As a rule, a change in flame size or shape easily recognized by eye, will alter the constituents or temperature of the stack gas and can be interpreted with the aid of a conventional CO_2 kit. To the engineer or fireman, incomplete combustion means fireside deposits, frequent cleaning, loss of capacity, and downtime. Let's add air pollution to that list, even though it may be invisible.

The imperfect flame has certain audiovisual characteristics that can be interpreted by a knowledgeable engineer in much the same way a doctor treats a patient according to the symptoms he observes. Fireballs or fireflies, for example, are sometimes seen escaping the main flame zone of an oil fire, and are the grossest example of poor fuel and air mixing, requiring immediate attention. They are flaming oil drops with liquid centers, caused by a damaged or encrusted atomizer. Where these smouldering droplets impact, they form hard carbon deposits. Fireflies can also be caused by carbon formation on the air diffuser or burner snout, which obstructs or alters air delivery to the preheat zone. The underlying problem in this case is why the carbon formed on the snout in the first place. Unfortunately, chronic carbon formation on burner heads, snouts, and air nozzles is often the result of certain inherent inadequacies in the design of older burners.

There are certain other conditions that cannot be brought into control by cleaning and adjustment. These have to do with the mismatching of the burners and the fuel, or incompatibility of the burner and combustion chamber. With this in mind, it might be well to consult first with factory representatives of the burner manufacturer in order to get some idea of just what you can hope to accomplish with a rehabilitation program. By all means, however, if it is a fact of life that the burner must be swung open once a shift to knock the whiskers off the air nozzle, then do it faithfully.

If burner design counts heavily on the radiation and conduction of heat from the refractory surfaces to diffuse oil droplets it is otherwise incapable of atomizing, operating at low–fire rates can be bad from a pollution standpoint, and very inefficient as well. Generally speaking, with such burners peak efficiency can be correlated with peak refractory temperature, which in turn can be inferred from the intensity of the glowing radiance immediately after shutdown. Nonradiance equates with nonperformance.

Modern burners have come to rely less on the radiation from combustion chambers. In the case of some boiler designs, refractory is installed merely to protect structural portions of the vessel from the destructive effect of high flame temperatures, and in another case primarily as a sound attenuator. This is possible because of improved burner design that permits precise mixture control in the preignition zone.

The most conspicuous symptom of incomplete combustion is smoke. Through the years the public has been conditioned to regard visible emissions as the most disgraceful and worst kind of pollution, when actually free carbon, which is the most obvious constituent of smoke, is one of the least harmful of air pollutants when compared with the oxides of nitrogen and sulfur. Even carbon dioxide itself which, along with water vapor, is the result of perfect combustion, is more harmful by volume. In a plume of smoke there are apt to be fewer unburned hydrocarbons, for example, due to the fact that in the fuel-rich atmosphere the dissociation of carbon implies that the lighter hydrocarbon compounds were combined with available oxygen in a very high-temperature environment, due to the absence of the flame-chilling effect of excess air, favoring the formation of CO_2. It would seem to make sense, then, that we operate at or near legal smoke, taking full advantage of whatever smoke-monitoring equipment we have to assist us in obtaining this optimum setting. Operators should be instructed in the proper procedure to follow whenever the audible or visual alarm indicates we have transgressed too far into the smoke range. Then either the operator or some other qualified person should take steps to reset the firing rate or fuel-air ratio accordingly.

The combustion of natural gas is relatively straightforward. Methane, the major constituent of the fuel, is an extremely stable hydrocarbon whose intermediate products of combustion do not figure prominently in atmospheric smog formation. For a given amount of fuel burned with a given amount of air, the products consist of a fixed mass of the four atoms, hydrogen, carbon, oxygen, and nitrogen. Furthermore, they appear in the stack gas as reasonably predictable compounds over a very wide range of fuel-air ratios, which can be attributed to the fact that, unlike oil fuel, none of the reactants exist in the combustion chamber in the condensed phase. There is little chance, therefore, of forming intermediate products that could pass through the reaction unburned.

The flame front is usually in intimate contact with the burner diffuser or gas annulus. The fuel and air are mixed in the chamber as a result of their relative mass velocities, and the diffusion of energy from and to the flame.

As compared to fuel-oil combustion, the tendency toward NO formation in the gas-fired boiler would seem to be greater because of the higher percentage of free oxygen customarily brought to the flame. However, this is undoubtedly due in part to a traditional apprehension over the presence of carbon monoxide in the products of a fuel-rich flame, and the unreliability of visual observations. Most fuel-air ratios set without the aid of instruments are exceedingly oxygen-rich. Experience has shown that, under these conditions, it is not unusual to find as much as 70 percent excess air when checked with a flue gas analyzer. A number of factors have a bearing on this enigma. One of these is that operators often do not realize that flame color has little or no relationship to combustion efficiency. Gas does not necessarily burn with a blue flame. Another factor having to do with the formation of carbon monoxide—which, incidentally, is the most widespread air pollutant—concerns the time-honored method of adjusting fuel-air ratio by watching the stack haze—forget it. It doesn't work with gas, because by the time the first faint haze appears there is already nearly 6 percent CO in the stack gas! CO is, of course, taboo since it is both poisonous and flammable under the right conditions.

Combination gas-and-oil-burner design is heavily influenced by the complex requirements of the oil fuel. Often a degree of gas-burner performance is sacrificed in the process. The simple expediency of providing an opening through the center of the gas-burner air diffuser so that the oil-burner gun can protrude, is an example. This configuration is nearly universally employed by boiler-burner manufacturers. It certainly seems a very natural and obvious method of getting the oil fuel into the combustion space, but it compromises gas-burner performance on low fire by impeding the diffusion process. On the other hand, the gas-burner annulus, which surrounds the oil-burner gun, does not adversely affect the performance of the oil burner. When burning gas, these burners operate with very lean low-fire rates. Any attempt to increase the fuel rate only produces CO, and ultimately smoke. Obviously a high percentage of the combustion air does not reach the primary reaction zone under these conditions. The air that is present but does not take part in the combustion process carries heat away, raises the stack temperature, and provides the free oxygen and nitrogen necessary for NO formation. In the final analysis, however, the heat release coefficient, which is the ratio of Btu input per cubic foot of furnace volume, is small on low fire. This is another way of saying net flame temperature is low, a condition which counteracts or at least does not fulfill the requirement for NO fixation.

The determination of the percentage of oxides of nitrogen or hydrocarbons actually present in the flue gas is not conveniently made. There is no way at present to read out these values directly from a sample withdrawn from the stack, as in the case of carbon dioxide. Chemical methods commonly used to determine the emission of oxides of nitrogen from stationary sources or from motor vehicles, are based on measurement of either the nitrite or the nitrate ion. Nitric oxide is first oxidized to nitrogen dioxide, and the latter is then absorbed in an aqueous reagent. The results are then expressed in terms of NO_2. Air–pollution ordinances often require a more complex testing procedure, based on colorometric measurements as described in Method 7 in *The Federal Register* of December 23, 1971, page 24891.

Similarly, hydrocarbons are measured according to the method described in Appendix E of *The Federal Register* of April 30, 1971, page 8198. A less precise analysis of total combustibles in the flue gas such as carbon monoxide, hydrogen, and hydrocarbons, may be accomplished by incineration with a measured volume of air or oxygen, usually in the presence of a catalyst. The percent of combustibles in the flue gas is then proportional to the measured heat released by burning, or it is proportional to the difference between the gross volume of the sample and the volume of its products of combustion; or it is measured by an analysis of the products of combustion of the sample, using either an absorption or conductivity apparatus.

No discussion of air pollution would be complete without at least alluding to the granddaddy of all pollutants—sulfur dioxide. Thousands of words have been written on the subject, which has become highly charged with political and emotional overtones. For of the realities we have discussed thus far, perhaps none is quite so grim as the fact that SO_2 control is big business. It costs the American public millions of dollars a year in increased costs of electrical energy and manufactured goods. One of the side effects of the Clean Air Act of 1971 is that low sulfur–bearing fuels, the bulk of which are imported to this country, are at a premium and in short supply.

One cannot help but wonder how long we, as a nation, can

continue to indulge ourselves in nebulous arrangements with capricious, even hostile, foreign governments thousands of miles across the seas, in the name of public welfare. Whether or not it is all worth it will remain a moot point. Regardless, I think we can all concur that the day has passed when the so-called automatic fuels could be left to completely unattended operation for long periods of time. At the same time, it would seem that a greater measure of sophistication is called for on the part of the operators of combustion systems, with respect to the interpretation of corrective action in order to do our part in the prevention of excessive oxidant formation. Nor is there anything wrong by simultaneously reaping the benefits—personal and otherwise—that will accrue as a result of more efficient fuel utilization.

21

Electrical Considerations

AUTOMATIC CONTROL SYSTEMS

When Thomas Edison ushered in the "Age of Light" on September 4, 1882 in New York City, he sounded the death knell for the in-plant steam engine. At the same time, the Edison System of electrical generation and distribution ultimately made possible the harnessing and application of steam energy to an extent never before possible. But it was a while in coming, as B. G. A. Skrotski, looking back to the turn of the century, many years ago editorialized in *Power,*

> . . . boilers stood in long rows, stoked by grimy men who shoveled more than six pounds of coal for every kilowatt-hour produced. Today, in clean, quiet, control rooms, fewer men guide the operation of vastly more powerful equipment in plants making a kwhr from less than one pound. The revolution, which so greatly increased the productivity of fuel and labor, began with the development of automatic firing. It came into full flower with the addition of automatic control. Mechanical firing made it possible to feed the hungry maw of a million pound per hour boiler; mechanical control made it possible to regulate the vast appetite of such a boiler, in response to ever-changing loads . . . Thus, in most plants, varying steam demand must be met by the unceasing vigilance of operators . . . or by the never-sleeping watchfulness of *automatic controls.*

Since earlier days, when man first began to think in terms of mechanical advantage to solve everyday work problems, he has extended the limit of his own brute force ten thousandfold.

In so doing he has learned to respect his electromechanical helpers, for they are like sullen beasts of burden, serving reluctantly, straining in the traces, looking for a chance to turn on their captors.

The primary consideration of the burner service person should be *operating safety*. The whole approach to developing a troubleshooting technique must be built on this basis. The consequence of every move must be carefully considered beforehand; not only as to personal safety, but for the safety of the entire installation. Above all, he must be an attentive observer, because the very nature of electromechanical equipment necessitates that for every action there follows a reaction. He should be able to predict in advance the *result* before taking radical action. If the reader infers that he should approach the big burners like a member of the Police Bomb Disposal Squad, he is correct; except he doesn't need the armorplate, just respect . . . and the confidence that comes with training and experience.

From the standpoint of personal safety, the danger of electrical shock is undoubtedly the greatest hazard associated with the operation of large burners. This is due in part to the prevalence of heavy–duty motors and electric oil heaters attendant with dual–fuel burners. The situation is compounded by the fact that motor starters, fuse blocks, terminal strips, and the like, are not housed in protective enclosures. That is, there is a real danger of coming into accidental contact with "live" high-voltage electrical conductors. There is no locking mechanism attached to the enclosure which requires the power be turned off before the cabinet door can be opened, as there is with fused disconnect switches, for example. Although a desirable feature, the necessity for access in order to troubleshoot electrical problems precludes its implementation. (See Figure 21-1.)

POLYPHASE MOTORS
AND THEIR CONTROL

Commercial/industrial burners from about two million Btu per hour, with motor horsepower from ¾, generally are wound for three-phase 208/240/480-volt, 60-cycle current.

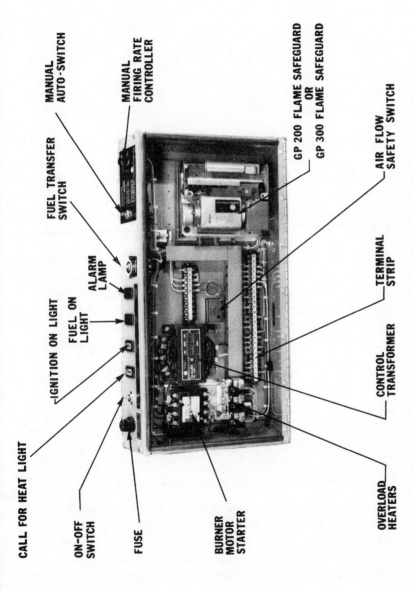

Figure 21-1. Dual Fuel Burner Control Cabinet (courtesy Peabody Gordon–Piatt)

The reasons are many, not the least of which is the basic simplicity of the polyphase motor. It needs no starting switch or capacitors and there is no auxiliary or starting winding. It can be easily reversed and is capable of handling higher starting torque than the single–phase motor. The basic principles involved in the operation of three–phase motors can be had from a limitless number of textbooks and service manuals on the subject, and should be required reading for anyone seeking to gain a well–rounded base from which to gain practical service experience.

The application of these motors to automatic fuel–burning equipment is straightforward, deviating only according to variations in additional switchgear in the *motor control circuit*. Everything the reader has learned about motor protection is valid. Basically, the motor control apparatus performs the following functions:

1. Allows the motor to be started from rest as and when required
2. Keeps the line current within prescribed limits during the starting period
3. Allows the motor to develop the required torque
4. Protects the motor against the effects of abnormal conditions
5. Protects personnel against electrical shock and other accidents
6. Allows the motor to be easily stopped either manually or automatically at the end of a process
7. Although not applicable to burners, in certain cases the control switchgear must be able to reverse the motor, control its speed, and apply a braking torque

The term *control circuit* as used in automatic burner–control technology has a different connotation than the term *motor control circuit* used in electrical language. The motor control-circuit function outlined above is primarily *protective* and passive. The term *control circuit* used in the frame of reference of a packaged boiler, on the other hand, denotes a much more complex and *dynamic* function. It involves not only motors but electric valves, ignition transformers, limit controls, and miscellaneous interlocking branch circuits. The control circuit, which monitors and commands the entire burner operating sequence, is separate and distinct from the heavy-duty *power circuit,* so-called, that furnishes the motive force for the drive motors, and the high wattage for heating oil. A control circuit is basic to all automatic fuel burners, regardless of size.

As stated above, on burners of relatively small size, the motors are single-phase and are operated from and at control-circuit voltage, there being no power circuit. Where the total amperage requirement exceeds the capability of the single-phase service, a separate three-phase power circuit is utilized for the heaters and/or motors, and the single-phase wiring is used as the control circuit.

The burner fan motor makes the largest demand on the burner electrical system. Air delivery to the combustion reaction requires approximately one horsepower per million Btu fuel input.

A typical 200-boiler-horsepower, forced-draft, low-pressure steam boiler with a combination No. 6 oil/natural gas burner, has the following electrical requirements:

Blower motor, hp	10
Oil pump motor, hp	.5
Oil heater, kw	7.5
Feed water pump motor, hp	.5

A 700-horsepower, packaged boiler of the same manufacture has a 30-horsepower blower motor which operates at 3450 revolutions per minute, and turns a backward-curved *impeller.*

The terms fan, fan wheel, blower, blower wheel, and impeller are synonymous. However, the term *backward-curved* denotes a particular type of fan configuration which affects the operating characteristics of the motor which drives it. Specifically, it takes longer to come up to full speed. As a result, the blower motor sustains the high starting current in-rush for a longer period of time than is typical for motor applications with which the engineer may be familiar. When it starts it sounds like it is winding up. By the same token, it coasts for a considerably longer time when turned off. Another characteristic of this centrifugal blower is that it is extremely shallow, and does not have a scroll–type housing. Therefore it is also known as a *caseless fan*.

The forward–curved fan wheel, where the blades are sloped in the direction of the rotation, is probably more conventional and is called the *squirrel cage* or sirocco–type fan. Typically, it turns inside a curved housing (scroll) and has a side air inlet. At 3450 rpm it comes up to speed almost instantly and shuts down promptly.

Although it is pointless to enumerate the advantages and disadvantages of the two types of fan wheels, inasmuch as nothing can be done about it once a particular burner has been selected and installed, it is worthwhile to list a few disadvantages of each with which the engineer must occasionally cope:

1. Motor protection is extremely crucial with the caseless fan, as will be seen later in the text.
2. The burner operating sound level can be objectionable with a high–speed sirocco fan.
3. An unbalanced (because of dirt accumulation or other reasons) caseless fan will cause premature bearing wear, shake the entire motor mount and boiler front on which the control cabinet is mounted so badly the controls literally fall apart.
4. An out–of–balance sirocco fan will eventually self-destruct and overload the motor.

RELAYING

In the field of technology the principle of the lever and fulcrum underlies the entire structure of mechanical engineering. In much the same way, the phenomenon of electromagnetic force is bedrock to control engineering. What the simple lever does for the engineer, the relay does for the circuit designer. It lets him apply a manageable force to manipulate a much larger and unwieldy force to his advantage. In addition, it allows the simultaneous control of multiple, incongruent circuits by the action of a single switch. Relays are used extensively in burner control as motor starters, contactors, and switching devices.

All relays consist of a pull coil and an armature, the latter being the movable portion carrying one-half of each pair of the electrical contacts. Coils may be dual-voltage or field-interchangeable, so that it is possible to energize the same basic relay form by the substitution of a 24-, 120-, 240-, or 480-volt coil as required.

When a relay is used as a motor starter (also called a magnetic starter) it has, incorporated in its design, thermal overload heaters and trip switches to provide overcurrent protection for the motor. The heater elements are located in at least two of the three "legs," and connected on the *load* side of the relay, just ahead of the motor terminals (T_1, T_2 and T_3), so that full-load current as drawn by the motor passes through them. The heat generated by any one of these elements when subjected to a current in excess of its rating is radiated to a heat-sensitive latch device which holds a spring-loaded switch closed in the motor-control circuit in series with the coil. As the latch moves from expansion, it allows the trip switch to pop open, effectively deenergizing the coil. The armature falls away from the coil, opening the multiple-pole switch in the motor-power circuit, stopping the motor. The trip switch must be allowed to cool and then be manually reset before operation can be resumed.

Figure 21-2 shows the application of a motor starter on a simple feed-water pump with a 230-volt, 3-phase motor. It is a basic motor-control circuit showing motor-overload protective devices with remote control accomplished by a float-operated switch. The motor-control circuit is *tapped* off the line ahead of the starter, so that the coil voltage is the same as the motor voltage. The overload trip switches, the float switch, and the coil are wired in series, so that the opening of any one switch deenergizes the coil, stopping the motor. This diagram illustrates the relationship between the motor-control circuit and the power circuit.

Like any mechanical switch, a relay (in this case a starter) has a *line* side and a *load* side; the contacts themselves being on the line of separation. Power enters on the line side and is energized or alive continuously, so long as the main disconnect switch is closed. The load side begins with its half of each pair

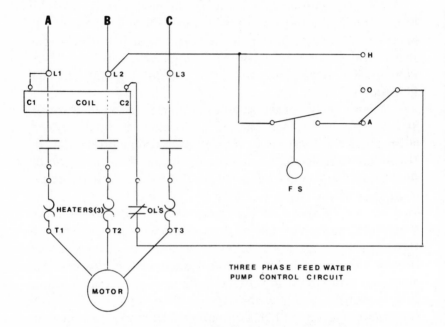

Figure 21-2. Three-Phase Motor Starter Schematic

of contacts and is energized only when the starter contacts are closed.

The motor-control circuit is energized and therefore alive continuously since it is connected to the *line* side of the starter and can be deenergized only by opening the disconnect switch. Even though an overload switch or the float switch might be open, care must be exercised since there is a *240-volt potential across the open switch.*

A three-wire, three-phase electrical service with an ungrounded neutral wire exhibits electrical continuity from line to line only. Therefore a multimeter would indicate line voltage between line A and line B, and line B and line C, etc. (across whatever pair selected), but not from line to the metal of the enclosure, called earth ground. A three-phase service with a grounded neutral *will* have an above-ground potential on two of the three lines, so be careful!

Single phasing is a condition where electrical continuity is lost between one line of the service and the other two, due to an "open" in one line. The open could be a broken wire, or a faulty connection, but more likely is due to a blown fuse. Single phasing is a serious condition which can cause costly motor damage.

Electrical codes universally require that each line (leg) of an ungrounded power supply contain a fuse ahead of apparatus such as motors, electric heaters, and the like. The fuses are there to protect the branch circuit, *not* the appliance (the magnetic starter or relay is assigned *that* duty).

Occasionally, fuses are installed that have too low an amperage rating yet stand up for years until one day, as a result of deterioration, one lets go and the power supply to the motor single-phases. If the motor is running when this happens, the motor will continue running, but at about half capacity, and start overheating. Once it stops it cannot restart. Instead, it will just hum and absorb the tremendous current in-rush until it burns the motor windings and they short-circuit (whereupon a fuse blows in a second leg), unless one of the overload heaters in the starter opens and saves the day.

Obviously the overcurrent rating of the thermal overloads must be sized carefully, taking into consideration the "nameplate rating" of the motor and the ambient temperature, so as to avoid nuisance trip-outs while at the same time maintaining enough sensitivity to respond quickly to a single-phase condition. An occasional nuisance trip is cheaper than a burn-out.

Power wiring should be sized so that there is a generous margin of safety between the trip rating of the overload heaters (which should be lower) and the recommended fuse size protecting the electrical branch circuit to the motor. Dual element (slow blow) fuses are recommended in the power circuit to 3450 rpm motors, especially those which do not come up to full speed immediately, if costly repairs resulting from single-phasing of the power supply are to be avoided.

It is worthy of note here, and will be discussed again later in the text, that remote fuel and water supply pump controls are technically *not* part of the burner control circuit. There is provision, however, in the control cabinets of large boilers for tieing in these so-called isolated circuits. Therefore care and good practice should be used in identifying these extraneous voltages and properly labeling same to insure the safety of all personnel who might not otherwise recognize them!

The form of relay called a *contactor* is similar to a motor starter, except that it does not provide motor protection. It is used for noninductive loads where pure relaying is all that is needed; that is, where an otherwise impotent power source can be made to operate a large and powerful electrical device like an oil heater by simply energizing an electromagnet, which in turn closes or opens a switch in another circuit to which the device is directly connected.

Switching relays are usually rated for relatively light duty, as compared with a starter or contactor. When in the deenergized mode they might have contacts that are normally open, normally closed, or multiple sets of each, depending on the intricacy of the switching function it is to perform. The switching relay, also called a *control relay*, might be designed to hold itself in the energized mode upon receipt of an impulse, even though the impulse was a fleeting one. A typical example of this application is an alarm-silencing relay used in conjunction with a pushbutton as shown in Figure 21-3. A purpose of this device might be to silence a very noisy alarm bell once it has attracted attention but before the problem that set it off can be readily corrected, such as a flame failure or a low water condition, for example. It is generally wired in such a way that all warning lights remain activated even though the audible alarm has been electrically disconnected, and the whole monitoring system, including the audible alarm, goes *back to the ready* upon activation of the reset button on the offending limit device.

Another important use for the switching or control relay is as a kind of electrical check valve. This might be a case where two hazardous conditions being monitored using a combination of warning lights might be required to set off a single audible alarm. Referring to Figure 21-3 (B), were it not for the control relay shown wired into the warning-light circuitry, the occurrence of either condition being monitored would light up both

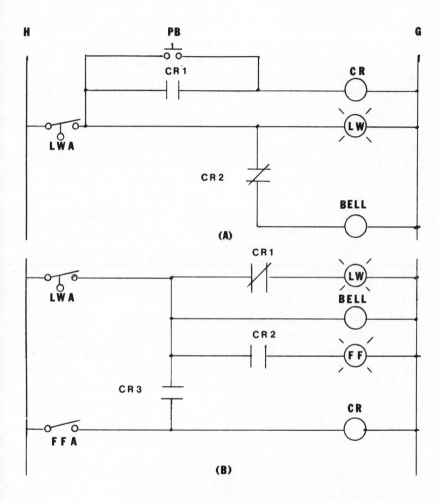

Figure 21-3. (A) Alarm Silencing Relay
(B) Relay as Check Valve

the flame–failure *and* low–water warning lights at the same time the audible alarm sounded, making troubleshooting considerably more difficult.

The *time–delay relay* is used where, for one reason or another, instantaneous switch action *is not* desired upon energization or deenergization of the coil. The delaying mechanism might be a pneumatic device connected to the relay armature, such as a piston which displaces air from a cylinder through an orifice, the area of which can be varied to slow down or speed up the action. The delay may be affected through the action of a bimetallic warp switch (or the principle of the *thermistor*). The latter is a resistor that allows current to flow only after a delay during which it has *warmed up,* and therefore cannot be used to obtain a time delay upon deenergization.

An important application of the time–delay relay is found in the low–draft switch. The device is designed to monitor air flow through the furnace. If the flow rate drops below a preset value, a limit switch opens and stops the burner operation. There are times, however, when due to gusty wind conditions, or rough lighting characteristics of particular burners, the draft falls below standard but for only a brief time. By using a time-delay relay with a nonadjustable fixed safe–time interval, the effect of the opening of the limit switch can be postponed and the burner operated through the rough spot into normal operation. If, on the other hand, the unsatisfactory draft condition persisted beyond the fixed safe–time interval, the limit switch would be allowed to stop the burner. The object being, of course, to reduce nuisance shutdowns from unsatisfactory draft conditions of momentary duration. In this sense the time–delay relay is not unlike the dual–element fuse that will take a momentary overload without melting, but will blow in case of a direct short circuit.

The most important and certainly the most complex relay in the control circuit is the *flame relay,* which works in conjunction with a flame detector in combustion control. Its function is to provide protection against ignition failure and to close the main fuel valve in case of loss of main flame. The detection system is part of a larger component known as a *programmer*. Figure 22-1 shows an early basic programmer that is still commonly found in the field.

22

Input Modulation

In chapter 7 we discussed the drive train and the motions involved in opening and closing the fuel valves and air dampers in proper relationship with one another. Whether the *driver* is an electric, pneumatic, or hydraulic controller, it responds to changes in the measurement of the medium being controlled. It does so *indirectly,* however, since the measuring device must translate a temperature or pressure reading into a signal compatible with the controller. Most engineers are familiar with recording instruments; whether they be recording volt/ampmeters, recording temperature, or recording pressure instruments, they all make use of a clock–driven chart and a recording pen. The curve produced by the action of the pen shows graphically *the motion of the measurement* over a given time interval.

If we illustrate the operation of a boiler by attaching a recording pressure instrument to the steam pressure line, the chart thus obtained might look like Figure 22-1a which represents the on–off operation of a fixed–input burner. The curve traces the movement of the steam pressure. Figure 22-1b represents the action of the fuel valve, which in this case is a simple solenoid valve. The vertical ordinates of chart **a** represent percent of scale (the scale could be degrees, pounds per square inch, etc.). The vertical scale of chart **b** represents percent of fuel valve travel. The horizontal scale for both graphs is expressed as time. It can be seen that valve action occurs only as the measurement crosses the *control point.* For all positions of the measurement above the control point the valve is closed, and for all positions of the measurement below the control point the valve is open. It follows, therefore, that the measurement of an on–off-controlled system must be continually cycling, and the fuel-valve operation intermittent. Operating steam pressure, in this case, will be an average of the cut–in and cut–out points of the controller.

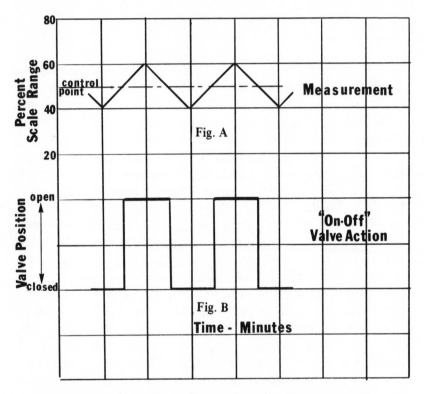

Figure 22-1. Motion of Measurement (courtesy The Foxboro Co.)

One step up in sophistication from the basic on–off system, is what is known as *low–high,* or *two-position control.* This firing–rate control method, in its simplest form, uses a metering valve in addition to the solenoid valve that can be throttled by the action of the driver. Instead of the fire going out when the operating control reaches its cut-out point, the solenoid valve is wired to remain open, and the operating control instead causes the firing-rate controller connected to the metering valve to drive to low-fire position. The firing rate thus varies from one extreme to the other in response to the alternate positions of the operating control.

The valve action curve would not be rectangular as in Figure 22-1b, but more saw-toothed and nearly parallel to the measurement curve. In addition to providing closer control than the on-off system, it offers the advantage of being able to light off the burner in low-fire position. Since the off cycles are reduced in number and duration, the standby loss is cut considerably.

PROPORTIONAL CONTROL

In each of the foregoing firing methods we had basically a two-position system. With proportional control, also known as *full modulation,* the fuel-metering valve *continues to move as long as the measurement is moving.* At any time the *amount* of valve movement is directly proportional to the *amount* of measurement movement, and in a direction to limit the deviation. The valve position always bears a fixed relationship to the measurement, and the peak value in valve correction occurs at the point of greatest measurement deviation, as long as the measurement does not move outside the *proportional band* of the operating control. The proportional band is the percentage of the scale through which the measurement must move to move the valve through its complete stroke.

Figure 22-2 is a graphical representation of the relationship between measurement and valve action where, for purpose of illustration, the valve action is not influencing the motion of the recorder pen. Rather, the curve shows only the change in valve position resulting from the measurement change. The driver can position the fuel-metering valve at any point between full-open and full-closed, which will proportion the delivery to the need as indicated by the operating control.

A typical and very popular modulating control circuit (Figure 22-3) consists of a reversible-capacitor-motor unit with an integral *balancing relay, balancing potentiometer,* and gear train, and an operating control which differs from conventional limit-type controls in that the electrical mechanism is a potentiometer rather than an electric switch.

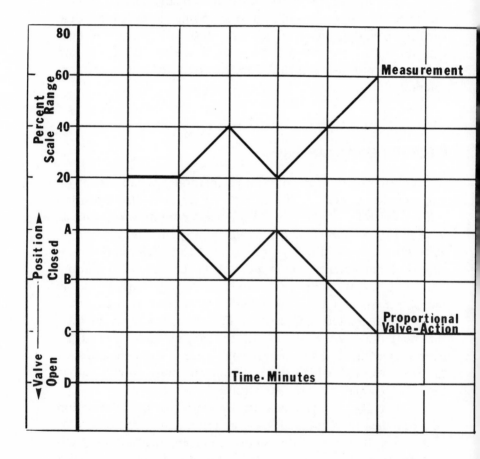

Figure 22-2. Proportional Control (courtesy The Foxboro Co.)

The potentiometer has a contact finger that moves across a wire-wound coil. The contact finger is moved much like a rheostat, by a temperature or pressure element of the control. Depending on the point of contact of the finger on the coil, a fewer or greater number of turns of wire are placed in series with the current flow to the balancing relay.

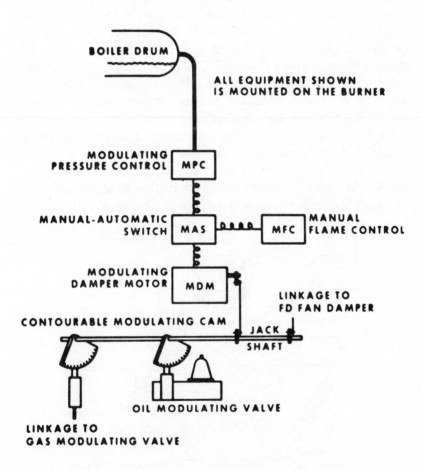

Figure 22-3. Electric Positioning Control System
(courtesy Cleaver-Brooks)

THE BALANCED BRIDGE CIRCUIT

Figure 22-4 illustrates how a balancing relay is constructed. It consists of two solenoid coils with parallel axes, into which are inserted the legs of a U–shaped armature. The armature is pivoted at the center, so that it can be tilted by the changing magnetic flux of the two coils. A contact arm is fastened to the armature so that it will touch one or the other of the two stationary contacts as the armature moves back and forth on its pivot. When the relay is in balance, the contact arm floats between the two contacts, touching neither of them. If coil C1 receives more current than coil C2 and thus becomes stronger, the contact blade moves to the left and completes the circuit between the transformer and the motor winding W1. Current also passes through current–limiting capacitor M to motor winding W2. The motor runs in the corresponding direction until the balancing relay breaks contact. When coil C2 receives more current than coil C1, the circuit is completed directly to motor winding W2 and the capacitor limits current to winding W1, resulting in motor rotation in the opposite direction.

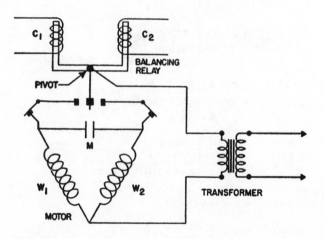

Figure 22-4. Balancing Relay (courtesy Honeywell)

Figure 22-5 represents a complete balanced–bridge, modulating–control circuit. Built into the motor is a balancing potentiometer. The potentiometer is electrically identical to the one in the operating control. It has a movable finger which is positioned along the coil by the motor shaft and establishes contact wherever it touches. The contact made by the balancing relay can only be broken if the amount of current flowing through coil C1 is made to equal that flowing through coil C2. This is brought about by the action of the motor–balancing potentiometer. As the motor rotates, it drives the finger of the balancing potentiometer toward a position which will equalize

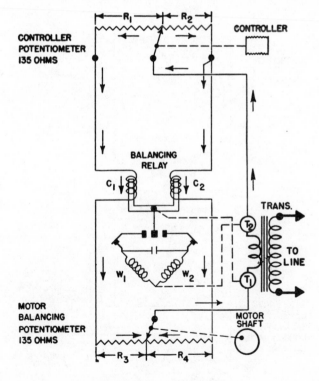

Figure 22-5. Balanced Bridge Schematic (courtesy Honeywell)

the resistances in both legs of the circuit. In the positions shown, the operating–control potentiometer finger and the motor–potentiometer finger divide their respective coils so that R1 equals R4 and R2 equals R3. Therefore R1 plus R3 equals R2 plus R4 and the resistances on both sides of the circuit are equal. Coils C1 and C2 of the balancing relay are equally energized, and the armature of the relay is balanced. The contact arm is floating between the two contacts, no current is going to the motor, and the motor is at rest.

Figure 22-6 shows an instantaneous condition in which the measurement has changed a small amount. As a result, the finger of the operating control has moved toward the right end of the potentiometer coil. The amount of resistance on both sides of the circuit is no longer equal (R1 plus R3 is greater than R2

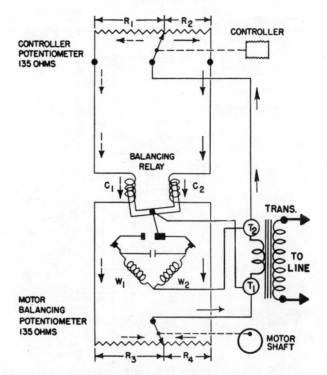

Figure 22-6. Balanced Bridge Schematic (courtesy Honeywell)

plus R4). The greater share of the current now flows through the right leg of the circuit, and coil C2 of the balancing relay exerts a greater force on the armature than does C1. The armature has rotated, making contact to the side of the circuit that sends current directly to motor winding W2. The motor is running in the corresponding direction and moving the motor-balancing potentiometer to a new position. When the motor–potentiometer finger reaches a position where R1 plus R3 equals R2 plus R4, the two legs of the circuit will rebalance; the contact made by the balancing relay will open, and the motor will stop in a new position.

Every time the measurement changes, the fuel–rate controller turns the valve until the finger of the motor–balancing potentiometer reaches a position which corresponds to the position of the finger of the operating control.

The system just described, for the most part, does a fine job holding the measurement within very close tolerance when operating conditions and the proportional band (range) of the operating control are such that the maximum offset (differential) is within permissible variations of the controlled medium. One important limitation of this system, however, which is referred to in ASME terminology as *constant speed floating,* is that the rotational speed of the drive motor is fixed. The fuel valve changes position at a constant speed, regardless of how fast the measurement is changing. It has a tendency to chase a widely swinging load, sometimes resulting in the performance characteristics of a two–position controller. On applications where there is sufficient leeway between the required control point of the medium and the maximum operating limit of the boiler, raising the operating control setting will reduce the *hunting* and afford a reserve or cushion to draw upon when the load peaks abruptly. Temperature– or pressure–reducing stations are then adjusted at points downstream, to control the medium as necessary for the proper end results.

23

Safe Operating Limits

We have already discussed the hazards attendant with electrical components and systems of the dual-fuel burner, as they relate to personal safety and motor protection. In addition to manipulating explosive fuel-air mixtures, it is a function of the automatic control system to prevent the rupture of the pressure vessel.

The immediate interruption of the firing cycle and extinguishment of the combustion process is mandatory whenever safe operating limits have been reached. Such *limit controls* are devices which prevent a control circuit from being energized if an unsafe condition exists, or deenergizes the control circuit if an unsafe condition occurs during burner operation. Limit controls require manual resetting before operation can be resumed, and fall into four categories:

1. Switches that must be closed at all times during operation to indicate safe conditions in the combustion chamber and flues, such as a combustion air-proving switch and/or low-draft switch.
2. Switches that must be closed at all times to indicate safe conditions within the boiler or heat exchanger, such as a high-pressure or high-temperature cut-out, or low-water cut-off.
3. Switches which must be closed for safe starting conditions, such as high- or low- fuel-pressure switches; and damper and valve position switches.
4. Switches that need not be closed during an attempt to start, but must close before a trial for ignition can be

made, such as an atomizing air–pressure switch on an oil burner or a combustion air–proving switch on a gas burner. The controls in this category are referred to as *nonrecycling interlocks,* because they either latch and stay in the open position when actuated or open the fuel–valve circuit of the burner causing a lock–out of the programmer due to flame failure. In any case operation cannot be resumed without the manual attention to a particular reset button, whether it be mounted on the individual limit control or on the programmer.

Operating controls, as a group, are similar to limit controls with which they are wired in series, except that they do not require manual resetting. When the medium they are monitoring deviates from the control point or cut–out setting an amount equal to a predetermined differential, the device reassumes the operating position automatically. As a rule, these controls are set at some safe operating value below the setting of the limit controls.

REGULATORY AGENCIES

The establishment of certain boundaries or limits within which a given boiler–burner unit is allowed to operate is based primarily on safety considerations. Criteria have been established over the years based on sound engineering principles tempered by solid experience.

Certain agencies exist, some governmental, some industry-sponsored, who function as regulatory bodies in the promulgation of standards and maintenance of laboratories for the examination and testing of devices and systems used in fuel-burning equipment. The following are some of the Listing Bodies and their function.

Underwriters' Laboratories

Underwriters' Laboratories, Inc., which was founded in 1894, is chartered as a nonprofit organization. It maintains and operates laboratories for the examination and testing of devices, systems, and materials related to life, fire, and casualty hazards, and to crime prevention.

Underwriters' Laboratories, Inc. is primarily concerned with the manufacture of equipment in accordance with established structural standards of safety. Having once inspected and approved a system or accessory, it is concerned only with the fact that the manufacturer continues to produce that equipment in conformance with the same specifications covering the model or models originally tested.

Field inspectors for Underwriters' Laboratories, Inc. do not police equipment installed on job sites, but restrict their activities entirely to periodic inspections of products coming off manufacturers' assembly lines.

Associated Factory Mutual

Associated Factory Mutual Laboratories (FM) is the testing laboratory of the eight Associated Factory Mutual Fire Insurance Companies. These companies specialize in protection for manufacturing plants and other large properties against fire, explosions, wind damage, and other types of losses (including loss of use and occupancy).

FM publishes many of its findings in manuals and bulletins. The laboratory publishes a monthly magazine on industrial fire protection which describes recent losses and their causes.

It also publishes a list of approved devices for industrial fire protection.

Each job is considered on its own merits, including:

1. Oven, dryer, furnace, or boiler construction.
2. Flame Safeguard control systems.
3. Fire protection equipment, sprinkler and alarm systems, etc.

Inspectors are located in field offices in major cities.

American Gas Association

The American Gas Association, established in 1925, is the testing organization of the American gas industry with laboratories in Cleveland, Ohio, and Los Angeles, California.

Any manufacturer of gas appliances or gas-appliance accessories may submit his products to the laboratories and secure certification of his designs upon compliance with the appropriate national standards. Upon such compliance the manufacturer is granted an Appliance Certificate or an Accessory Certificate and is permitted to display the trademarked Laboratories' Certification Seal or trademarked Laboratories' Certification Symbol on the appliance or accessory.

Certification of an appliance or accessory is granted only upon compliance of its design with national standards, and then only for the balance of the calendar year during which it was certified. Certification is renewed for the succeeding year contingent upon a satisfactory examination of production models at the manufacturer's plant. The design of all appliances and accessories must also be reexamined at least every five years under the latest standards.

Canadian Standards Association

The Canadian Engineering Standards Association (CSA) was incorporated under the Dominion Companies Act in 1919 as a nonprofit, nongovernmental organization to provide a national standardizing body for Canada. In 1944 Supplementary Patent Letters were granted extending its activities to a broader field of standardization and changing its name to Canadian Standards Association.

The CSA Testing Laboratories, inaugurated in May, 1940, is a division of the Canadian Standards Association, and is recognized as a testing and investigating agency by inspection authorities and by fire marshals and fire commissioners throughout Canada.

The CSA Laboratories investigate by test and examination, electric products that are submitted for approval for compliance with pertinent CSA codes and standards. When a product complies with the related requirements, a report is prepared and forwarded to members of the CSA Approvals Council throughout Canada. If two-thirds or more of the inspection authorities indicate the equipment is acceptable, it is listed as approved.

The Laboratories provide a Certification Service for other types of products.

Industrial Risk Insurers

The Industrial Risk Insurers (IRI)—formerly Factory Insurance Association—is composed of member stock insurance companies. IRI is concerned with all phases of fire protection and other perils insured against by its members.

Generally, IRI accepts Underwriters' Laboratories, Inc. listing as evidence of device acceptability, but approves or disapproves each job on its own merits, including:

1. Oven, dryer, furnace, or boiler construction.
2. Flame safeguard control systems.
3. Fire–protection equipment, sprinkler and alarm systems, etc.

Inspectors are located in field offices in major cities.

The home office is in Hartford, Connecticut, where a laboratory is maintained. The laboratory is used primarily for demonstration of all types of fire–prevention equipment, including flame–safeguard equipment.

Improved Risk Mutuals

Since 1921 Improved Risk Mutuals (IRM) has been providing vital underwriting and protection service for policyholders through 17 member companies and their agents. Field engineers and inspectors, known as "field representatives," are assigned to survey and inspect properties, and when warranted to make practical recommendations that will assist the property owner in minimizing the possibility of loss. These men report to the underwriting department with factual information for each risk surveyed or reinspected, evaluating insurability of the risk.

The engineering department prepares and provides for IRM policyholders, practical loss–prevention folders, booklets, manuals, information sheets, and kits covering construction features, welding, heating, electrical, cooking, and cold–weather hazards, the safe handling of flammable liquids and gases, fire and intrusion alarms, and automatic sprinklers. IRM's publications covering general and specific hazards are now in use in industry and in various universities offering fire engineering courses.

A fully–equipped laboratory is maintained at the home office to provide fire–prevention and fire–protection training for IRM field men, engineering personnel of member companies, and independent insurance adjusters.

The American Society of Mechanical Engineers

The American Society of Mechanical Engineers (ASME) set up a committee in 1911 for the purpose of formulating standard rules for the construction of steam boilers and other pressure vessels. This committee is now called the Boiler and Pressure Vessel Committee.

The Committee's function is to establish rules of safety governing the design, the fabrication, and the inspection during construction of boilers and unfired pressure vessels, and to interpret these rules when questions arise regarding their intent. In formulating the rules, the Committee considers the needs of users, manufacturers, and inspectors of pressure vessels. The objective of the rules is to afford reasonably certain protection of life and property and to provide a margin for deterioration in service so as to give a reasonably long, safe period of usefulness. Advancements in design and material, and the evidence of experience have been recognized.

The Boiler and Pressure Vessel Committee deals with the care and inspection of boilers and pressure vessels in service only to the extent of providing suggested rules of good practice as an aid to owners and their inspectors.

The rules established by the Committee are not to be interpreted as approving, recommending, or endorsing any proprietary or specific design, or as limiting in any way the manufacturer's freedom to choose any method of design or any form of construction that conforms to the Code rules.

In the formulation of its rules and in the establishment of maximum design and operating pressures, the Boiler and Pressure Vessel Committee considers materials, construction, method of fabrication, inspection, and safety devices. Permission may be granted to regulatory bodies and organizations publishing safety standards to use a complete Section of the Code by reference.

Where a state or other regulatory body, in the printing of any Section of the ASME Boiler and Pressure Vessel Code, makes additions or omissions, it is recommended that such changes be clearly indicated.

The National Board of Boiler and Pressure Vessel Inspectors is composed of chief inspectors of states and municipalities in the United States and of provinces in the Dominion of Canada that have adopted the Boiler and Pressure Vessel Code. Since its organization in 1919, this Board has functioned to uniformly administer and enforce the rules of the Boiler and Pressure Vessel Code. The cooperation of that organization with the Boiler and Pressure Vessel Committee has been extremely helpful. Its function is clearly recognized and, as a result, inquiries received which bear on the administration or application of the rules are referred directly to the National Board. Such handling of this type of inquiry not only simplifies the work on the Boiler and Pressure Vessel Committee, but expedites action on the problem for the inquirer. Where an inquiry is not clearly an interpretation of the rules, nor a problem of application or administration, it may be considered both by the Boiler and Pressure Vessel Committee and the National Board.

It should be pointed out that the state or municipality where the Boiler and Pressure Vessel Code has been made effective has definite jurisdiction over any particular installation. Inquiries dealing with problems of local character should be directed to the proper authority of such state or municipality. Such authority may, if there is any question or doubt as to the proper interpretation, refer the question to the Boiler and Pressure Vessel Committee.

The American Society of Mechanical Engineers does not "approve," "certify," "endorse," or "rate" any product or construction and there shall be no statements or inferences which might so indicate. A manufacturer holding a Code Symbol and a

Certificate of Authorization may state in advertising literature that its products "are built in accordance with the requirements of the ASME Boiler and Pressure Vessel Code," or "meet the requirements of the ASME Boiler and Pressure Vessel Code."

The ASME Symbol shall be used only for stamping and nameplates as specifically provided in the Code. However, facsimiles may be used for the purpose of fostering the use of such construction. Such usage may be by an association or a society, or by a holder of a Code Symbol who may also use the facsimile in advertising to show that clearly specified products will carry the symbol. General usage is permitted only when *all* of the manufacturers' products are constructed under the Rules.

National Fire Protection Association

The National Fire Protection Association (NFPA) was organized in 1896 to promote the science and improve the methods of fire protection and prevention, to obtain and circulate information on these subjects, and to secure the cooperation of its members in establishing proper safeguards against loss of life and property by fire. Its membership includes over two hundred national and regional societies and associations, with headquarters in Boston, Massachusetts, and over twenty thousand individuals, corporations, and organizations. Anyone interested may become a member.

The NFPA in the course of fire–safety activities issues many publications on all aspects of the subject. Compilations of various NFPA standards are issued annually in the following National Fire Codes:

Volume 1. *Flammable Liquids and Gases*
Volume 2. *Combustible Solids, Dusts, Chemicals and Explosives*
Volume 3. *Building Construction and Equipment*
Volume 4. *Fixed Extinguishing Equipment*
Volume 5. *Electrical*
Volume 6. *Transportation*
Volume 7. *Mobile Fire Equipment, Organization, Management*

24

Flame Detection and Programming

The programmer (in up-to-date parlance referred to as the *Flame Safeguard* control) functions together with operating, limiting, and related interlocking controls, to program or schedule each starting, running, and shutdown sequence of the burner. The flame detection circuit of the programmer monitors both pilot and main flame presence, and does not permit the main fuel valve to open unless a pilot flame has been established and *proved*. Proved means that it has been recognized by the light-sensitive, optical-scanning device which is also part of the detection circuit.

Over the years it has been well-established that the safe operation of automatic fuel burners requires the positive establishment of an ignition source prior to the opening of the main fuel valve. Explosions result when this one-two sequence is reversed. The widespread use of fully-automatic burners firing gas or oil, or both, demanded better protection from the hazards of flame failure. Thermally-actuated, stack-mounted flame detectors were far too slow in response to dangerous conditions, especially where high firing rates of gas or oil were involved.

Although the development of the *photoelectric cell* provided a means of actually viewing the flame and could respond to the loss of flame within a matter of seconds, it was only applicable to oil burners since these cells are blind to nonluminous (gas) flames. On combination fuel burners, or oil burners with gas pilot burners, a flame rod had to be used in conjunction with the photocell. In spite of the installation and maintenance problems associated with these systems, they were well accepted and find limited application even today.

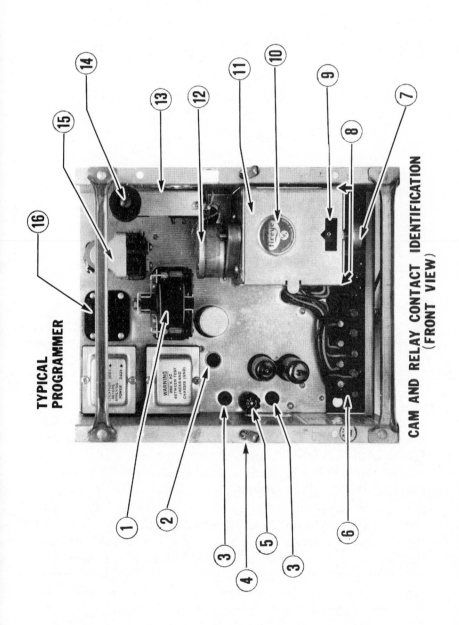

TYPICAL PROGRAMMER

CAM AND RELAY CONTACT IDENTIFICATION
(FRONT VIEW)

PART NO.	PART NAME
1	MASTER RELAY
2	TEST ATTENUATOR PIN
3	D.C. VOLTMETER TEST JACKS
4	CHASSIS RETAINER SCREW (BOTH SIDES)
5	FUEL VALVE FUSE
6	TERMINAL BOARD
7	CAM KNOB
8	TIMER COVER
9	SEQUENCE INDICATOR
10	CAM SWITCH ASSEMBLY (INSIDE)
11	PROGRAMMING TIMER ASSEMBLY (INSIDE)
12	PROGRAMMING TIMER MOTOR
13	LOCKOUT SWITCH
14	RESET BUTTON
15	FLAME RELAY
16	A.C. LINE PLUG AND VOLTAGE SELECTOR SOCKETS

Figure 24-1. Early Programmer

A serious shortcoming of the photocell, which is responsive to steady light radiation, is that it can be made to respond falsely when subjected to light energy from artificial as well as natural sources. For instance, the red glow of a hot combustion chamber can "fool" it, with possible disastrous consequences.

The development of the *photoconductive cell* in the late 1940s marked a significant breakthrough in flame–detection technology. The single element of the cell is coated with lead sulfide, which is sensitive to invisible (infrared) radiation present in *all* flames. It is a semiconductor whose electrical resistance instantaneously changes in accordance with the amount of infrared and visible radiation it receives. Another advantage to the photoconductive circuit is that it is exclusively responsive to modulated radiation within its view. It will not accept the steady signal which might result from a high resistance short circuit, or from viewing hot refractory. When a DC voltage is impressed across the lead cell and a series resistor, the fluctuation of the cell resistance corresponding to the fluctuation of flame radiation produces a corresponding fluctuation of voltage across the cell. This voltage is what constitutes the *flame signal* and is fed to an amplifier. The amplifier is tuned to accept a certain frequency of the flickering signal only, and the conditioned voltage is used to energize the flame relay of the programmer.

Although the infrared (lead sulfide) flame–detection system responds only to flickering infrared radiation, it can respond to the infrared rays emitted by a hot refractory, even when the refractory has visibly ceased to glow. The refractory's otherwise steady signal can be made to fluctuate if it is reflected, bent, or blocked by smoke or fuel mist within the combustion chamber. Therefore, care must be taken in the application and check–out of an infrared flame–detection system to ensure its response to flame only. The maximum recommended ambient temperature for the lead–sulfide–cell assembly is 125°F.

ULTRAVIOLET FLAME DETECTION

The ultraviolet flame detector is a cathode ray (CR) tube. Gas filled, it is sensitive to extremely short–wave light (ultraviolet) radiation; it cannot be fooled by the radiation from hot refractory.

When ultraviolet radiation enters the tube and strikes the broad surface of an area called the cathode, electrons are emitted and attracted to another terminal called the anode. Passage of electrons through the gas ionizes the gas and renders it conductive.

Once a gas–filled electron tube becomes conductive it will continue to conduct as long as a voltage is applied across its terminals, even though the radiation which triggered it ceases. In flame–detector applications, however, the electronic amplifier, to which the tube is connected, interrupts the voltage many times per second, so that the tube must reestablish conductivity each time. Of course, it can do so only if a flame is present. The tube is capable of detecting the ultraviolet radiation present in all flames.

There are a few installation and service instructions peculiar to the UV detector. The detector should be located as close to the flame as possible—18 inches or closer—but not so the ambient will exceed 200°F at the sight tube. To increase sensitivity, a quartz lens union may be used. The quartz lens permits location of the detector tube at twice the above recommended distance. The scanner must not sight the spark from the pilot igniter, or any part of the burner that can reflect the light energy from the spark to the scanner. The maximum available ultraviolet radiation is located in the first third of the visible flame, counting from the burner head. If it is necessary to view two areas to obtain a reliable flame signal, two UV scanners may be installed and wired in parallel.

SEQUENCE CONTROL

In addition to affording a means of protection against the hazards of flame failure, the programmer acts as a master sequence controller, and provides a central junction point for all the electrical circuits of the burner.

For the purpose of discussion now, and for ease in troubleshooting later, it is convenient to divide the time frame of the automatic operation of the burner into an *on cycle* and an *off cycle*. The on cycle is further divided according to the events or steps which must be taken before the main fuel valve opens. Hence we have the *starting* sequence and the *running* sequence.

The steps or events which make up a typical starting sequence are as follows: Start the burner motor, and/or draft fan motor; position the air dampers for prepurging of the combustion space; return the air damper to low-fire position; turn on the spark igniter and light the pilot burner; open the main fuel valve; turn off the pilot burner.

After the pilot burner is turned off, the first action of the programmer, as the running cycle begins, is to release the firing-rate controller to automatic control. Until this point, the operating pressure or temperature control was bypassed or overridden by the switching action of the timer in the programmer.

The timer mechanism consists of multiple leaf switches actuated by cams driven by a tiny synchronous motor. The switches operate in a nonadjustable timed program to control all external loads except the flame–failure alarm. The timer motor is started and stopped by actions of various relays, certain external switches, and its own contacts. The position of the cam shaft is indicated by a drum–type dial which is imprinted with a numeral corresponding to the step in the sequence, or the actual words "trial for ignition," main flame," "purge," etc.

The programmer consists of two basic components: the chassis containing the moving parts, and the frame or base containing the terminal strip to which the field wiring is attached. The frame is permanently connected to the burner control cabinet and prewired by the burner manufacturer so that the connections are duplicated on his main terminal strip. The chassis plugs into the frame or base so that it can be removed and replaced without disconnecting any wiring. Tip jacks are also provided for conveniently checking flame signal strength.

Understanding the operation of the relays on the programmer chassis has been facilitated somewhat by the standardization by two of the major control manufacturers of the functions they perform. (See Figure 24-2.) Whether designated 1K, 2K, 3K, or RL1, RL2, RL3, their functions are equivalent.

Number 1 relay's function is to act as a master relay, or load relay. The firing cycle can neither begin nor continue if it is not energized. It is responsive to the action of all the limit controls and interlocks. Relay number 2 is the flame relay, and is energized in response to the presence of the pilot or main flame. Relay number 3 is the interlock relay, and is initially energized by the starting interlocks and then kept energized by the running interlocks.

The function of the safety lockout switch (LS), or just plain safety switch (SS), is to prevent the automatic starting of a burner–operating sequence when there has been a previous failure to ignite or loss of flame. In addition, the safety switch will lock out upon the loss of combustion air, atomizing air, or due to high or low fuel pressure, according to the circuit design of the particular boiler and the fuel in use at the time. The failure of relay 3 to pull in, or the dropping out of relay 3 after it was initially energized, will prevent ignition.

The safety switch consists of a bimetallic warping bar, a heating element, a set of electrical contacts, a latching arrange-

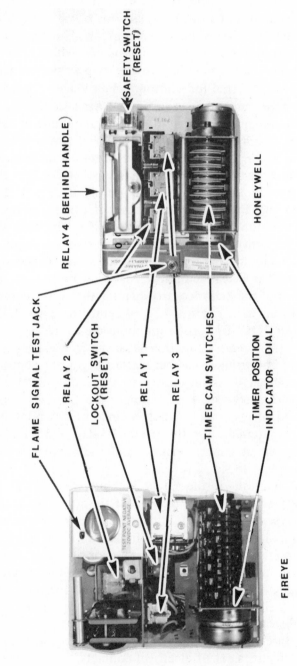

FLAME SAFEGUARD CONTROLS

SAFETY SWITCH (RESET)

RELAY 4 (BEHIND HANDLE)

HONEYWELL

FLAME SIGNAL TEST JACK

RELAY 2

LOCKOUT SWITCH (RESET)

RELAY 1

RELAY 3

TIMER CAM SWITCHES

TIMER POSITION INDICATOR DIAL

FIREYE

Figure 24-2.

ment, and a resetting means. When electrically energized, the element conducts heat to the warping bar which, after a preset period, moves to open the electrical contacts. The mechanical latch holds the contacts open until manually released or reset.

The electrical contacts of this device are wired in series with the coil of relay 1, the deenergization of which prevents operation of the pilot and main fuel valves, as previously described. The safety switch is actually a single-pole, double-throw device (SPDT) so that when in the locked-out mode it completes a circuit to the alarm terminal on the terminal strip. A visual or audible alarm can be connected between this terminal and the neutral or ground wire of the control circuit if desired, and will function whenever the burner goes into lockout.

Some programmers have a test-run switch incorporated in the internal wiring to the timer motor. This makes it convenient for the engineer to make adjustments at various stages in the program. For instance, adjustments to the gas pilot flame and scanner viewing angle, that require several minutes, can be accomplished by opening the test switch during the ignition period. This does not bypass any safety devices, it merely disconnects the timer motor from the control circuit. If the flame relay does not prove the establishment of the pilot flame, for instance, the safety switch will eventually lock out.

In burner control terminology, the term "flame failure" has become so ambiguous as to be almost meaningless. Of the many conditions which can cause a safety lockout, actual loss of flame is of lesser common occurrence than the breakage of a belt, for instance, resulting in the loss of atomizing air which exhibits the same symptom—flame-failure alarm. This has come about as a result of increased emphasis by insurance underwriters on so-called safe-start conditions. Compliance by control manufacturers with the new requirements gave birth to whole families of controls differing from one another according to a dash number or two. Not only will they fill a book by themselves, but it would be redundant to reproduce the many and varied wiring diagrams and check charts, since they are readily available through authorized wholesalers and rebuilders.

Programmers without test–run switches employ other methods to temporarily stop the timer motor in accordance with the manufacturer's instructions.

The comparitively recent introduction of so-called intelligent microprocessor-based integrated burner management systems offer features beyond the capability of conventional electromechanical programmers previously described. In addition to sequence control and flame supervision, this new generation of programmers provide status indication, first-out annunciation, self-diagnostics, and energy conservation.

25

Introduction to Troubleshooting

ELECTRICAL PROBLEMS

Among the highest paid technicians in any trade are the trouble-shooters—the problem solvers. As a group, they like problems, because problems have solutions and coming up with the answers is the name of the game. The successful players have a bag full of answers, and are eagerly looking for problems to try them on. There is, however, an old axiom: Before we can solve a problem, we must establish what the problem is.

The problems burner men encounter can be arranged in two classes: *starting problems* and *running problems*. Broadly, a starting problem is one that occurs as the result of some malfunction at the initiation of the operating cycle, before the main fuel valve opens. A running failure can be regarded as caused by some circumstance occurring *while* the fuel valve is open. The situation is seemingly complicated by the fact that both types of failures often result in the same symptoms.

It is generally not obvious to the service man (without making a trial run) at what stage of the operating cycle the failure occurred. Before any attempt is made to restart the burner, however, certain preliminary checks should be made, primarily for safety reasons, and secondarily, to investigate as many potential causes of starting problems as possible *external* to the burner itself; the reason being that *starting problems are more common* causes of flame failure symptoms than are running problems. From the safety standpoint, the technician must always remember that every lock–out of a safety device carries the implication that some potential or real danger threatens, and for him to attempt to restart the burner indiscriminately is foolhardy. Treatment of the problem in a serious, careful manner is, therefore, mandatory.

Every service problem is *affected* by some *cause,* so that what the troubleshooter is greeted with on arrival at the job is an *effect.* What he must do, then, is work backwards like a detective—from the effect, to the cause, to the problem. The single most important thing he can do in his problem–solving procedure, is to find out all he possibly can about the *effect.* It is not enough to know that the burner is not running; he must find out *when* it stopped, and *how* it stopped. All these things are effects of different causes, and lead to different problems.

Obviously, the person who knows most about the effect, is the operator of the burner. He sees it day in and day out when it *is* running. Don't put him down, even if he is only the sweeper. Question him in depth. Maybe this effect has been coming on for days, and may have been preceded by unusual noises or actions that will provide a clue. Perhaps the burner went off before and he didn't bother to call because he was able to get it going himself. If so, have him go through the procedure he used to start it *in detail.* Overlook no moves on his part, even if he only hit it with his broom. Find out where he hit it, and how hard. If he pressed a reset button or buttons, which one did he press first, which one next, etc. One button causes one effect, another something entirely different. The path to the problem may well be determined at this crossroad. Encourage the man to talk, and let him volunteer his bag of answers. After all, at this point he is the man closest to the problem.

There are certain things experienced engineers know about the installations they maintain. They *know,* for instance, whether the burner utilizes forced draft or induced draft; the type of burner setting, a packaged unit or a conversion from some other fuel; if it is a combination burner, what the standby fuel grade is; the approximate input; type, brand, and model designation of the flame safeguard system; general conditions of the boiler room and auxiliary equipment; operating gauge readings, standing and running, etc. There are, of course, many more important facts about these installations programmed into the engineer's memory bank, and a good many written down, perhaps in a notebook, for future reference. For to clutter the memory with all the detail that *could* be important is impractical. "The secret to remembering, is knowing what to forget," is still a good axiom, with one modification—"the secret to remembering, is knowing what is of importance everyday, and what can be looked up when necessary."

ENGINEER

When we say a man is *experienced,* what we really mean is that *he has made his share of mistakes.* Facetious though this may sound, it is true; for as the old saying goes, "Show me a man who has never made a mistake, and I'll show you a man who has never done anything."

There are ways, though, to keep the mistakes to a minimum. One way is to profit from the experience of another. For a fledgling apprentice, there is no substitute for the learning opportunity the company of an accomplished journeyman affords. It is extremely helpful for a trainee to be able to see a burner he may be called upon to service when it is operating normally; how it looks, how it sounds, and how it *reads out.*

LOCATING THE PROBLEM

. . . A pump coupling shears, the flow of feed water stops . . . a boiler is in danger of structural damage . . . the float mechanism in the water column trips a limit switch, stops the burner and signals LOW WATER . . .

Although a problem may be a mechanical one, such as a sheared coupling, it will nearly always manifest itself *initially* as an electrical problem, since in any case we must interrupt an electrical circuit in order to stop the burner. As we have seen, electricity is the prime mover, and in large measure the status of the engineer as a troubleshooter hinges on his mastery of the fundamentals of electrical circuitry. That is where it's at, as the expression goes.

When we refer to a particular problem as *external* to the boiler, we mean that it is not caused as a result of a malfunction of the boiler or a burner component, but the failure of one of the *utilities* or auxiliaries connected to the boiler package. For instance, in the case of utilities, the lack of electricity or of one of the fuels (either pilot fuel or main fuel) will cause a shut-down—as the failure of the feed-water pump illustrated the point in the case of an auxiliary.

In the absence of an audiovisual alarm that would indicate the opening of a limit control, such as a low-water cut-off, or low fuel-pressure switch, for example, it would be necessary to determine whether the burner is being held off and prevented from starting because of an open switch in some limit device, or whether the control circuit is even energized. A blown control-circuit fuse obviously would have stopped the burner immediately, since the fuel valve, motor-starter coil, and all the limit controls are in this circuit. The programmer timer dial would have stopped indicating the stage it was in when the fuse blew, just as a stopped clock indicates the time of day it was when it stopped. This in itself offers a clue as to where to begin to look for *short circuits.* In order of most likely causes of burner inter-ruptions, however, a blown control-circuit fuse ranks near the bottom of the list.

SINGLE-PHASE CONTROL SYSTEMS

As noted previously, one of the safety requirements of a mod-ern burner electrical-control system is that it be limited to 120 volts single phase, with one leg grounded, and that all switching be done in the *hot* leg. Where a control circuit is not supplied from a conventional single-phase lighting panel, but from a step-down transformer tapped off two of the three phase legs of the power circuit, it is possible to have an ungrounded con-trol circuit. Since the two legs of the control circuit originate at the secondary winding of a transformer, there is no continu-ity from the circuit to ground; only from leg to leg, unless one leg is mechanically bonded to the metal of the burner or boiler setting.

Overload protection for such transformers is provided by a fuse in each leg of the *primary* circuit; sometimes there is no fuse in the secondary or control circuit. The fuses in the primary circuit are sized according to the maximum VA rating of the *secondary* circuit, however, as follows: If the maximum safe current rating of a 120-volt control circuit is established at 15 amperes, and it is to be supplied by control-circuit transformer, the operating VA rating of the transformer would be 1800 (VA equals volts times amps, disregarding power factor). Dividing the primary voltage, which let's say is 480, into the VA rating would net the proper fuse size—in this case 3.75 amps. If the power-source voltage was 240 instead, and the VA rating the same, the fuse size would work out to 7.5 amperes (1800 ÷ 240).

An ungrounded circuit is difficult to troubleshoot because we cannot use the metal of enclosures or other parts of the boiler-burner as the neutral conductor. By proper grounding of one leg of the control circuit, the metallic parts of the electrical system, the metal of control enclosures—indeed the metal of the burner itself—form one huge, contiguous envelope containing the current conductors. Grounding one lead of a test meter to any clean, unpainted metal surface of the boiler or its appurtenances in effect *picks up the neutral.* Using the other lead of the meter to touch various points in the *hot leg,* the meter will indicate line voltage wherever the point of contact is *live* or energized. In this way, by making a series of continuity tests along the path of current flow, checking each limit switch terminal and each splice point, the *open* is found where the meter indicates zero voltage. The location of the open determines the next course of action by the troubleshooter, just as the finding of the open low-water cutoff switch led to the discovery of the sheared feed-water pump coupling in the example in the preceding chapter.

OBSOLETE CONTROL CIRCUITS

There are many boiler–burner units in service today dating back more than 20 years that have unsafe control systems by modern standards. The fuel valves, ignition systems, and programmers operate on 240 volts, and in so doing present some special problems for the troubleshooter.

Instead of one leg of each appliance, such as a valve or transformer, being connected to a common wire which is a grounded neutral, the common is one live 120-volt leg of a 240-volt system. The hot leg, which runs through the switching devices and ultimately to the other side of each appliance, originates as the other 120-volt leg of the 240-volt supply. Each leg is individually fused, and line-to–ground voltage is 120 (ground being any metal enclosure or burner part). Herein lies one of the problems, for although fuses may be rated the same, seldom if ever will both blow at the same time under the same conditions.

With only one fuse blown, the circuit is open but *still alive*, and if not careful when testing with a neon–type pocket tester (popular among burner service men), an erroneous conclusion can be made that *both* fuses are all right. Such a tester will glow when testing either side of a blown fuse in a 240-volt system, if one lead of the tester is grounded. True, it will glow less brightly than when testing across the 240-volt line, but often this fact is not easily recognized. The voltage on the load side of the blown fuse is *feedback* or return voltage from the other 120-volt leg, through the appliances and back to the (blown) fuseblock. Depending on the resistance characteristics of the load, the voltage will be less than 120 but sufficient to light a neon tester.

Under similar conditions, it is actually possible to hold a relay coil or valve solenoid energized with less than 120 volts even though they are nominally rated at 240 volts. This can occur where a short circuit has welded one leg of the control circuit to the metal of some enclosure, blowing only one fuse. For this reason it is an extremely unsatisfactory control system, since it is not *fail–safe*.

For continuity testing, a voltmeter will give more dependable results than a test lamp when working with an ungrounded circuit. When checking a limit switch which is open, one terminal will register 120 volts to ground, and the other something less than 120, depending on the load being controlled. If the switch is closed, the readings will be identical. This is due to the fact that one side of the switch is connected directly to one 120-volt leg of the control system, whereas the other terminal has the load in series with it and the other (common) 120-volt leg. When the switch is closed, it is as though it is not there. It is as if you are merely testing at a new point on the same conductor, hence the same readings on both terminals.

When checking out a series limit circuit by means of a test lamp, a 240-volt bulb must be used together with a little different procedure. The first step is to determine the relative intensity of the bulb when reading 120 volts as compared with 240. This can be done by checking leg-to-leg and leg-to-ground at the fuseblock. At one-half voltage the lamp is markedly dimmer than at full 240 volts. When continuity testing a limit switch, a similar difference in intensity will be noticed if the switch is open; on one terminal the glow will indicate half voltage, and on the other it will glow even duller. If this difference is not easily discerned, using the test lamp to *shunt* around the switch may prove a better technique. In this method, one lead of the tester is *not* grounded; instead the leads of the lamp are each connected to the respective terminals of the switch. The bulb lights, although at less than full brilliance, if the switch is *open,* and does not light if the switch is closed.

When testing by the shunt method, it is recommended that a neon lamp be used. It has no filament and therefore no electrical continuity through it; whereas a conventional bulb can act like a high-resistance ground. Conducting enough electricity through it to cause a relay to pick up or chatter can be disconcerting to the troubleshooter, and the arcing can be injurious to the relay contacts.

VISUAL INSPECTION

Where the cause of the burner failure is not obvious, the programmer and its terminal strip is the logical place to begin investigating because of the master function it performs as the control center for burner operation. A visual inspection of the safety switch and reset button would be a first step to determine whether it has *locked out on safety* and is preventing the burner from starting.

The burner operator should understand its operation and learn to recognize its normal or running mode, as well as how it looks when locked out. This is not always easy, since most modern programmers have semienclosed safety switches, and all that can be seen clearly is the red reset button. Fortunately, they also have an alarm terminal which, although it may not be connected to a remote signaling device, becomes live when the control has locked out on flame failure. Table 25-1 is a terminal and relay comparison chart for the Fireye control Model 26CF6 5022, and the Honeywell R4140L 1006, which have been selected for discussion in this text because they meet most or all requirements of the various regulatory agencies (UL, FM, IRI, CSA, IRM, ad infinitum) and are commonly found in the field.

Table 25-1. Terminal Comparison

Terminal Number		Circuit or Function
Fireye 5022	*Honeywell R4140L 1006*	
L1	L1	Line voltage, hot to limit controls
L2	L2	Common, or neutral line
13	4	From limit controls to interlocks
3	16	From preignition interlocks
P	3	From running interlocks
M	8	Blower MS, and to low–fire switch
D	13	From low–fire switch
8	15	From high-fire switch
5	5	10–second interrupted ignition
6	6	15-second interrupted ignition
7	7	Main fuel valve(s)
A	9	120–volt alarm
10	11	Series 90 modulator, common*

*Honeywell M941 or M936 Modutrol motor   *(more)*

Table 25-1. Terminal Comparison (concluded)

11	12	Modulator, automatic
12	14	Modulator, low (closed damper)
X	10	Modulator, high (open damper)
S1	F	Scanner (flame detector) connection
S2	G	Scanner connection (grounded)**
	Relay and Timer Identification	
RL	1K	Master (load) relay
RF	2K	Flame relay
RA	3K	Interlock relay
–	4K	Load relay (extension of 1K)
K	M	Timer contacts, K9-1 or M10B (example)

**Fireye signal voltage, normal 20 D.C.
Honeywell signal strength, 2¼-3½ microamps

NOTES:

1. To test the C-series controls for flame signal, a 10,000 ohms per volt or greater D.C. voltmeter should be used.

2. To check the 4140–series flame safeguard, a Honeywell W136A multimeter (or equivalent) is required, in addition to a meter connector plug (PN 117053). The meter should have a 0–25 microampere test range.

3. To test line voltage terminals, set the meter on the 0–300–volt A.C. scale and use the test prods with or without alligator clips as necessary.

CONTINUITY TESTING

Use of the terminal strip should be made after it is determined that the programmer is *not* in safety lockout, and before removing limit control covers and shooting in the dark. One of the consequences of modern design, however, is that when either of the programmers under discussion is installed in its frame, its terminal strip is inaccessible. Therefore the chassis must be removed before certain *static* tests can be made to determine the problem; loss of continuity (an open) through the limit controls or preignition interlocks, for example.

The master switch should be opened before attempting to remove the programmer chassis.

The respective controls may be removed by loosening one screw. Honeywell uses a conventional threaded screw, centered near the top of the chassis. Fireye is similar, except that it is a quarter–turn, zeus–type fastener. Both controls swing down and out from a slip–in lower hinge mount. The only wires that need to be disconnected are those plugged into the meter jack(s) where applicable.

Once the chassis has been removed (and placed in a safe place), the master switch can be turned on. Using the Honeywell 4140 for the sake of illustration, the following voltage tests can be made carefully:

Between Terminals	*Indicates*
L1-L2	Voltage, control circuit power supply is on (minimum 102 volts)
4-L2	a) No voltage, an open limit control or broken wire or connection
	b) Voltage, limits closed and ready
16-L2	a) No voltage, one of the starting interlocks is open, or broken wire, etc.
	b) Voltage, preignition (starting) interlocks closed and ready

If in going through the above tests it is determined that the limit–control circuit is open, it then becomes a matter of checking each device and the interconnecting wires and connections. Remembering that, by definition, the opening of a limit control indicates an unsafe condition, the cause of the trip should be investigated and *corrected* before the burner is put back on the line.

STARTING (PREIGNITION) INTERLOCKS

Starting interlocks are switches which must be closed for safe starting of the burner. Most typical is the valve–closed (proof–of–closure) switch, which is associated with the actuator of the main fuel valve(s), and required by certain code authorities. On combination fuel burners, the gas/oil selector switch bypasses nonapplicable interlocks, such as low oil temperature when burning gas. However, proof–of–closure switches must be made (closed) on the alternate fuel valve as well as the applicable fuel valve in order to make a successful start. Furthermore, they must remain closed during prepurge, or a safety shutdown and lockout will occur. At a certain point in the program, usually a few seconds before a trial for ignition is made, the programmer automatically switches control of the interlock relay (see Table 25-1 for identification) from the starting to the running interlocks. If the interlock relay drops out (is deenergized) at any point in the starting or running cycle of the burner, a safety shutdown will occur.

If all the tests indicate satisfactory continuity, the problem may be in the programmer itself. It is difficult if not impossible to trace a circuit through the entrails of a programmer without the aid of the manufacturer's bulletin or schematic diagram covering the specific model of control in question. Even controls of the same series or group differ radically from one another by virtue of a different digit or two in their model numbers.

Since it is a rare control cabinet that contains, in its proper place, all the service information and schematic diagrams the troubleshooter needs, it is pretty much up to the engineer to maintain a personal library of instruction sheets and bulletins covering the programmers he is likely to encounter. Some useful publications are listed below.

Detailed Instruction Sheets, Wiring Diagrams, and Check Charts

Programmer Model	Form Number
Honeywell:	
R4150A, B, and X	95-6255-2
R4150G	95-6895-1
R4126	95-6336
R4140L	60-2339-2
BC7000	60-2529
Cleaver-Brooks:	
CB40	C9-768
CB20	C9-767
CB70	CB18-6363
Fireye:	
26RJ8 6070	CP-59
26RJ8 6080	C-30
26CF6 5022	C-14
26CF6 5023(A)	C-15
E100	E1001

EMERGENCY SITUATIONS

The most critical situation a service man can come upon, which is almost in a class by itself, is one where there has been a flame failure accompanied by malfunction of the safety–shutdown system or fuel valve, and unburned fuel is either present in the combustion chamber, or has overflowed to the occupied space. The first consideration in a case like this is preventing ignition of the accumulated fuel and second, the *manual* closing of the fuel–supply emergency valve, and finally, the ventilation, dilution, and subsequent removal of the fuel accumulation. *He must not throw any electrical switches;* the arcing thus caused could be the ignition source needed to cause an explosion. Instead, he should close only the manually–operated valves or cocks provided to stop the fuel flow. When it can be determined that no dangerous level of fuel concentration is present in the boiler room, electrical disconnects can be opened.

In automatic commercial and industrial heating systems, the intermittent operation of the burner often takes place with no one in attendance. Consequently, if the main fuel valve leaks or does not function properly when the burner is supposed to be off, fuel will leak through the burner into the combustion chamber of the furnace. Leakages of this kind occur most often in installations where fuel is continuously supplied under pressure to the main fuel valve. However, they can also occur in oil–burner installations with integral pumps, which have long prepurge and postpurge cycles during which the fuel pump is running while the fuel valve is scheduled to be closed. The resulting danger of exploding the fuel in the furnace when normal ignition takes place has been a long–standing problem in the industry.

26

The Operating Sequence

When the initial inspection of an inoperative burner system indicates the safety switch of the programmer *is* in the locked–out position, and a preliminary inspection of the combustion space and fuel valves verifies the absence of unburned fuel or vapor (in the case of oil), a trial run can be made in an effort to pinpoint the problem as either in the programmer itself or elsewhere. With the burner switch on, all limit and operating switches and starting interlocks closed, pressing the reset button on the safety switch will initiate the operating cycle.

The engineer's attention should be concentrated on the programmer during the trial run, rather than on the burner and its functions, for the interaction of the main components of the programmer (load relay, flame relay, interlock relay, and timer dial, etc.) will tell the story. In fact, on the first run he should not be concerned with making visual observation of the gas pilot flame, or even the main flame. The flame–detection system should be considered capable of confirming flame presence until determined otherwise. By familiarizing himself beforehand with the normal operating sequence of the programmer, and carefully observing the operation of the relays in relation to the particular position of the timer dial during the trial run, deviations may become apparent that will dictate his next step.

TYPICAL BURNER OPERATING SEQUENCE

Again citing the Honeywell R4140L (Figure 24-2) as typical, since it complies with requirements of insurance underwriters such as Industrial Risk Insurers (IRI) and Factory Mutual

Insurance Association (FM) and certain other codes, the following is a description of the burner operation from startup through shutdown. No attempt is made to correlate the action of the fuel supply system or feedwater system, except for those controls that directly affect the action of the programmer. Referring to Figure 24-2 (page 242), the legend on the timer dial indicates the position of the timer and stage reached in the operating cycle. The bar graph shown in Figure 26-1 relates the dial indicator to the timing of dial rotation. This sequence makes reference only to the dial indication and not to the actual time involved. These timings do *not* represent elapsed time, since the timer is interrupted and governed by other components during a normal cycle, such as the high–fire switch (damper–open proving switch) and the low–fire (low–fire start) switch, and the contacts of the purge time extender which may be required by code.

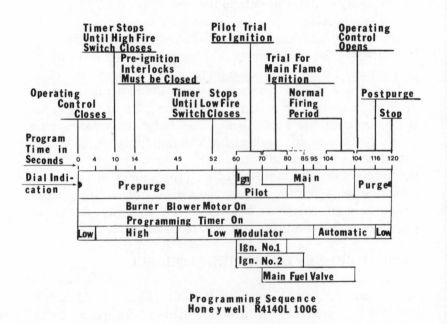

Figure 26-1. Program Sequence

With the limit controls closed, and the preignition inter-locks satisfied, when the burner switch is turned on, power is routed through the limits and interlocks to terminal 3. Relays 1K and 4K are energized. The timer starts from the standby (DOT) position, and the burner (blower) motor starts. The heater in the safety lockout switch begins to heat; PREPURGE begins, and is indicated on the timer dial.

Four seconds into the program, terminals 10 and 11 are powered and the modulator (damper motor) begins to move toward high (open) position, which allows full flow of air through the combustion chamber and flues, When terminals 10 and 11 are powered the modulating pressure or temperature control and the manual flame control (where applicable) are bypassed and have no control over the modulator. When the combustion air proving switch and other running interlocks make, relay 3K pulls in and the safety switch stops heating. Continuity through the starting and running interlocks allows the sequence to continue. If any of these are not closed at this time, or if they subsequently open, relay 3K will drop out. The timer will complete its revolution to the starting position and a safety lockout will occur.

The blower–motor–starter interlock is wired into the cir-cuit to prove that the starter is energized and to interrupt the circuit if the starter be deenergized for any reason (as discussed in the section under three–phase motors). When oil is fired with an air–atomizing burner there is a pressure switch to prove ade-quate compressed air, a low–oil–temperature switch and a high-oil–temperature switch in the running interlock circuit. In the gas mode, the low–gas–pressure switch and the high–gas–pres-sure switch must be closed to prove sufficient but not excessive gas fuel pressure.

At ten seconds into the program, the timer stops until the high–fire (open damper) switch closes. Existing IRI requirements and/or others require additional prepurge time beyond that pro-vided by the programmer. This is accomplished by the use of a separate time–delay relay. The timing of this relay is adjustable from 1 to 200 seconds, and is field set according to code or in-surance requirements. The purge timer coil is energized through the contacts of the open damper switch as the damper approaches open position. The open damper switch may be located inside the auxiliary switch section of the mod motor, or as a damper–actuated proximity switch. When the purge timer contacts close, a parallel circuit is established to keep the damper motor open. The motor stays in the open position until the number of seconds set on the purge timer have expired, at which time the holding circuit is broken and the mod motor returns to low–fire position. As soon as the low–fire start switch (which may also be located inside the mod motor or on the damper linkage system) closes, the programmer timer restarts and the program continues. Elapsed time 51 seconds.

At 57.5 seconds the safety switch heater begins to heat again, in anticipation of a trial for ignition. Up to this point in the program if the flame relay (2K) should pull in for any reason, 3K will drop out and the timer will complete its revolution and the programmer will lock out. Dial indication is "IGN PILOT"; elapsed time is 60 seconds.

The ignition transformer and gas pilot valve are energized from terminal 5 or 6. As soon as the pilot flame is detected, the flame relay (2K) is energized. The low–fire, high–fire, and test/run switch on the programmer are bypassed at 66 seconds.

At 70 seconds the timer dial will indicate "MAIN" and the trial for pilot ignition ends. Flame must now be established or the flame relay (2K) will drop out, 3K will drop out and lockout will occur in about 30 seconds. If relay 2K is energized, terminal 7 will be powered and the main fuel valve(s) will open.

At 80 seconds terminal 5 deenergizes (end of 10–second trial for ignition).

At 95 seconds terminals 11 and 12 are powered and the mod motor is "released to automatic." The modulating (series 90) pressure or temperature control can now position the mod motor (also referred to as the firing–rate control motor) according to load demand.

At 100 seconds terminal 6 deenergizes (end of 15–second trial for ignition).

At 105 seconds the programmer timer stops. System is in the run mode.

NORMAL SHUTDOWN

The burner will fire until steam pressure or water temperature in excess of the setting of the operating control is generated. When that happens, relays 1K, 3K, and 4K drop out. The timer restarts; dial indication is POST PURGE. Main fuel valve(s) close, and when the flame goes out relay 2K drops out.

At 116 seconds terminals 11 and 14 are energized, driving the mod motor to low (damper–closed position).

At 120 seconds the timer stops at the DOT, terminal 8 is deenergized and the blower (burner) motor stops. End of cycle.

WARNING

The cause for loss of flame or any other unusual condition should be investigated and corrected before attempting to restart the burner.

Typically, the field service of a programmer is limited to cleaning contacts, replacing amplifier tubes, and/or amplifier modules. No manufacturer will accept as a trade–in a control that has had surgery in the inviolable area of resistors, capacitors, and printed circuitry; it is beyond the scope of training and experience of the technician, and to attempt repairs in this section will invariably void all warranties.

There are two general groups of contacts in the programmer: relay contacts and timer contacts. Like most contacts, they occasionally fail to open, fail to close, and are susceptible to dust and dirt. In the case of airborne contamination, dust–proof gasketed enclosures can be provided to greatly reduce the problem. In addition, a self–cleaning action known as *wipe,* is designed into the mating leaves to which the contacts are attached. Instead of a simple abutting when two contacts meet, wipe involves a butting, sliding action which burnishes the contact surfaces.

Arcing, which is a natural phenomenon whenever an electrical circuit is broken, accounts for some of the so–called dirt found on contacts. The dirt is actually an oxide of the metal the contacts are made from. By using a metal whose oxide is a conductor of electricity, such as silver or tungsten–alloy, the blackening due to arcing interferes very little with the switching function. Low–voltage contacts (20–30 volts), on the other hand, are much more affected by airborne dirt. Small dust particles often build up enough mass to resist proper functioning of contact points, especially at the low wattages with which we are dealing. For that reason, programmers with low–voltage starting and running interlock circuits have been obsoleted by line–voltage (120 volt) models.

CONTACT CLEANING AND ADJUSTMENT

The manufacturers offer the following advice regarding cleaning the contacts in their respective programmers.

Honeywell

Field cleaning of relay and timer contacts is *not* recommended. If they must be cleaned, use *only* Honeywell pressurized contact cleaner, Part No. 132569. Honeywell's chemical analysis laboratory has found this cleaner to be acceptable for this task. Directions for using this cleaner are printed on the can.

IMPORTANT

1. Do not clean contacts unless absolutely necessary.
2. Use only Honeywell contact cleaner. Do not use any other type of contact cleaner.
3. Use utmost care to avoid bending the contacts or changing their specifications or configuration in any way.
4. Do not use abrasive material to clean contacts.
5. Do not use hard paper, such as a business card to clean contacts.

CAUTION

Open the master switch before removing the relay/ timer cover or before cleaning contacts. Line voltage may be present on most contacts when power is on.

Honeywell's laboratory tested other contact cleaners but did not approve them for these reasons:

1. The solvents could deteriorate plastic parts and wire insulation.
2. The cleaners leave an oily residue which will collect dust and dirt. This residue will also break down to form various carbonaceous products. Either result will cause early contact failure.

Do not use an abrasive (burnishing tool, sandpaper stick, file, etc.) to clean contacts. Use of an abrasive can cause early contact failure for these reasons:

1. Some relay and timer contacts are plated with gold for increased reliability. Burnishing can quickly remove the plating.
2. The radii or points of the contacts are designed with specific shapes to best serve the intended functions of the contacts. Burnishing can rapidly alter these contact configurations.
3. Use of an abrasive loosens fine particles of the contact material which adhere to the surface of the contact, thus increasing its resistance.
4. Contact specifications (contact pressures, pressback, and gaps) are carefully controlled during manufacturing to ensure maximum contact life. Burnishing can easily change these specifications.

IMPORTANT

Blackened M4A, M6B, or M11B timer contacts is due to normal deposits of impurities caused by breaking an inductive load (ignition transformer). Tests on returned programmers have shown that the deposits are not heavy enough to cause ignition failure. Determine *exactly* at what point in the operating sequence the trouble occurs and follow the applicable trouble-shooting procedure carefully. End of instructions.

ECA (Fireye)

All contacts are designed with adequate wiping action for self–cleaning under normal conditions and the switching assemblies are covered for protection against abnormal atmospheres.

Should contact cleaning be required, use a burnishing tool or fine crocus. *Never file, or sandpaper, or apply liquid or aerosol spray cleaners.* End of instructions.

WARNING

Only qualified servicemen should attempt to service or repair flame safeguard controls.

HOUSE BRANDING

So-called "proprietary versions" of well-known flame-safeguard controls are quite common in the field. Usually, a proprietary control is specially designed, constructed and labeled to meet the burner manufacturer's requirements. Generally it has been deliberately bastardized so that it fits only a specific burner's control cabinet or frame. Consequently, the end user's source of a replacement control is limited, to say the least.

Competition and ingenuity being what it is, however, both major control manufacturers have kits available which circumvent the other's proprietorship. They even supply kits to circumvent *their own* proprietary controls, and maintain detailed cross-reference charts and diagrams to show how to do it.

27

Starting and Running Problems

STARTING PROBLEMS

The Pilot Flame Does Not Light

When during the trial run, it is determined that the pilot flame did not light on schedule, troubleshooting of the ignition system is in order. Oddly, perhaps, there is very little new under the sun when it comes to methods used to automatically ignite volatile fuels.

Concepts embodied in the design of automatic ignition systems for large gas and oil burners were established nearly 50 years ago, and have come down through the years virtually unaltered. It bears repeating now that one of the prerequisites of good burner performance has always been *a dependable ignition system*. Regardless of the degree of sophistication the flame–safeguard system affords in the prevention of explosions, frequent nuisance shutdowns due to the malfunction of an ignition component cannot be tolerated. Nuisance shutdowns are preferred to explosive light–offs, of course, and usually are symptomatic of an inherently undependable ignition system, or poor adjustment. Such inconveniences can be aggravating and expensive in terms of downtime. There is something basically wrong when a burner requires an inordinate amount of preventive maintenance in order to ensure dependable, smooth ignition.

Early in chapter 2, when describing the combination fuel burner ignition system, it was pointed out that the gas–electric pilot burner types in common use today are generally blue–flame burners, which are also referred to as premix or partial premix type burners. An electric spark is used to light the fuel, which may be oil or gas, main burner or pilot burner. Some codes and ordinances require a gas–electric pilot ignition system on oil burners with inputs in excess of 20 gallons per hour. Gas burners with inputs in excess of 2,000,000 Btu per hour are similarly required to have interrupted pilots. An *interrupted pilot* is one which is on only long enough to light the main flame, as contrasted with an *intermittent* ignition system which is on at all times during which the main burner is operating. A third type, called a *constant ignition* system (also referred to as a standing pilot), which is on continuously even during off cycles of the main burner, is used on some smaller gas commercial boilers and the majority of domestic gas space heaters and water heaters that operate with natural draft.

Direct–spark ignited oil burners are very similar in ignition methods, and even afford a degree of parts interchangeability. Burners that use a gas–electric ignition system, on the other hand, have custom–designed pilot burners exclusively. Consequently, each manufacturer's pilot–burner configuration precludes parts interchangeability from brand to brand. Needless to say, each seems to have its own built–in peculiarities as well.

The major difference between the spark ignition of an air/oil dispersion and the spark ignition of a gaseous fuel mixture is in the location of the electrodes relative to the fuel. This gives rise to service problems that are also distinctly different. Although each system uses a step–up transformer to supply the electrical potential necessary to create the spark, and the primary side of such *ignition transformers* are connected to the burner control systems identically, the secondary circuits differ in output voltage, number of conductors, and grounding method.

A semiliquid, turbulent oil spray is much more difficult to ignite than a premixed, relatively placid gas stream and, consequently, requires a hotter spark. The spark must also be elastic and strong enough to be *bowed* by the combustion air stream as it rushes by the electrodes. For this is a basic design principle: locating the electrodes in the air stream just outside of the spray pattern, where they cannot be wetted by the oil yet close enough so that the spark can be blown into the atomized mixture. On such systems, two electrodes are customarily used to establish the air gap which a 10,000–volt spark must bridge. Virtually all domestic oil burners, and many commercial–industrial No. 4 oil burners, use this method. In the latter case, the spark voltage may be 12,000 to 15,000 volts. Bunker C, or No. 6, oil burners almost exclusively use the gas–electric pilot ignition system.

The spark potential of the gas–electric ignition system is seldom more than 6,000 volts, and only one electrode is used. One side of the ignition transformer secondary circuit is grounded to the burner metal, and only one high–voltage conductor is brought to the pilot burner. The electrode itself, and occasionally even a portion of the conductor, is mounted right in the gas stream, since wetting by the fuel is not a problem. However, it does make it vulnerable to fouling and erosion from other causes. By virtue of the immersion of the electrode in the gas stream, certain phenomena that occur in the process of gas combustion must be taken into consideration. The spark gap is adjusted between the single electrode and the metal of the burner housing, since actually it has been made one of the conductors when one side of the 6,000–volt secondary was *grounded* to it.

Every current, however small, generates heat. The energy present in the spark, expressed in watts or kilowatts, may be computed by multiplying the voltage across the arc by the current flowing in the circuit. The relationship between electrical energy and heat is, in turn, given by the expression:

$$1 \text{ kwh} = 3{,}413 \text{ Btu.}$$

An ignition system with a conventional ignition transformer whose secondary has a nameplate rating of .020 amps at 6,000 volts, would have the potential necessary to generate 408 Btuh in a spark as follows:

6,000 volts $\times$ .020 amps = 120 watts
120 watts $\times$ 3.4 Btu/watt = 408 Btuh.

The actual temperature and color of the spark depends upon arc length, arc voltage, composition of the metal elec-

trodes, and constituents present in the gaseous medium surrounding the electrode(s). In the case of gas igniters, which actually arc in the fuel, certain deficiencies in the composition of
the gas/air mix cause cratering, rapid erosion of the electrode,
light carbon dusting of the electrode and grounded surfaces, arc
instability, and in extreme cases collapse of the spark due to
carbon bridging of the electrodes. An improperly sized electrode
for a given current density, may lead to tip erosion. If the current is proportionately too high for the tip area, the electrode
tip may melt. As a rule, however, a smaller diameter electrode renders the spark more stable. The gap across which the
spark must bridge is customarily set as follows:

For 10,000–volt ignition systems, 3/16 to 1/4 inch
For 6,000–volt ignition systems, 1/8 to 3/16 inch.

Oil igniters are not affected by the composition of the
fuel/air mix. They are fouled, however, by raw oil droplets that
stray from the air stream and impinge on them. In their exposed position, they are easily disrupted by careless handling,
and their porcelain insulators are often cracked and broken in
this way. Then too they are easily short–circuited by accumulations of soot or carbon, a condition aggravated by their position close to the flame front.

The flame temperature produced is a function of the relative proportion of the gas and air. More importantly, the mix
should be adjusted to produce a neutral flame, which is neither
rich nor lean, neither *carburizing* nor oxidizing. For with the
carburizing, or excess gas flame, the hydrocarbon dissociates
and free carbon is deposited in very fine form. As the carburizing effect of the flame increases, the flame temperature drops
and the amount of carbon deposited on the electrode increases.
A decrease in flame temperature reduces ionization, lowering
spark temperature also. In addition, the carbon coating on the
electrode acts as a heat shield, which causes cratering of the
electrode tip. Since the carbon envelope has a melting point
some 1,000 or more degrees higher than a typical nickle–alloy
electrode, the pressure of the expanding gases and of the electron stream blows the vaporized metal toward the outside sur-

face of the electrode. The higher temperature at the center of the electrode results in a lower surface tension at that point, in comparison with the carbon-insulated perimeter. As a result, more metal is lost from the center of the electrode than from its perimeter, and a tiny crater forms on the tip. Over a period of operation under these conditions, the depth of the crater will increase significantly, and eventually a carbon bridge will form. The bridge, which has a diameter approximating that of a human hair, forms from the edge of the crater to the carbon deposit on the burner surface. This of course acts as a short circuit, prevents the establishment of an electric spark, and results in a safety shutdown.

RUNNING PROBLEMS

Running problems are broadly defined as those which occur at times during the burner running cycle when the main fuel valve is open. Typically, the burner is discovered by the attendant to be off on safety lockout for no apparent reason. After a checkout, the burner is cycled and performs normally through several trial runs, only to fail again several hours or days later. In discussing pulsation and concussion, the transient nature of some of the intermittent burner problems was emphasized. *Unpredictability* would seem to be the key word associated with running failures.

In any electrical or electronic device, transitory troubles are not uncommon. Because of the fleeting nature of such problems as those caused by momentary shorts or opens in such components as coils, capacitors, and resistors, the actual cause may be hard to determine. For example, the difficulties may last only while the faulty component is passing through a certain temperature range or occur only when a certain temperature is reached. Sometimes, as in the case of combustion safeguard controls or programmers, substituting a new vacuum tube, scanner cell, or amplifier module will help isolate the difficulty. Repeated lockouts or flame failures could additionally be caused by one or more of the following:

a. High ambient temperature (higher than 125°F)
b. Supply voltage variations, plus 10 or minus 15 percent
c. Electrical overloading of contacts
d. Marginal or unsteady flame signal
e. Short cycling of the burner

One of the first things the troubleshooter should try to establish is whether or not there is any pattern to the interruptions that can be associated with the time of day, the time of peak load, or the time of low load. Of course, what we are trying to do is determine whether or not we are actually dealing with a running failure; that is, if the main fuel valve *was* open and everything else in the go position at the time of failure. This is where we must round up as many witnesses as possible, and listen carefully. If the problem occurs repeatedly at times of peak load, odds are it is a running failure. Conversely, during times of low load the burner could be expected to cycle on and off more and be prone to fail during the ignition sequence, for as we have seen in discussing the mechanism of the electric spark, an undependable ignition system on a burner that cycles frequently can be trouble.

Figure 27-1 shows two versions of a portable test instrument that was developed as a service tool to pinpoint the cause of nuisance safety lockouts. The larger model combines a flame signal meter which reads DC volts or microamperes, and a miniaturized diagnostic annunciator. When left attached to the appropriate terminals of a programmer, an amber neon lamp lights up to indicate an ignition (starting) failure, and a red lamp lights to indicate a main flame (running) failure whenever the programmer goes into safety lockout. It measures approximately 3 by 6 by 2 inches and weighs only 12 ounces. It is affixed to any ferrous metal surface by means of magnetic anchors attached to the case.

Depending on the indication by the annunciator, the troubleshooter can rule out all of the controls and other components not associated with the symptom and concentrate his efforts on those devices that could cause the starting or running failure, as the case may be. By the same token, the instrument does not

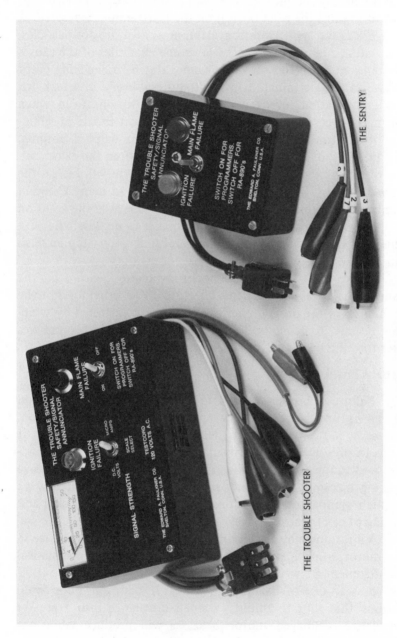

Figure 27-1. Diagnostic Annunciator

require that he be present when the failure occurs, since it stays energized until the reset button on the programmer is reset.

Excessive heat, vibration, dampness, dust or soot particles, fluctuating fuel pressures, etc., are some examples of the causes of transient problems. It often comes down to checking every screw on the terminal strip for tightness, every interlock for proper operation, every wire, splice, and so on. Even when through process of elimination you are down to the programmer itself, trial and error substitution of various plug-in units, and cleaning of contacts is all you can do. Often the exasperating result is that somewhere along the line you will hit on the answer, but by that time you will have tried so many things in combination, you will not be sure which one was the solution to the problem. Unfortunately, this makes us no wiser the next time the situation arises, unless a careful step-by-step analysis can be made in critique.

Where there is a multiple boiler installation, each using the same model programmer, the question of whether or not the problem is *in* the programmer can be quickly answered by swapping chassis from one boiler to the other. If the problem moves over too, the trouble is definitely in the programmer.

VIBRATION

Failure of burner and control components due to vibration caused by unbalanced motors or driven units is fairly common. Excessive motor vibration is detrimental in several respects. It tends to produce structural insulation failure of the motor windings and causes premature bearing failure. In addition, excessive shaking transmitted to other metal surfaces either directly or through sympathetic vibrations, can cause excessive arcing and pitting of electrical switchgear mounted thereon.

Vibrations may be produced by an electrical unbalance in the motor, a mechanical unbalance in the motor, a mechanical misalignment between the motor and load, or by the load itself —such as an out-of-balance fan wheel. In addition, poor foundations that vibrate amplify a small unbalance into a greater unbalance. Damaged motor bearings will produce vibrations that can usually be detected by the noise they make.

Vibrations can also be caused by aerodynamic phenomena associated with motor–driven combustion air fans that run at a constant speed but whose air flow is varied at the inlet or outlet by a damper mechanism. Where the energy of excessive turbulence or eddy currents in the area of impellers or dampers is transmitted to the burner windbox, plenum, or breeching, and ultimately to the motor itself, it can result in premature bearing failure also.

The ball joints of control rods and linkages which are connected to vibrating surfaces wear out quickly, and can affect the fuel/air ratio they regulate. In addition, the gear–reduction modutrol motors that drive such fuel–rate control systems and their delicate potentiometers, can be ruined by excessive vibration of their bases. In extreme cases, *remoting* or removing them to some more stable surface may be necessary if the vibration is basically due to an aerodynamic unbalance.

Because of the nearly universal code requirement that the burner be in low–fire position prior to ignition, any malfunction of the control system that does not allow proper positioning of the fuel–rate controller or damper motor will prevent a start–up. The low–fire start switch, which closes only when the fuel–rate controller is in the low position, is a starting interlock which is wired in such a way that either the entire starting sequence of the burner is prevented, or the opening of the main fuel valve is blocked. Any mechanical failure of the drive motor or jamming of the valve–control–linkage system that prevents the return of the controller to the low–fire position similarly will result in an aborted light–off if the low–fire start switch does not close on schedule.

The balanced bridge system is designed to produce a level temperature or pressure measurement curve over a wide range of burning rates. This necessitates a degree of delicate instrumentation which can only be achieved at the expense of rugged dependability. The potentiometer, by virtue of its construction, is one such instrument. The movement of the slide wire eventually wears the pot coil with which it is in contact. Coil life is foreshortened still more by airborne abrasives such as dust and soot. The latter, which in reality is carbon and a conductor of electricity, seems to burn between the slide wire and the coil, overheating and fatiguing the windings. The potentiometer in the operating control is particularly susceptible to soot. The enclosures of these controls are not designed to be dust tight, and in a boiler room where a film of soot covers everything, you can be sure some will find its way to the pot coil. Slipping a plastic bag over the control enclosure and tying it closed around the bulb well or pigtail will help reduce service calls on this account.

When the very fine winding of the pot coil in the operating control burns through, the fuel-rate motor begins to hunt. That is, it makes very wide swings either side of the set point instead of following the load. Once the coil wire has broken, the balance is destroyed and the controller acts like a two-position device. The slide wire, in effect, must jump from one portion of the coil to the other, across the break.

On process boilers where the steam demand is relatively steady, the slide wire will narrow its movement over a very few turns of the coil winding, concentrating the friction wear and hastening coil failure, unfortunately a fact of life that must be lived with.

Excessive external vibration transmitted to the instrument will also accelerate coil failure. Dirty or worn contacts in the balancing relay that results in erratic drive-motor operation and a corresponding wide pressure or temperature fluctuation so that the slide wire must continually move to compensate, also increases unnecessary wear.

28

Microcomputer - Based Integrated Combustion Control System:

Some of the most overworked buzz words in modern technology are "state-of-the-art." Nowhere are they more flagrantly applied than in the electronics industry. "Solid State" are two more gems that conjure up the image of a kernal-sized chip of plastic containing all the switchgear formerly housed in a 10-foot square panel board. Printed circuit boards and miniaturized load relays are embodied in the current generation of programmers of both major manufacturers whose safeguard systems we have been studying. As a result, a measure of rugged dependability has been sacrificed in the interest of sensitive instrumentation. It is extremely important, for example, to provide proper fuse protection for these controls and to be sure the connected loads do not exceed the terminal ratings listed. Also, when installing a new or replacement programmer it is mandatory to perform a static checkout of all the wiring circuits before installing the control on the subbase, to avoid irreversible damage to the printed circuit boards and/or load relays.

Although the plug-in concept is not new to combustion control technology, dividing the Flame Safeguard function into separate circuit boards (subbase, programmer module, and amplifier module) was innovative. In case of failure of a particular module the whole control need not be replaced. From the stocking jobber's point of view the universal chassis, which can accept a number of different program modules and various amplifiers to accomodate infrared or ultraviolet scanners, photocells, or flame rods, was a good thing because it reduced his inventory. It doesn't mean much to the service technician or end user, however, as we well see.

Some of the burner control systems touted today as the latest things are neither state-of-the-art nor all-solid state. The transition from electromechanical switching systems to 100% solid state circuitry is still evolving in our industry, and many combustion safeguard systems are technically obsolete when they leave the drawing board. Manufacturers have been slow to incorporate the latest space age technological developments. For example, the microcomputer has been used in industrial process control for 10 years, yet the synchronous clock motor driven timer (trade name Telechron) has only recently been replaced by a solid state timer (see the Preface to this book). Line (120 volt) loads are still being switched on and off by old fashioned control relays with open contacts in "state-of-the-art" devices.

"Self-diagnostics" and "first-out annunciation," are terms describing functions associated with microprocessor- (microcomputer) based combustion control systems. The microprocessor tests itself and associated hardware with comprehensive safety routines *hundreds of times per second*. Any malfunction detected will cause a safety shutdown, and the programmer will announce what it has found, when it found it, and what it has done about it. It may communicate with us in words or in alphanumeric code. It could even call us on the phone in an emergency; or on command, give us a status report; or talk to our "mainframe" computer.

SELF-DIAGNOSTICS

The ability of the programmer to distinguish between field (external) and system related (internal) faults facilitates trouble shooting the cause of a safety lockout or failure of the burner to start. When the system "indicates" it has detected an internal fault and shuts itself down, however, it's not always obvious which of the modular components is at fault. The subbase, programmer chassis, amplifier, scanner, and interconnecting wiring, are all suspect. Unless the display module specifically directs you to the amplifier, for instance, you are going to have to make some trial and error substitutions. If you don't have the spare components on the shelf, you are going to have to call in a service contractor who does. There is no way to circumvent or defeat the purpose of the programmer to "fail safe."

FIRST-OUT ANNUNCIATION

In addition to reporting the cause of a safety shutdown related to the flame supervisory system, all field input circuits are monitored at the load terminals to ensure system ability to recognize the true status of the limit controls and interlocks. In addition, the programmer provides for short circuit and excess current detection on the pilot and main fuel valve circuits. The programmer will de-energize all fuel valve circuits within four seconds following a flame failure or at the end of a pilot "trial for ignition" period if no flame is detected. The alarm circuit is energized following a safety lockout. The programmer will lockout and display the appropriate message or code if the high-fire purge switch remains open longer than 3 minutes during prepurge. If the control has finished the prepurge cycle, the firing rate controller has driven to low fire position and the low-fire start-switch remains open after 3 minutes, the programmer will lockout and display the appropriate code or message, and energize an alarm circuit.

(ECA) FIREYE FLAME-MONITOR

The Fireye Flame-Monitor is a microprocessor-based burner management control system with self-diagnostics, non-volatile memory, and a vocabulary of 42 different messages which scroll out on the message center to provide the operator with status, first-out annunciation, and failure mode information. On a safety shutdown, the message center will advise the operator that the control is in "lockout" and scroll a message indicating the cause as well as the position in the sequence of operation it occurred. The 18 terminal wiring base allows for many functional circuits including multiple interlocks (such as high-fire purge switch, low-fire start switch, air flow, and fuel pressure switches) pilot ignition circuit, and main fuel valve. The Flame-Monitor uses the same wiring base as the Fireye C Series and D Series controls and is designed to be interchangeable with most models without extensive rewiring.

The Programmer has an eight-character read-out display. Messages that are greater than eight characters in length will scroll on the display from right to left. If power is interrupted during a lockout, when power is reapplied, the control will maintain its status and reason for lockout display information. Additional features of this control are: a constant flame signal read-out, eliminating the need for a DC voltmeter; a run/check switch which allows the operator to stop the program sequence in any of four different positions, or drive the firing rate controller to low fire mode during the running cycle; read-out of main-fuel operational hours and complete cycles.

The Fireye E 100 Flame-Monitor consists of the universal chassis, display module, mounting screw, and dust cover. The programmer module slides into the tracks on the chassis just behind the display module and engages the contact pins. The amplifier module slides down behind the programmer, then the mounting screw is inserted from the front, and the assembled control is ready for installation in the wiring base. The dust cover may then be put on. Programmer modules are designed to fit only in the proper slot. They cannot be snapped into place if inserted in the wrong location. Do not force them.

The Fireye E 300 expansion module provides increased interlock supervision capability of the Flame-Monitor System. The expansion module connects to the Flame-Monitor by means of a ribbon cable and expands the standard 42 display messages of the Flame-Monitor to include an additional 31 diagnostic messages. By wiring any of 16 interlock switches (three recycling and thirteen running) into the expansion module, the Flame-Monitor will automatically act as a first-out annunciator for these interlocks. In addition, a fuel change-over circuit (for dual fuel burners) is standard.

HONEYWELL BC7000

In addition to automatic burner sequencing and flame supervision, the BC7000 microprocessor-based burner management system provides status indication, first-out annunciation, self-diagnosis, and energy conservation. It mounts on the same subbase as the R4140 and R4150 conventional programmers, in most instances without rewiring. Since combustion safety is the main task of the BC7000, sixty percent of the running time of the microcomputer is devoted 15 different but overlapping safety routines. More than 400 safety checks are performed every second that the BC7000 is in operation to check the performance of the total burner control system (microcomputer operation, program memory and execution, timing functions, input signals, logic operations, and output commands). Faults associated with either the flame detection subsystem, plug-in program module, or system chassis are isolated and reported by the multi-function display as a three-digit fault code. The multi-function annunciator display also shows the elapsed time during prepurge, ignition trials, and postpurge sequences. If a safety shutdown occurs during a timed period, it provides the time in sequence when it occurred. The hold/fault code and the time are alternately displayed. The annunciation and diagnostic display comprises three system hold codes and 28 fault codes consisting of two numerals preceded by the letter H or F accordingly. Each system is supplied with, and should have posted near it, a complete list of diagnostic codes. In addition, Honeywell makes available a wallet-sized plastic card listing the diagnostic codes.

Light emitting diodes (LED's) mounted on the front of the programmer provide positive visual indication of the program sequence: STANDBY (power on), PREPURGE, HOLD, IGN TRIAL, FLAME ON, RUN, POSTPURGE, and through the illuminated reset switch, safety shutdown (lockout). In addition, the BC7000 has a triple function test switch, which enables the operator to halt the sequence of operation at the end of PREPURGE, or during IGNITION TRIAL. Placing the switch in TEST position during the RUN cycle drives the firing rate controller to low-fire mode.

ENERGY CONSERVATION

Unnecessary and wasteful purge related heat losses are significantly reduced, according to Honeywell, by the program intelligence of the BC7000 computerized burner control. Energy saving prepurge (ESP) is a field selectable feature which prevents blower operation at start-up until the air damper reaches the purge position (high-fire purge switch closed). This prepurge sequence change is said to save 300,000 Btu per boiler horsepower annually on cycling boilers in typical heating applications. Energy saving intelligence also teminates burner/blower operation and energizes the alarm whenever the high or low purge switch fails to close after a 3-minute delay.

29

Support Systems

The grey area of involvement by the plant engineer with the operation of the whole boiler package, and the development of a boiler–room sense, comes about partly because the challenge is there and partly in self–defense. Recognizing the fact that the operation of the "power house" necessitates a division of responsibility, it is important also that he appreciate there can be no sharply defined areas of responsibility. As pointed out in the Boiler and Pressure Vessel Code of the American Society of Mechanical Engineers, "prior to taking charge of any unit, operators should recognize the definite responsibility which they inherently assume for handling any operating emergency which may arise."

Although as a group power engineers are primarily responsible for the operation of the combustion equipment, mishandling of this equipment probably results in more boiler failures than the next two causes—overpressure, and weakening of the structure. In fact, mishandling of combustion equipment can very well precipitate the last two conditions, for firing rate not only has a relationship to the load–carrying ability of the boiler, but the integrity of the pressure vessel itself.

Although the accumulation of soot, slag, and scale on the internal heating surfaces of the pressure vessel is not regarded as hazardous, in the sense low water level or overpressure is dangerous, buildup of these materials has a long–term detrimental effect on boiler metal.

Soot and slag accumulation on the fireside of the heat exchanger can be corrosive, and it retards heat transfer into the water. Scale encrustation on the waterside not only interferes with heat absorption, in the extreme it causes hot spots, called *bagging,* which is structural distortion due to overheating.

Fuel-oil conditioning and feedwater treatment are vital preventive maintenance procedures that not only protect the investment in plant and equipment, but pay dividends in operating efficiency.

FUEL OIL ADDITIVES

There are certain operational shortcomings inherent in the combustion of residual fuel oils that in the past did not greatly diminish their economic attractivenesss to industrial and commercial consumers. Today these oils, especially No. 6, are essentially by-products of refining processes designed primarily to yield gasoline, jet fuel, home heating oils, solvents, and other vital domestic products. So we are dealing, frankly, with the heavy ends remaining after the extraction of more valuable products from the raw petroleum and the final product contains the bulk of the impurities naturally present in the various crudes. Even though it is of comparatively poorer quality, industry has always felt it more acceptable to contend with, and where possible, deal with the problems associated with the use of this oil, than pay a significantly higher fuel bill. Nowadays of course there are factors at work that limit to an ever-increasing extent that freedom of choice; fuel shortages, import quotas, air-pollution ordinances, to name but a few.

One of the most controversial subjects concerning the firing of residual oils is the use of additives to correct the precombustion and fireside problems inherent in the burning of oil. There are at least as many *formulas* as there are chemical suppliers, and it would seem that each has the right answer. Basically the problems associated with the utilization of heavy oils fall into two categories: problems that occur primarily as a result of the storage and handling of the oil, and those associated with the buildup of the by-products of combustion on the furnace walls and flues of the boiler.

Certain chemical reactions take place when the oil is heated and cooled repeatedly, and when it is exposed to air during transit. Although some sludge may be present in the fuel when delivered, it is most commonly formed in the storage tank after delivery, and then precipitates out in the warmer areas of the oil–transport system to interfere with the proper delivery of fuel to the burner. Some of this sedimentation results from the aging of unstable components of the oil—a kind of slow oxidation—which is aided by the presence of relatively minor quantities of water. The water acts as a *catalyst* affecting the instability of impurities, and serves to *agglomerate* the heavy oil, rust and dirt, into a viscous emulsion. This type of colloidal dispersion can be largely controlled by preventing unnecessary contamination of the oil in the first place, as by surface water. As we have seen, it is characteristic of all catalysts, even in minute quantity when subdivided into colloidal size, that they present a very great surface area to the reacting substances.

Additives especially compounded by reputable chemical manufacturers to control specific problems are available to consumers. These additives are scientifically developed catalysts which when mixed with the oil, either speed up or arrest certain chemical and/or nonchemical reactions of the various components. Sludge stabilization, for instance, requires an additive that has the ability to:

1. Actively emulsify limited amounts of water with the oil
2. Extend the solubility of certain components of the residual oil to retard subsequent precipitation
3. Disperse sludge and dirt particles present, and hold them in suspension until they can either be filtered out or consumed in the combustion process
4. Solubize and homogenize the mixture to prevent the formation of a heavy gummy mass on the tank bottom.

Another type of additive acts as a detergent, which has just the *opposite* effect from the emulsifier just described. Instead of holding the impurities in suspension, it breaks the surface bond between the molecules in dispersion so that they coagulate, or group together in clots (still microscopic, however).

When they become large and heavy enough, they precipitate out and settle on the tank bottom. Obviously this type of additive should not be used where sludging is the problem, for it is designed for use where it is more important to keep atomizers and other close-tolerance orifices clear of sediment. You can see, hopefully, how it is possible to inadvertently work at cross purposes with yourself, *when you don't read the label,* so to speak. This has been known to create chaotic, though temporary, problems where additive brands have been mixed without due regard to the consequences. Unfortunately many chemical industries are vitally interested in catalytic research, and consequently additive formulas and the way in which they work are sometimes closely guarded trade secrets.

An operating engineer was once overheard to say, "Each time the boiler is opened for inspection and cleaning, it is a bit like attending an unveiling; you are never quite sure what you are going to see. Everything you did right or wrong, is there before your eyes." Indeed it can be quite disconcerting to find the boiler flues full of thick black soot, but aside from the filthy job it is to remove, it is the least difficult to handle of all the fireside deposits. In fact, the light, fluffy character of true carbon black, which might result from an oxygen-poor natural-gas flame, for instance, precludes its existence to any great depth in most mechanical draft boilers; the gas velocities are so high as to carry this type of accumulation out as fast as it forms. As a matter of fact, once the oxygen deficiency has been corrected, the hot gases of the clean flame will consume much of the loose soot that does not blow through. For this reason, operators of combination fuel boilers often run for a month or so on gas before opening the boiler for cleaning, after a long hard winter on oil.

Vanadium slag is the toughest and most troublesome deposit to remove. Many a mechanical tube cleaner and air brush have been ruined before resorting to old-fashioned hammer and chisel. Ironically, the problem potential of this and other impurities present in fuel oil is on the increase, due to the improved refinery processes that yield more gasoline per barrel of crude, and more sophisticated boiler designs that permit higher operating temperatures and pressures.

Although the normal ash content of the hydrocarbon constituent of residual oil is only .1 to .5 percent, other elements in the mixture undergo certain thermal decomposition during the combustion reaction, and precipitate as molten matter or solid particles. Sodium and vanadium, for example, melt at relatively low temperatures, thus compounds composed of these constituents are molten and sticky in areas where temperatures correspond to their fusion temperature. Conditions in the furnace and first pass of the average fire-tube boiler of modern design are generally conducive to the formation of slag containing vanadium constituents. Complexes containing these elements promote deterioration of refractories also by penetrating into the porous surfaces. Since the slag expands and contracts at a different rate than the refractory, eventual weakening and spalling of the brickwork results, especially under conditions imposed by intermittent firing.

Sulfur is the best-known impurity in residual fuels. I dare say every school child has heard of its gaseous form, sulfur dioxide. At room temperature sulfur is a yellow, odorless solid. It can also exist as a liquid under certain conditions, and burns with the fuel oil to form a colorless, stable, toxic gas that is roughly twice as dense as air. Readily soluble in water, it forms sulfurous acid which is extremely corrosive to boiler metal. In addition to sulfur dioxide, approximately 4 percent of the sulfur oxidizes to form sulfur trioxide, which quickly unites with other basic oxides such as the calcium and magnesium also present, to form sulfates. Together they account for nearly 50 percent of the total fireside accumulation, and are basically colorless and scaley. Hand brushing removes such encrustations with little difficulty, so long as the boiler is dry and preferably warm. When allowed to absorb moisture, as during a summer shutdown, the scale becomes more corrosive, extremely sticky and difficult to remove. When, for one reason or another, a boiler must stand idle for a long period, it should be thoroughly brushed and cleaned first to minimize fireside corrosion.

TREATMENT

A widely applied approach to the slag problem is use of a liquid chemical catalyst containing either an alumina or dolomite derivative that raises the melting point and corresponding fusion temperature of the sodium–vanadium complex, so that it passes through the boiler as a dry ash.

Corrosion in the cooler zones of the boiler is controlled by inhibiting the formation of the sulfur trioxide which decomposes with the water vapor to form sulfuric acid. Another method neutralizes the sulfuric acid as it forms. It is interesting to note in this connection, that in the industrial preparation of sulfuric acid by the so–called contact process, divanadium pentoxide is used as a catalyst in the initial step involving the oxidation of sulfur dioxide to sulfur trioxide. How it works is still in dispute, but the general belief is that the catalytic action is dependent upon the ability of the vanadium to have various oxidation states. One suggested mechanism is that the solid vanadium adsorbs a sulfur dioxide molecule on the surface, gives up an oxygen atom to convert the sulfur dioxide to the trioxide, itself reducing to divanadium tetroxide. The tetroxide in turn is restored to the pentoxide by reaction with the oxygen. The point here is that catalytic reactions, especially those involving solid/gas interfaces, are not very well understood *even by chemists* at the present time. While we as burner technicians and operating engineers are primarily interested in the oxidation of the hydrocarbon constituent of the fuel, it is obvious that parallel reactions take place simultaneously that are every bit as intricate, if not more so than the fundamental combustion reaction, and we must at least appreciate if not understand them.

WATERSIDE PROBLEMS

Although boiler water conditioning is not normally part of the routine maintenance that concerns the burner technician, deficiencies in this area by those who are responsible create problems for them. What goes on inside the boiler during the evaporation process has been the subject of countless thousands of books and papers. Records show that such knowledge existed earlier than 150 B.C., yet the abstract nature of the physico-chemical relationship of the many constituents involved continues to mystify many operators. As a result, *boilers get out of control,* as chemists say when the recommended concentration limits are not maintained and difficulties arise in the form of poor steam quality, scale buildup, corrosion, pitting, or embrittlement of metal surfaces.

An erratic water level is a typical condition that represents a loss of control that directly concerns the technician. Since the float-operated switches that control the burner and feed-water pump motors reflect such surging or priming, as it is called, it results in the shortcycling of these units which in turn causes them to lose control. In addition, the rapid banging in and out of their respective relays could cause the trip-out of an overload heater due to stored heat energy. The starting inrush of current through the heater time after time gives it little opportunity to cool between cycles.

The bobbing up and down by the water in the gauge glass of a steam boiler is not normal; it is unsatisfactory, and *can be controlled.* It is due to the fact that most impurities—dissolved, suspended, or otherwise—tend to accumulate just below the surface of the boiler water. This overconcentration interferes with the liberation of the molecules from the surface of the water— the *steam release,* as it is called. The whole area is churning, puffing, and snorting like a pot of boiling oatmeal, instead of permitting a smooth transition from water to steam. Unfortunately it is difficult to spot such a condition by analyzing boiler water samples, unless taken from a surface blow-down line, for the problem is not one of total concentration but of overconcentration in a localized area. It occurs usually at times of peak steam demand, when top to bottom temperature differences within the boiler are greatest.

The remedy is the surface blow-down, which in effect skims the surface, and readjustment or elimination of the constituents that formed the concentration; cutting oil for instance that got into the system as a result of new piping work, or an overdose of feedwater chemicals without adequate blow-down. It is emphasized that skimming is more effective even than draining the boiler completely, because in the draining process some if not most of the impurities adhere to the water walls and tube surfaces, only to be launched into the fresh water as the boiler is refilled.

Erroneous water levels are another, although less common, problem. This is a case where the gauge glass, for one reason or another, is not indicating the true height of the water in the boiler. Correspondingly, the low–water safety control and feed-water pump control, which are usually mounted on the same water column, are rendered unreliable or worse—useless. Mud accumulation in the float chamber of the low–water cut-off can prevent the float from dropping with the water level. Scale and sludge buildup in the piping that connects the water column to the boiler shell can isolate the level control completely. That is why plugged tees and crosses are used instead of elbows in such piping, so that it can be reamed periodically. Most boiler inspectors require the opening and inspection of all water-level controls at least annually.

Steam leaks from packing nuts, try cocks, and fittings at the top of the water column or gauge glass will make the water level in the column ride higher than it actually is inside the boiler. Try cracking open the upper test cock if you doubt it. As a result, there is less water above the top tubes of the fire–tube boiler than normal, and should be corrected.

Good practice dictates that the control of fire– and water-side conditions is a joint effort of the operator, chemist, and burner technician. The degree to which the venture is successful can be measured in years of dependable and economical steam generation.

The checklist on the following pages is useful in setting up a boiler preventive maintenance program.

PREVENTING FURNACE EXPLOSIONS

The National Fire Protection Association Standard 85 lists three situations which are typical examples of conditions favorable to boiler–furnace explosions:

1. An interruption of the fuel or air supply or ignition energy to the burner, sufficient to result in momentary loss of flame, followed by restoration and delayed reignition of an accumulation;

Table 29-1. Boiler Checklist

NOTE: This is a general list. Items shown are in random order, not necessarily ranked by importance and may not apply to a particular boiler.

ITEM TO BE CHECKED OR TESTED	*DAILY*	*WEEKLY*	*MONTHLY*	*SEMIANNUALLY*	*ANNUALLY*	BRIEF COMMENTS
1. Boiler water level	X					Proper operating level. Pump on—pump off levels.
2. Boiler blowdown	X					Or as prescribed by
3. Water column blowdown	X					your water treating
4. Visual flame check	X					company.
5. Water treatment						As recommended by a reputable feed water company.
6. Analyze water sample	X					
7. Pressure (or temperature) Burner "On"	X					For any variance from
8. Pressure (or temperature) Burner "Off"	X					normal setting.
9. Feed pump pressure		X				
10. Feed water temperature		X				
11. Flue gas temperature	X					
12. Fuel Supply		X				
13. Oil burner pressure	X					Variations indicate
14. Oil supply pressure	X					dirty strainers or fuel
15. Oil supply vacuum		X				pump wear; leaks.
16. Oil temperature (preheated fuel)	X					
17. Gas pilot pressure	X					
18. Housekeeping	X					
19. Check for leaks, noise vibration, unusual conditions, etc.	X					
20. Atomizing air pressure	X					
21. Water level—Expansion tank		X				Hot water system
22. Burner maintenance		X				Depends on type of burner, fuel, etc. See burner manual.
23. Tight closing of fuel valve		X				Flame extinguishing characteristics
24. Combustion analysis (CO_2)		X				
25. Flame safeguard		X				Per manufacturer's recommendation

Table 29-1. Boiler Checklist (concluded)

ITEM TO BE CHECKED OR TESTED	DAILY	WEEKLY	MONTHLY	SEMIANNUALLY	ANNUALLY	BRIEF COMMENTS
26. Fuel and air linkage		X				
27. Water pump			X			Packing glands, coupling, etc.
28. Duration of water pump run			X			Indication of wear
29. Water strainer			X			—or as experience dictates
30. Oil pump			X			Packing gland, seal, drive, etc.
31. Oil strainers/filters			X			—or as experience dictates
32. Air cleaner			X			
33. Indicating lights, alarms			X			
34. Low water cutoff operation		X				Test under normal firing conditions—not shocked by rapid blowdown
35. Operating & limit controls			X			
36. Safety & interlock controls			X			
37. Belts			X			Tension and condition
38. Clean low–water cutoff				X		⎰ or as required by
39. Remove all plugs in LWCO and piping				X		⎱ insurance company
40. Circulating pump			X			Packing glands, seals, couplings, etc.
41. Remove and clean oil preheater				X		—or as usage indicates
42. Flue gas leakage		X				Gasketing, etc.
43. Hot spots		X				Paint discoloration
44. Breeching					X	Clean as required
45. Refractory				X		Spalling, cracking
46. Fireside surfaces				X		To be cleaning
47. Waterside surfaces				X		Scale, mud, pitting
48. Safety (or relief) valves						As recommended by insurance requirements
49. Lubrication						Per manufacturer's recommendations
50. Seasonal lay–up or standby						As recommended by water consultant

2. Fuel leakage into an idle furnace and the ignition of the accumulation by a spark or other source of ignition;

3. Repeated unsuccessful attempts to light-off without appropriate purging, resulting in an accumulation of an explosive mixture.

The NFPA states further that an examination of numerous reports of boiler-furnace explosions suggests that the occurrence of small explosions, furnace puffs or near misses, has been more frequent than usually recognized.

Human error is charged as the cause of the majority of furnace explosions. Improper design of equipment, obsolete control systems or the failure of the fuel cut-off system to function when unsafe conditions occur are some contributory causes.

The imminence of the danger is punctuated by the following quotation from *Honeywell Flame Tips,* Vol. 5, No. 6:

> A cubic foot of natural gas (or about ¾ ounce of fuel oil), properly mixed and vaporized and confined, has the explosive equivalent of a stick of dynamite. A burner firing at full input into a properly designed and sized combustion chamber takes about 8 seconds to fill the chamber. If light-off occurs with the chamber 1/3 or less full of fuel (about 2.66 seconds at high fire) the result is a puff. If light-off occurs with the chamber more than 1/3 full, the result is a substantial explosion.

In order to reduce the possibility of an explosion due to the accumulation of fuel in the furnace, regulatory agencies and code enforcement authorities have established certain safety precautions. One such precaution is the requirement that the combustion-air fan be operated a predetermined length of time during the start-up cycle before the ignition source is turned on and the fuel valve opened, in order to purge the combustion space of fuel before ignition takes place. This is referred to as the prepurge period of the burner operating cycle. As a result, the emphasis of contemporary automatic burner operating control design has been on longer prepurge periods in the hope of diluting any explosive mixture which may have accumulated in the furnace. By flushing large quantities of air through the combustion space and flues it is felt that all of the combustible mixture will be carried out the stack before pilot light-off is scheduled.

FUEL FLOODING

Statistical data is meager on the number of incidents of oil fuel flooding which occur annually. Perhaps this is due to the fact that insurance companies do not usually cover losses because of damaged equipment and downtime unless an explosion or fire has taken place. Consequently, the cost of removing fuel oil from a furnace, cleaning up the mess, and reconditioning the boiler-burner setting following a fuel flood must be borne by the owner. In addition, there is the possibility of being fined for polluting nearby rivers and streams if the oil finds its way to the boiler room floor drains.

Experience shows that fuel flooding happens more often than furnace explosions. In large burner installations using heavy Bunker C fuel oil, main fuel valves are prone to stick or hang partially open. Wear and tear from the abrasive action of the oil, varnish and sediment accumulations on valve plungers and seats, are some of the reasons valves fail to close securely. Leaks of this kind occur most often where fuel oil is supplied under continuous pressure to the valve. At typical pumping rates it takes but a short time to put several hundred gallons of raw oil into the firebox of a tightly-gasketed boiler.

Another safety precaution required by regulatory bodies such as the National Fire Protection Association and the Factory Mutual Insurance Association, is an interlocking electrical control switch to insure that the main fuel valve is in the closed position before the burner can be started. Called a proof-of-closure switch, automatic fuel valves are available with this feature but can only be used on modern flame-safeguard systems that have the special preignition interlock circuitry to accommodate them.

MINIMIZING HUMAN ERROR

A *safety shutdown* is the act of stopping burner operation by shutting off all fuel and ignition energy to the furnace by means of a safety interlock or interlocks and requiring a manual restart. Some of the unsafe conditions that will cause a safety shutdown of a modern burner are:

1. Under– or overpressure in the fuel supply
2. Undertemperature (No. 5 and No. 6 fuel oil)
3. Loss of combustion air supply
4. Loss of or failure to establish flame
5. Loss of control system actuating energy
6. Power failure
7. Low water level
8. Loss of atomizing medium in the case of oil burners (steam or air supply, for example).

Typically, any or all of the above conditions give the same indication—the flame–safeguard system will stop the burner. To the boiler fireman it is not immediately obvious what has happened. Faced with dropping steam pressure and loss of the load, he is under great stress to get the boiler back on the line. This is when a cool head must prevail.

The temptation to bypass or manually override an interlock calls for good judgment based on a thorough understanding of the device in question and the consequences of the action. The person charged with the responsibility of placing the system back on the line safely must read and analyze every indication, every symptom. There is no room for guesswork, especially if a fuel–rich condition exists in the furnace. Human errors in judgment are kept to a minimum when all of the available facts surrounding an incident or condition are known. Unless there is a diagnostic annunciation system with read–out devices that indicate the failure resulting in the trip or alarm, someone will have to troubleshoot the system. When a troubleshooter must sort through the electrical circuitry and controls involved in all eight conditions enumerated above, the chances for a quick and correct diagnosis of the cause of a safety trip are nil.

HANDLING THE OIL-FLOODED BOILER

Manufacturers of modern oil- and gas-fired boilers provide a number of methods to gain access to internal areas. Pressurized boilers, in particular, generally employ tightly-gasketed front and rear *heads* that can be swung open for inspection and cleaning of firesides. Their davit-type suspension or watch-case hinging facilitates fast and easy access to furnace, fire tubes, tube sheets, and refractories.

Such well-sealed boilers do not customarily have under-fire combustion-air intakes, so that when a flooded condition is discovered belatedly the oil is found to have accumulated to the point where it either flows out of the windbox or fills the furnace and spills out the fire-inspection port. Obviously, when this happens there are many gallons of oil in the boiler. They are *hot* gallons that may be burning on the surface. Where there is no flame, which is usually the case, the heat in the oil is not a problem except for the possibility of it splashing on someone during its removal. Since this type of malfunction most often occurs during a period when the boiler is unattended, by the time it is discovered things have generally cooled down to below the ignition temperature of the oil.

Preliminary Steps

First, prepare a dike of *speedy dry* around the boiler at least 2 inches high and 6 inches wide—we don't want any oil getting into the floor drains. Next, avail yourself of several empty 55-gallon steel drums and a portable oil pump with a plastic hose, and a piece of soft copper tubing for use as a suction line.

If the oil is dripping from some fitting fairly high up on the boiler, *do not* attempt to open the boilerhead or swing out the burner. Instead, with the portable pump set up and *primed,* place a large pail beneath the fire-inspection port. Place the suction line of the pump in the pail and the discharge line in one of the barrels. If oil flows from the port when you open it, you will be able to prevent a worse mess by starting the portable pump. Once flow has stopped, you may be able to snake the copper tubing into the furnace through the inspection port and remove most of the oil. Scotch-type boilers, where the first pass of fire tubes is below the furnace, will test your ingenuity when you try to figure how to get the oil out of these tubes without opening one of the heads. This is where the speedy-dry dike comes in. You may have to resort to opening the boiler a crack or so, catching as much of the oil as possible in a pail the way you did when you first opened the fire-inspection port. Be prepared to take several gallons of oil from the gas train of a combination fuel boiler as well.

Cleaning Up the Mess

Once the raw oil has been removed, the next operation is to dry the firesides as best you can. Swabbing, and mopping speedy dry over and through the passages is effective. You may consider a hot-water wash, but it adds to an already messy situation that might raise havoc with the floor drains, and care must be taken not to soak the brickwork. The gas train will undoubtedly have to be dismantled and cleaned. Renew all gaskets that were oil soaked and repair or replace the defective fuel-cutoff valve components.

Call the Fire Department

Before you close the boiler preparatory to lighting off, it is advisable (in come cities mandatory) that you put in a call to the Fire Department for inspection and standby. It's nice to have them around, just in case; especially since at this point it is anybody's guess how wet the inside of the breeching and stack might be. The officer in command will usually station his men and equipment in anticipation of a chimney fire after surveying the situation and consulting with you. Advise him to set up one or more smoke ejectors in the boiler room.

There is usually plenty of acrid smoke when you first light off, because it is almost impossible to get all the oil out of the refractory and insulating material. If, in your judgment, the material is porous and obviously heavily oil soaked, it may be advisable to strip it out and replace it, for once a fire gets started under or behind a refractory it could be troublesome, especially in a dry–base firebox boiler. An oil–soaked refractory acts like a lampwick and will keep a flame burning as long as oil vapor is present. The controlled burn–off procedure is primarily concerned with preventing the accumulation and explosion of such vapors. Once you commit yourself to a light–off, keep the flame lit *at all costs*, and you need not fear an explosion. Don't be dismayed by smoke and pungent fumes emanating from the gasketed joints; the flames cannot get outside the boiler. Besides, the Fire Department is there. Set the firing rate controller in the low-fire mode.

BE SURE THERE IS PLENTY OF WATER IN THE BOILER, THE AUXILIARY SYSTEMS ARE ENERGIZED, AND THERE IS A HEATING LOAD SUFFICIENT FOR A REASONABLY LONG FIRING CYCLE.

Assume a four-hour operation as necessary to place the boiler back into unattended automatic operation. But before it is put back to work, it is advisable to cool it four to six hours and reopen for cleaning and inspection of the firesides. Wire brushing of the secondary surfaces while the boiler is warm will undoubtedly be in order.

Bibliography

Cotton-Lynch. *Chemistry, An Investigative Approach.* New York: Houghton-Mifflin, 1968.

Daniels-Alberty. *Physical Chemistry.* New York: Wiley, 1966.

Depuy-Rinehart. *Introduction to Organic Chemistry.* New York: Wiley, 1975.

Hamell-Williams-Mackay. *Principles of Physical Chemistry.* New York: Prentice Hall, 1966.

Vacek, L. C. *The Enjoyment of Chemistry.* New York: Viking, 1964.

Garard, J. D. *Invitation to Chemistry.* New York: Doubleday, 1969.

Cobine, James Dillon. *Gaseous Conductors.* New York: McGraw-Hill, 1941.

Arzimovich, L. A. *Elementary Plazma Physics.* Lexington, MA.: Xerox College Publishing, 1965.

Allen, J. E. *Aerodynamics.* New York: Harper-Row, 1963.

Rossi, B. E. *Welding Engineering.* New York: McGraw-Hill, 1954.

Smeaton, R. W. *Motor Application and Maintenance Handbook.* New York: McGraw-Hill, 1969.

Steam, Its Generation and Use. New York: Babcock and Wilcox Company, 1927.

Steiner, Kalman. *Oil Burners.* New York: McGraw-Hill, 1937.

Kogan, Zuce. *Correcting Oil Burner Deficiencies.* Chicago: Zuce Kogan Associates, 1941.

Heating, Ventilating, Air Conditioning Guide. New York: American Society of Heating, Refrigerating, and Air Conditioning Engineers, Inc., 1960.

Research Conference Proceedings on Distillate Fuel Combustion. API Publication 1701. New York: American Petroleum Institute, 1962.

A Survey of Components For Use With Air-Atomizing Oil Burner Nozzles. API Publication 1720. New York: API, 1961.

Design of Blue Flame Oil Burners, Utilizing Vortex Flow or Attached Jet Entrainment. API Publication 1723A. New York: API, 1965.

Henein–Patterson. *Emissions From Combustion Engines and Their Control.* Ann Arbor, Michigan: Ann Arbor Science Publishing, 1972.

Lewis–Pease–Taylor. *Combustion Processes, Volume Two. High Speed Aerodynamics and Jet Propulsion.* Princeton, NJ: Princeton University Press, 1956.

Hutchinson, J. W., ed. *Handbook of Control Valves.* Pittsburg: Instrument Society of America, 1971.

National Engineer. Various articles published during the last 20 years. Chicago: National Association of Power Engineers.

Power Magazine. Various articles appearing in handbooks and supplements, dating back more than 20 years. New York: McGraw-Hill.

Fundamentals of Gas Combustion. American Gas Association Laboratories. Arlington, Virginia: American Gas Association, 1973.

Electric Control Circuits. Engineering Manual of Automatic Control. Minneapolis: Honeywell, Inc. 1954.

Index

Abatement
    air pollution, 180, 196–206
    smoke, 9, 94, 112, 180, 202, 295
Abbreviations, 15
Activated complex, 150, 162
Activation, level of, 150
Additives
    fuel oil, 282
    feed water, 286
Aerodynamic effect, primary air, 119
Aerodynamic unbalance, fan, 273
Agencies, regulatory
    American Gas Association (AGA), 230
    American Society of Mechanical Engineers (ASME), 233
    Associated Factory Mutual (FM), 230
    Canadian Standards Association (CSA), 231
    Factory Insurance Association (FIA), see IRI, 232
    Improved Risk Mutuals (IRM), 232
    Industrial Risk Insurers (IRI), 232
    National Fire Protection Association (NFPA), 235
    Underwriters' Laboratories (UL), 229
Air
    atomizing systems, 106, 145–146
    clean, standards, 176, 198
    cleaner, 140, 146
    combustion, 2, 15, 167, 211
    composition of, 167
    compressor, 135
        lubrication of, 140
    damper drive systems, 125
    envelope, 119, 154–158
    excess, 1, 148, 169, 171

Air (continued)
    infiltration
        into furnace and flues, 174
        into idle boilers, 193
    interaction with oil, 136
    nozzle, 117, 201
    oil interface, 138
    Pollution, Realities of, 196–206
    primary, 9, 117, 136
        aerodynamic effect of, 119
        capture velocity, 153
    pump, 138–146
        Cleaver-Brooks, 140
        Orr and Sembower (Gast), 145
    purge, 106, 224
    register, defined, 7
    secondary, 9, 117
    supply, boiler room, 194
    theoretical, for combustion, 167
Air pollution, 180, 196–206
Air requirements
    for boiler room, 194
    for combustion, 167
Alarm
    flame failure, 216
    low water, 216
Alkanes, family of, 149
American Gas Association, 230
    recommendations, 180
        limits of flammability, 160, 287
American Petroleum Institute (API), 92
American Society of Mechanical Engineers (ASME), 233
Annulus, gas, 7, 186
Annunciation, first-out 277
Annunciator, diagnostic, 271, 276
Arc
    of rotation, cranks and levers, 58–65

Arcing
  at electrical contacts, 261, 272
  at ignition electrodes, 266-269
Aspiration, of fuel in air, 9
Atmospheric
  gas burners, 10
  pressure, effect of, 14, 77-80
Atomization, 9, 152
Atomizers, types, 98, 114-124
  distortion of, effect, 200
Atomizing
  air, oil burner, 120
  air, systems, 106, 135-146
  oil, principles of, 110-113
    effect of centrifugal force, 116
Attenuation, combustion noise, 159
Autoignition, 9, 150, 200
Automatic control systems, 207
Auxiliary systems, 248
  isolated electrical circuits, 216
  support systems, 281

Backpressure
  in fuel flow systems, 22
  in furnaces, 161-164
  valves, 87
Baffles, 159
Bibliography, 299
Blowers, fans, impellers, 10, 15, 211
Bodies, regulatory, 229
Boiler(s)
  breeching, 10
  care checklist, 289
  cleaning, 163, 176
  combustion rates, 183
  design, 163, 184, 189
  flues, 10, 15, 163, 184
  heating capacity vs rating, 172, 184,
    185
  heating surface, 172
  oil flooded, handling of, 292-296
  packaged, 10, 14, 35, 164, 176,
    193, 210
  pressurized, 10, 174, 292
  room air supply, 194
  room sense, developing, 281
Bridge, balanced circuit, 224
Burner(s)
  aerodynamics, 5, 12, 119

Burner(s) (continued)
  cleaning, 176, 201
  configuration, 5, 204
  control circuit, 210
  dual-fuel, introduction to, 1
  fans, 211, 272
  gas
    atmospheric, 10
    blue flame, 8, 204
    luminous flame, 8, 152
  head, 7
  ignition systems, 265
    spark electrodes, 268
    transformer, 12, 267
  oil
    air atomizing, 7
    gun type, 6, 154
    high pressure, 120
    low pressure, 120
    pressure atomizers, 120
    rotary cup, 94, 106, 114
    steam atomizers, 120

Canadian Standards Association, 231
Carbon
  as a heat source, 5, 145
  bond with hydrogen molecules, 150
    with other carbon molecules,
      150
  compounds as intermediates, 148
  content in the various fuels, 149
  ignition temperature, 148
  oxidation in the combustion reac-
    tion, 149, 152
Carbon dioxide
  as a product of combustion, 147,
    154-158
  in flue gas analysis, 165-176, 201
  relationship to excess air and carbon
    monoxide, 177-180
  ultimate for various fuels, 168
Carbon monoxide, 177-180, 204
Catalytic effect
  of combustion chamber walls, 160
  of fuel oil additives, 282-284
  of water on oil, 282-284
Cause/effect relationship in troubleshooting, 246, 275-279
Cavitation, pump, defined, 83

Cell, photoconductive, 238
Centrifugal force, effect of in oil drop-
    let formation, 116, 122
Chamber, combustion
    as a combustion catalyst, 160
    as a refractory, 159
    as an insulator and muffler, 159
    as it contains the flame, 6
Characterized valves, 54
Chemical, chemistry
    colloid, defined, 112
    equilibrium, 197
    fuel oil additives, 282
    mixtures and solutions of fuel and
        air, 6, 111, 165
    reactions, 150
    test methods, air pollution, 205
    water treatment, 286
Chimney(s)
    available draft, 189
    determining sizes, 189
    performance, 191
    static draft, 194
    the, and its Effect On Modern Boil-
        ers, 187–195
    theoretical draft, 188
Circuit, electrical design, 211, 275-279
Circuit(s)
    balanced bridge, 224
    burner control, defined, 210
        obsolete, 250
    extraneous, 216
    isolated, 216
    motor control, defined, 209
    oil piping, 77
    power, three phase, 208
    printed 275-279
    transformers, 249
    ungrounded, 250
CO (see cCarbon Monoxide)
CO2 (see Carbon Dioxide)
CO$_2$ kit, 177, 201
Coal, relative combustion efficiency, 2,
    5, 207
Code, fault 276
Coefficient, valve (C$_V$), 136
Coil, magnetic pull, 213
Coke trees, 119
Colloidal dispersion
    of oil droplets in air, 111
    of smoke and other solids in pol-
        luted air, 112

Colloidal dispersion (continued)
    of sludge in oil, 283
    surface chemistry, 113
Coordinating Fuel and Air Input Rates,
    57-67
Combustion
    activated complex, 150, 162
    activation, level of, defined, 150
    adjustments leading to compaction
        of the flame, 158
    air, composition of, 167
    air inlet to fans, 2, 94, 212
    air required for, 15, 167, 184, 211
    air, theoretical excess, 165
    analysis, 165–171
    chamber, 6, 158-160, 184
    complete, 167
    control, 275-279
    efficiency, defined, 1, 172
    energy balance, 171
    gas, 160, 203
    heat of, 152, 171
    incomplete, 147–149, 161, 181
    index, 172
    instability, 161–164
    losses, 171
    oil, 147, 200
    perfect, 167
    process, physicochemical, 9, 150
    pulsation, 162
    principles of, 147
    programmer, 219–227, 275-279
    reaction time
        oil, 152
        gas, 160
    reactive center of equilibrium, 162
    stoichiometric, 167
    system, 164
    wave propagation, 181
Compaction, flame volume, 8, 158
Components of total pressure, 20
Compressors, air, 135
Condensation, flue gas, 161
Conduction of heat energy to pressure
        vessel walls, 152
    retarded by soot, 172, 182
Conservation, energy, 280
Continuity testing, 249-256
Control(s)
    automatic fuel changeover, 51
        systems, 207
    balanced bridge, 224, 273

Control(s) (continued)
  burner, 210
  circuit transformers, 249
    ungrounded, 249
  combustion sequence, 240, 257, 275-279
  constant speed floating, 227
  contact cleaning, 262
  firing rate, 125, 219
  flame safeguard, 236, 275
  full modulation, 2, 227
  house branding, 264
  interlocks, 225, 229, 240, 255
  limit, defined, 228
  motor, 213
  low-high, 220
  low-draft, 218
  obsolete circuits, 250
  operating, defined, 229
  photoelectric, 236
  point, setting, 219
  pressure, 219
  programming, 281, 236, 275-279
  proportional, 221
  proprietary versions, 264
  recording, 236
  relays, 216
  single phase, 248
  staging, 127
  temperature, 219
  typical system, 217
  vibration, effect of, 272
Controllers, 219
Conversion, units of measure, 15
Corrosion, boiler fireside, 161, 181, 281
Cranks, rods, levers, 57-67
  excessive wear, 272
Diagnostics, self, 276
Diagnostic annunciator, 270
Diodes, light emitting (LED's) 279
Diffuser, burner, 7
Dispersion, oil droplet, 7
Dissociation and decomposition of hydrocarbon molecule, 152
Domestic oil burners, 154
Draft [also see Chimney(s)]
  available, defined, 189
  control, 193
  defined, 189
  excessive, 183

Draft [see also Chimney(s)] (continued)
  factors, 189
  gage readings, 190
  induced, 10, 174
  low, switch, 218
  mechanical, 10, 174
  natural, 10-11
    fundamentals of, 187-194
  theoretical natural, 188
Drive train, 57-67
Droplet, oil formation, 7, 9, 12, 14, 110-113, 116-124, 135, 147, 155, 200-202, 268
  residence time required, 8, 153

Efficiency
  boiler, 2, 172
  combustion, 172
  steady-state, 172
Electrical Considerations, 207-218
  continuity testing, 214, 253-256
  diagrams and checkcharts, 255
  fuse testing, 248-251
    time-lag, 215-218
  horsepower requirements, 211
    burner fan types, 211
  isolated circuits, 216
  shock hazard and personal safety, 207
Emergency situations, handling of, 256, 288-296
Emissions, visible from stacks, 9, 180, 202
Engineer, the, as troubleshooter, 208, 247
  as observer, 201, 208
Energy conservation, 280
Errors, human, minimizing, 293
Energy balance, defined, 171
Equivalent feet of pipe in
  gas line sizing, 24
  oil line sizing, 84
Excess air, 1, 148, 154-158, 167
Excess oxygen, 147, 169
Explosion hazard, 160, 236, 246, 265

Factory Mutual Insurance Association (FM), 288

Fan(s)
  aerodynamic unbalance, 273
  caseless, 212
  centrifugal, 211
  combustion air, 10, 15
  impeller types, 211–212
    disadvantages of each, 212
  noise, 212
  scroll, 212
  sirocco (squirrel cage), 212
  vibration from, 212, 272
Fault codes, 276
Feed water pumps, 214
Filters (see Strainers)
Fireye, 236, 242, 251, 263, 277
Firing rate
  control, 219-227
  controller, 2, 21
  control methods, 125
  staging, 128
  turndown ratio, 185
First-out annunciation, 277
Flame
  appearance of, 12, 153, 201
  blue, 8, 9, 12, 152
  color, 12, 152, 204
  compaction, 8, 156, 158
  decomposition, 152
  Detection and Programming, 236-244
  failure, 243
  fireflies, 119–201
  front, 12, 121, 155, 176, 203
  generated motion, 11
  impingement, 12
  ionization, 268
  luminous, 8, 152
  monitor, 277
  observation, 153–155, 177, 201
  pulsation, 162
  retention, 153–160
    head, 12
    magic grid, 155
  safeguard, 236, 275-279
  signal, defined, 239
    measurement, 253
  stabilization, 7
  temperature
    gas, 268
    oil, 152
  Volume Dynamics, 147–164
  volume per unit input, 8, 153–155
  vortex, 12

zone, 6, 7, 14, 27

Flow
  Fundamentals of Fluid, 14
  compressible fluids, 15
  control valves, common types, 54–55
  measurement, 16
  Pitot tube, 20
  resistance to, 7, 70
  through nozzle or orifice, 7
  valve characteristics, 51–56
Flue Gas Analysis, 165–176
Flue gas data, interpretation of, 177–186
Friction loss, through pipes and fittings, 23–31, 84–86
Fuel(s), the, 149
  air flow rate, Cardinal Rule, 51
  air interface, 11, 14, 135, 155
  air mass flow rate, ideal, 161
  air ratio, harmonizing, 51
  aspiration into the air stream, 10, 12
  burning rates
    gas, 161
    oil, 152
  calorific value
    gas, natural, 160
    oil(s), 93
  changeover, automatic, 51, 57, 278
  flooding, 79, 282-287
  pressure regulation, 14, 39, 86
  rate, input controller, 21
Fuel oil
  additives, 282
  blended, 73
  calorific value, 93
  classification of, 73, 91
  gravity, API, 92
  heavy ends, 181, 282
  maximum (ultimate) CO_2 values, 168
  piping, 68–70, 77–90
  pour point, defined, 73, 105
  preheating, 72-75, 101–109
  pumps and strainers, 80
  residual, 73
  sludge treatment, 283
  storage, 73–76
  surface tension, 9, 121

Fuel oil (continued)
  transport systems, 73–76
  vaporization, 100
    temperature of, 152
  vapor phase, 6
  viscosity, defined, 70
    compensation and control, 91–109
  weight per gallon, 93
Furnace(s)
  defined, 8
  explosions, prevention of, 288
  length, comparison, 8
  pressure, 14–17, 25, 35, 174, 186
    factors affecting, 16, 184
  submerged, 163, 164, 189
  volume, 163
  water cooled, 163
Fuses, checking, 215, 250, 275

Gage(s)
  draft, 190
  pressure, 88
  vacuum, 77–81
Gas(es)
  atmospheric burners, 10
  burners, 1–8, 10, 152, 204
  calorific value, 160
  classification of, 160
  combustion of, 111, 160, 177–180, 204
  explosions, cause and prevention, 160, 185, 282, 288
  flammability, limits of, 160
  flue analysis, 165
  flue data interpretation, 177
  mains, 23
  natural, 1, 149, 160
    composition of, 166
  pipe sizing, 23–31
  pressure
    available, 16, 25
    net regulated, 25
    regulators, 18, 19
      selection and performance, 39
      spring selection, 40
  propagation rate, 161
  train, described, 18
    over and undersized, 38

Gas(es) (continued)
  utility company, policies as to service pressure, 25, 43
Gasification, 9, 113

Hazard(s)
  electric shock, 207
  explosion, 160, 219, 265, 288
  rupture of pressure vessel, 228, 275
Head, burner, 7
Heat loss (see Energy balance)
Heaters
  motor overload, 215
  oil, 101–109
  safety switch, 107
Honeywell, 252, 257-263, 279-280
Horsepower, boiler, defined, 185
House line, 23, 39
Human error, minimizing, 291, 293
Hydrocarbon(s), 9, 147–152
  combustion of, 149, 165
    activation, 150, 162
  decomposition, 152
  in atmosphere, 199
Hydroxyl radicals, 149

Igniters, 13
Ignition systems, 266
  source energy, 12, 151
  temperature, defined, 148, 150
Illustrations
  air atomizer detail, 139
  air pump, 141
    module, 143
    interior, 144
  annunciator, diagnostic, 271
  atmospheric gas burner, 10
  balanced bridge schematic, 225-226
  boiler(s)
    battery, oil piping schematic, 88
    four pass design, 17
    modern dual-fuel, 11, 82
  chimney performance curves, 191
  CO_2, O_2, air, relationships, 170, 178
  control, early programmer, 237-238
  cranks, levers, gear ratios, principles of, 59
  dual-fuel burners, 3, 4
    control cabinet, 209

Illustrations (continued)
  dual-fuel burners (continued)
    modern boiler room, 82
    packaged boiler, 11
  electric positioning control system, 223
  external sensing line, PRV, schematic, 49
  flame retention head, 8
  flow characteristics, valve curves, 53
  flow chart, valve coefficients, C_V, 36
  flow vs pressure drop, gas piping, 37
  flue gas, four pass travel, 17
  fuel flow schematics, oil, 69, 88, 126, 132, 133, 137
  fuel oil controller, 71
  fuel oil field piping, typical, 72
  gas flow vs pressure drop, 37
  gas piping, typical, 26
  heaters, oil
    in tank, 104
    steam/electric, 102
    water, safety, 103
  hollow flame pattern, 154
  linkage systems, fuel/air control, 6, 59, 61, 64, 67, 72
  low-fire start, oil flow schematic, 126
  lube oil reservoir, Cleaver-Brooks, 142, 144
  magic grid, 156
  Maxiltol PRV
    210 series, 42
    straight-through series, 46
  metal grid, expanded, 157
  motion, the measurement of, vs valve action, 220, 222
  nozzle(s)
    air atomizing, 136
    bypass, 131
    high pressure, 121
    multiple, 129
    variflow, 131
  oil heaters, 102–104
  oil pressure loss, standard pipe, 85

Illustrations (continued)
  overtravel linkage, 67
  pressure regulating valve(s)
    gas, 19, 49
    oil, 69, 88, 126, 132, 133, 137
  program, sequence of burner operation, 258
  programmer, early, 221
    modern, 241
  proportional control, 222
  relays
    balancing, 224
    typical schematics, 217
  rotary oil burner(s)
    Cleaver-Brooks, 118
    Petro, 115
  standard gas train, 18
  standard pitot tube, 20
  strain release mechanism, 67
  tank heaters, 104
  three-phase motor wiring schematic, 214
  uniform motion, levers, rods, and cranks, 61
  valve action vs motion of measurement, 220-222
  viscosity/temperature relationship, 76, 99
  viscosity valve, Ray Burner, 97
Impellers (see Fans)
Improved Risk Mutuals (IRM), 232
Infiltration, air
  into boiler settings, 174
  through idle boilers, 193
Inherent flow characteristics, valves, 52
Instruments, flue gas analysis, 177, 201
Insurance company requirements, 18, 229
Interlock(s), 228, 229, 255, 274-279
  high and low damper position, 129, 130, 258
  low oil temperature, 108

Jackshaft, 5, 51, 62, 224
Jet entrainment effect, 11
  of oil in air stream, 138

Kit, CO_2, 177, 201

Lead sulfide (PbS) cell, 238
Leverage ratio, 63
Levers, rods, cranks, 57
Light-emitting diodes (LED's), 279
Linkage, drive, fuel/air ratio control, 5, 51
    overtravel, 65
    phase angle, defined, 62
Listing bodies, 229
Load demand, 2
    heating, 238
Loop, oil circulating, 87
Loss, standby, 193
Low-fire start
    defined, 2
    in sequence control, 106, 123-125, 193
    mode, 278
Maintenance, preventive, 176, 183, 200, 282
    air pump, routine, 140-146
Manifold, gas, 7
Manometer, 20, 22
Metering, 89
    nozzles, 122
    valves, 122
Methane, 149, 167
Micron, 110
Microprocessor, 277
Mixtures, fuel/air, defined, 111
Mode, firing
    variable, fixed, on-off, full modulation, 2, 224
Module, program 275, 278
Modutrol motor, 221-227
Molecular reactions, 111
Monitor, flame, 277
Monoxide, 177-180, 204
Monoxor, tester, 179
Motion, the measurement of, 219
Motion, uniform
    firing rate control, 221-227
    linkage drive system, 5, 51, 62, 65
Motor(s)
    control circuit, 208, 210
    drives, 57, 60-63, 240
        arc of rotation, 57, 63, 67, 72, 223
    modutrol, 57, 60-63, 223
    overload protection, 215, 287
    polyphase, 208
    single-phase, 215

    timer, program, 240
    vibration, 272
National Fire Protection Association (NFPA), 235, 288
Natural draft, fundamentals of, 187-194
    theoretical, defined, 188
Nitrogen
    contained in combustion air, 167-169
    contained in stack gases, 169
    oxides of, 196, 205
Noise
    combustion attenuation, 159
    fan, combustion air, 212
Nozzle(s), oil burner, 7
    air atomizer, 106
    classification of, 120
    markings, ratings, 122
    multiple, 127
    pressure atomizer, 105, 121
    return flow, 130
    spray patterns, 122
    variflow, 130

Odors
    from stack gases, 181
Oil (see Fuel Oil)
Oil burner(s)
    atomizer types, 120-135
        principles of atomization, 110-113
    classification of, 110
    combustion process, 9
    furnace requirements, 8
Oil entrainment in the air stream, 138
Oil firing rate control methods, 125-134
Oil flooded boiler, how to handle, 292-296
Oil heaters, 101-109
Oil, lubricating, compressor consumption, 145
    recommended grades, 145
Oil temperature, low cut-out, 108
Openings
    boiler room air supply, sizing, 194
Operating gage readings, 246
Operating safety, 208, 292-296
Over firing
    causes of, 183
    hazard of, 184

Oxidants, 149
  level in atmosphere, 198
Oxides of nitrogen, 196, 205
Oxygen, excess, 169, 177
  analyzer, 177

Paraffins, 149
Particulate matter, in stack gases, 180
PbS (lead sulfide) cell, 238
Perfect combustion, 167
Phase angle, firing rate control system, 248
  law of, 60
Photochemical reactants, 180
Photoconductive cell, 222
Physics, elementary of centrifugal force, 58
Pilot burners
  types, 13, 266
Pipe(s), piping
  capacity, 23–31, 28, 68–70, 77–90
  equivalent feet of, 23, 84
  friction loss, 23–31, 28, 68–70, 77–90
  gas
    house line, 23, 39
    mains, 23
    train, 18, 38
  pressure loss, 23–31, 28, 68–70, 77–90
Pitot tube(s), 20
Pollution, air, 180, 196–206
Polyphase motors
  control, 208–212
Potentiometer, defined, 238
  excessive wear, 273
Power circuit, 211, 213, 249
Pre-ignition interlocks, 255
Pressure
  atmospheric, 14
  available gas, 25
  differential, 21, 25, 43, 50
  drop, 8, 21, 43
  furnace, 14–16, 186
  gas, 16
    intermediate, 28
  measurement, 15
  net regulated, 22

Pressure (continued)
  regulators, regulation,
    gas, 18, 39
    oil, 86
  relief, ten commandments of, 88
  safe operating, 109
  static, velocity, defined, 7, 20, 21
  total, 20, 22
  vessel, 8, 228, 275
Preventive maintenance, 176, 183, 200, 282
Printed circuits 275-279
Products of combustion
  intermediate, 148, 181
Programmer, 2, 19, 224, 275-280
  field service, 261
Propagation, flame defined, 110
Proportional control, 238
Pulsation, 161–164
  defined, 162
  puffing, 105
Pump(s)
  cavitation, 83
  horsepower requirements, 86
  oil, 80-82
  positive displacement, 96
    defined, 80
  slippage, 80
  staging, defined, 86

Radiation, from flame
  infrared, 222
  ultraviolet, 223
Rate control, firing, 57, 125, 219
Ratio, turndown, 131, 185
Reactants, defined, 113
Reaction, chain, 149-152
Realities of Air Pollution, 196
Reducing valves, selection and performance, 39
Refractory material, 159, 202
  catalytic effect of, 160
Regulations, insurance company, 18
Regulator
  draft, 193
  gas, 18, 19
  oil, 86
Regulatory agencies, 229
Relays, relaying
  balancing, 142

Relays, relaying (continued)
  contactors, 107, 216
  control relays, 216
  flame, 219
  programmer, 219
  switching, 216
  time delay, 218, 259
Rotary oil burner, 94
Running problems, defined, 269

Safe operating limits, 228
Safety, operating, 208, 245, 255, 279, 281
  lock-out, programmer, 225, 252, 257, 277
  minimizing human error, 291
  personal, 208
Safeguard, flame 236, 275-279
Saybolt, oil viscosity measure, 70
Scaling, waterside, 286
Scanner (see photoconductive cell)
Secondary air, 9, 117
Self diagnostics, 276
Sensing line, external, PRV, 48
Sequence control, 240
  operating, 257
Shunt, method of testing control circuits, 251
Signal, flame, 222
Single-phase motors, 208
  control systems, 248
Single-phasing, 215
Slag, 180
Sludge, 284
Smog, 9, 94, 112, 180, 202, 294
  abatement, 180
  density measurement, 182
  monitoring, 182
Solids, in boiler water, 287
Solidstate, technology, 275
Solutions, chemical, defined, 111
Soot, 9, 112, 180, 281
  losses due to accumulation, 181
  treatment for, 282
Sound, combustion
  attenuation, 202
Spark, electric ignition, 266-269
Specific gravity, 30, 70
Speed, burning, 8, 152, 161
Spray, atomizers
  oil cone, 127
  methods, 98, 114-124

Spring selection, PRV, 40
Square feet of heating surface, defined, 185
Squirrel cage fans, 212
Stack(s) [also see Chimney(s)]
  emission data, 166
  losses, 181
  stub, 183
  temperature, 171, 172, 189
  visible emissions, 9, 180, 202, 295
Staging
  firing rate control, 128
  fuel oil pumping, 86
Standard(s)
  clean air, 176, 198
  commercial, oil, 92
Standby losses, 171, 221
Starting and running problems, 186, 245, 265, 274-279
  defined, 269
Steady-state efficiency, defined, 172
Steam
  heaters, oil, 101–109
  pressure relief, 108
  properties of, 175
  quality, 107
  release, defined, 287
  trap, 108
Stoichiometric combustion, 167
Suction
  lift, defined, 77
  oil lines, 79
    sizing, 84
Sulfur, 166, 168, 181, 285
  in products of combustion, 205
Surface, boiler heating, defined, 185
Surface tension, oil, 121, 127
Suspended solids, in boiler water, 107, 287
System(s)
  electrical control, 207, 274-279
  oil transport, 68
  support, 281
Switches
  auxiliary, 128
  low-fire start, 273, 277
  motor overload, 215
  proof of closure, 254
  safety lock-out, 225, 274-279
  test/run, 237

Tables
  boiler checklist, 289
  boilers, tubular, furnace pressure, 17
  bypass nozzle, delivery rates, 134
  CO_2, ultimate for various fuels, 168
  combustion, intermediate products
    of, 148
  cfh multipliers for other specific
    gravities, 30
  cfh multipliers for 10% pressure
    drop, per 100 feet of pipe
    length, 30
  cfh for other lengths, 30
  equivalent length of fittings
    gas, 24
    oil, 84
  furnace pressure, tubular boilers, 17
  gas piping capacity, 29
  gas train, under-, oversized, 38
  gravity/density/heating value by oil
    grades, 93
  gravity/temperature relationship, 98
  Maxitrol PRV spring selection, 40
  pressure drop capacity Maxitrol
    210 series PRV, 41, 44
    straight-through series, 47
  pressure regulating valve(s), 41, 44,
    47
  programmer, combustion control
    terminal comparison, 253
  properties of saturated steam, 175
  simplex oil nozzle delivery rates,
    123
  steady-state efficiency, 173
  steam, properties of saturated, 175
  terminal comparison, programmers,
    252, 274-279
  tubular boilers, furnace pressure, 17
  ultimate CO_2, various fuels, 168
  valve coefficients, C_V, 33
Tank heaters, 104
Temperature(s)
  ignition, oil, 152
  intermediate products of combus-
    tion, 152
Ten commandments of pressure relief,
  88
Terminal strip, burner, 252, 275-279
Terminology, burner, 2-13

Test methods
  air pollution, 205
  combustion, 165
  continuity, electrical, 253, 275
  piping, oil, 91
  suction, vacuum, 80
Time–delay relays, 259
Time–lag fuses, 218
Time, residence, oil droplet, 153
Total pressure, components of, 20
Train, gas, 18
Transformer
  control circuit, 249
  ignition, 12, 266
Transmission, power, 58
Transport, oil system, 68
Trap, steam, 108
Treatment, fuel and water, 281
Troubleshooter, diagnostic annunci-
  ator, 270
Troubleshooting
  introduction to, 245
  problems, 245-247, 274-280
    gas piping, 27
    oil pumps and suction lines,
      79–83
Turndown ratio, 131, 185

Ultraviolet flame detection, 222
Underwriter's Laboratories, 229
Ungrounded electrical circuits, 250
Uniform motion, law of, 63

Vacuum
  available, 85
  suction lift, 77
Valve(s)
  anti-syphon, 78, 83
  backpressure, 87
  butterfly, 21
  bypass, 125
  capacities and flow measurement,
    32
  characterized, 60
  check, 78, 83
  coefficient, C_V, 32
  fire, 83
  flow characteristics, 51
  flow control, common types, 54

Valve(s) (continued)
  foot, 82
  gas pressure reducing, 18, 39
  gate, 55
  globe, 56, 83
  hunting, 43
  inherent characteristics, 43–45, 53, 56
  oil metering, 95–100, 130
  solenoid, 12, 107, 125–134
Vapor phase, 5–6
Vaporizing oil burner, 5, 73
Vapors, oil, 80, 292, 295
Velocity, oil capture, 7, 153, 155
  oil droplet relationship, 34
Ventilation, boiler room, 194
Venturi effect, 9, 139
Vessel, pressure, 6, 8, 15, 108, 228
Vibration, 272
Viscosity, oil
  as a function of flow, 94
  compensation and control, 89, 95, 97

Viscosity, oil (continued)
  defined, 70
  effects of, 70
  temperature relationship, 75, 98
  valve, 96
Visible emissions, 9, 180, 202, 295
Voltage, feedback, 251
Volume
  flame dynamics, 7, 147–164
  furnace, 8, 163
Vortex
  combustion air, 14
  flame, 12
Water level, erratic, 287
Water/oil heaters, 103
Water treatment, 286
Water vapor, 147, 165
Wave, combustion, 151

Zone
  flame, 7, 14, 27
  premix and heating, 12, 153, 200